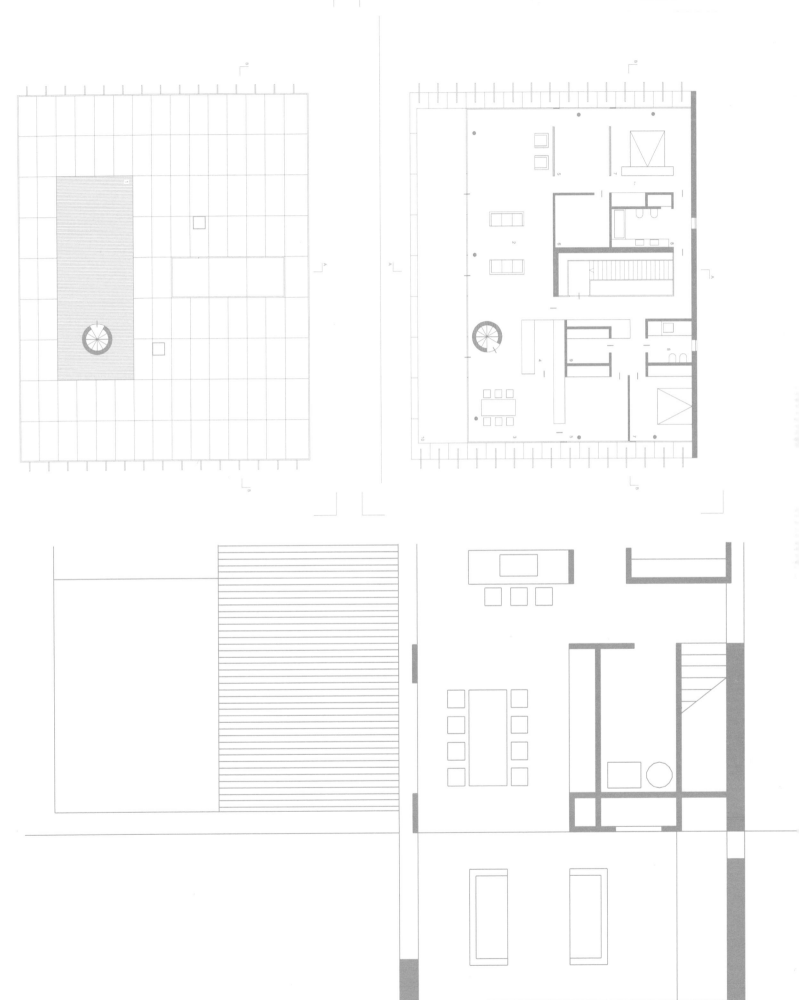

CONTEMPORARY

Home Design

CONTEMPORARY
Home Design

70 PLANS AND PROJECTS

Wolfgang Bachmann

Arno Lederer

Schiffer Publishing Ltd®

4880 Lower Valley Road • Atglen, PA 19310

Contents

Challenging lots, restrictions, and conditions

Building in the countryside

Hillside lots, complicated substructures — great views

Small homes, economical solutions

Introverted or one-way orientation

Unusual shapes: geometric order or free compositions

Conversions, attachments, fitting into grown environment

Separable floor plans for granny flats, guests, office space

3-bedroom kitchen bath balcony — floor plans as an adventure

Wolfgang Bachmann

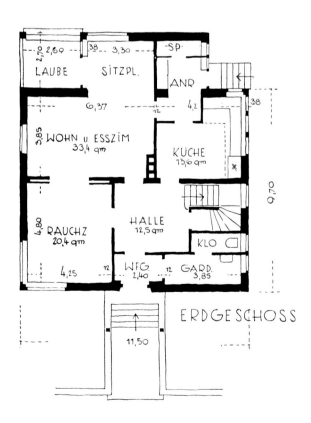

The freestanding single family home is regarded as a timeless dream project; only the floor plans have changed. Example from the early 1930s by Emil Freymuth, Munich.

The innocence of the home-builder is gone. If you open a home or living style magazine or thumb through the real estate sections of newspapers, you are confronted with floor plans. The sales effort is not only aided with photorealistic ideal perspectives and florid real-estate prose, but those small drawings are part of it too. For the layman, they are proof that this is about architecture which someone has recently designed for him, and that he is getting his money's worth. Based on the floor plan, he can already arrange the furniture and also suggest changes or discard offers — which makes him a quasi-partner in matters related to planning. He learns that his furniture is way too large if it is drawn according to scale, that the dining room should not have a direct access to the bathroom even if it may be convenient at times, and that, absent an expensive basement, an endless amount of storage space has to be planned for. Floor plans, particularly of single-family homes, are the essence of architecture. They provide space for family life and they reflect how the members of a household stand in relation to each other, where they meet, retreat, get out of each other's way.

Rudolf Steiner expected that the architecture he invented would have an educational effect — this is essentially applicable in reverse for even the most basic row house layout, if it stands in the way of the family's needs.

Designing

Back when I was studying, designing floor plans for homes was regarded as a treat next to the many dry obligatory tasks. You didn't have to get into the details of industrial or cultural architecture — a home was pretty obvious: on the one hand, the non-perfect architecture one grew up with, and on the other hand, the future architecture, which hopefully one could build according to one's personal ideas. No design courses were required to develop a floor plan. It was sufficient to walk through the rooms with a yardstick, move a chair here or there or open a door, and the ideal size became obvious.

No question, the design projects for the different courses were still intricate and challenging. The lots were narrow, or located next to noisy streets or on humid slopes facing north, the floor plans had to be child-friendly or women-friendly, for single parents or the handicapped person. (Today one would add "sustainable" into the task formulation.) More than anything, within the context of the student revolution of the 1960s the design of freestanding homes or even mansions was impossible to conceive. It was essentially all about high-volume, individual, and affordable living space which was at once a quite realistic goal but on the other hand, as would be seen later, a rather unsatisfying solution as well. This was not about custom-designed dream homes but about spicing up the usual product with refinement, providing a sense of generosity even to the smallest of places, finding new solutions for essential functions and, despite the systematic agglomeration, creating a variety of individual solutions and fitting them into a single design. The issue was the run-of-the-mill city, not the lakefront or oceanfront lot.

The design professors pointed to appropriate examples of contemporary building which certainly deserved to be improved. Others insisted on facts and formulas, national norms and regulations, sunlight incidence diagrams, and second escape routes. Irrefutable design planning was intended to eliminate the student's pie in the sky ideas. Hence the rule was to save on technical installations. The kitchen and the guest lavatory always featured a common wall for installations, that was a rule of thumb! The assistants knew this much even without ever having built a house. It was essential to justify the design with fictional life experience. Thus, for example, the professor sought refuge in the question: where does the worker go first when he gets home in the evening, tired and exhausted? Response: the kitchen, to the fridge to get a cold beer. Hence it is logical to place the kitchen close to the entrance. This of course was easy to challenge for us students, by providing our professor with a different scenario: the working stiff comes home and the first thing he does is to push his lady into the bed, so the bedroom has to be close to the entrance! The professor did not want to provide personal experiences in this case.

As we have said already, floor plans are layouts for living, in the best sense of the word. For the German philosopher and author Gernot Böhme, the primary topic of sensuality is not the object or thing but the atmosphere. The first impression is not the subject or object but rather the mood of a room and its affective tonality. This might sound like a quixotic alibi for a client who is looking forward to a certain standard of features for his hard-earned home budget. The worst-case scenario in this case would be the understanding that a badly-located, inconvenient, expensive, and energy-wasting home is not worth the trouble and the stress on his family.

Experiencing

There are unchanging features of habitation. However, every epoch has its own concepts. While looking at the seventy architectural designs presented in this book you encounter common features which repeat as if planned. Today, the word "room" elicits some resistance, so architects utilize "area" to describe the rather casual boundaries of space between kitchen, dining, and living. Why do clients prefer this solution? Does it seem to be more spacious? More democratic if the preparation of dishes does not involve hours of confinement? But this might preclude the experience of new spaces. Moving from the dining table to the living room couch is not that enticing when you only move three yards within the same room. And the arrangement known from hotels with the sink or bathtub/shower in the bedroom, indicates a lack of prudishness rather than the yearning for new spaces.

However, it must be noted that architects today are challenged to come up with ingenious soulutions, particularly for small homes. As much as the examples are different from each other, you can sense their atmospheres, can recognize the floor plans which are closest to your own idea of living. Even in the case of a standard 3-bedroom-kitchen-bath-balcony home, it is always worth it to change the arrangement of items in order to achieve the best living space possible. For an author who is used to forming an opinion after one visit to the home, it is an unexpected expansion to view houses from the viewpoint of the architect and of the residents, to understand their unique features, and to describe them. After a few days of work it turned, rather surprisingly, not into a confusing indifference but into a kind of comparative forensics. What distinguishes a design? How do the rooms react to their intended functions? Are there any fixed places, areas to be interpreted, cozy corners, passages to cheer you up? Which direction would you prefer to move in? Where do you want to sit, rest, work, chat with friends and family? Should it be on a single level or do stairs, galleries, bridges, and offset levels constitute the culmination of home architecture? Which solution is best: orthogonal, organic, symmetrical, or fractal? How would you feel inside of it? During the day, when it is getting dark, with lighting? In June, in November?

One of the results of the excursions through the many designs was this: there isn't really a single floor plan which one can not come to like. But there is also none of them where one would want to move in right away. Of course there are a lot of them to try out! This might lead to finding out what works for you. Layouts and floor plans inevitably prompt the client and the architect to move, rearrange, turn, open, divide, annex, reduce — to change. No time for getting bored. Your chips, please. Make your move!

Tradition, modernism, or experiment — the variety of building

Arno Lederer

In the 1950s Willy Hagara sang about a "small house with a garden, but mine; what else do I need to be happy?" Only a few of those who are thinking about building today will know this song, much less the singer, who actually became the owner of a sizable villa when he was older due to an inheritance. The wish for a personal home seems to be ever-present. Despite the complaints about land use, urban sprawl, and the accompanying problems for city planning, many people dream of their own home, of nice architecture set into green surroundings. It is not quite clear whether this is due to the flight into privacy, or the wish for independence — perhaps it is simply the enthusiasm for architecture.

However, this does not involve the grand architecture at all, the kind that belongs to the canon of art and cultural history: from Palladios's *Villa Rotonda* to the homes of modernism such as the *Villa Savoye* by Le Corbusier, Frank Lloyd Wright's *Fallingwater,* or Mies van der Rohe's *Farnsworth House* (image on page 12) and Werner Sobek's *Glashaus R 128*. It is not about the financial or the engineering aspect either, which architecture cannot do without, that is, everything that's expressed in numbers. However, building your own home offers the opportunity to create your own microcosm. For this reason many describe it as a second, slightly-larger dress or suit which the homeowner is purchasing. Architecture provides this additional value when compared to purpose-based building. Thus the home acquires a level of meaning which reflects the individual imagination of its owner.

What our homes say about us

If you take a walk on a weekend through one of the typical single family home neighborhoods you will notice, independently of the design qualities, how the owners have tried to give the exterior of their homes an individual look despite the fact that most cities require a uniform look dictated by the applicable building codes. Just by looking from the street, it becomes clear whether one takes care of the property, whether the applied form language is oriented toward historic examples or elements of classic modernism, whether the building is based on ecological premises or acquires an experimental character through the use of unusual materials. In other words, all these homes allow to make conclusions about the individual owners. They express wealth, modesty, educational level, and societal standing. For this reason there is the saying that architecture is a mirror of society.

"Show me your home and I can tell who you are." As a matter of fact, the face of a home tells more than we tend to think. An apparently historical door from the home improvement center, perhaps advertised as an exquisite contribution to the regional style, manufactured and distributed by the thousands, is certainly neither historical nor related to the local culture. It is not even a copy like a fake Rolex watch, which is at least very similar to the original. It is merely a testimony to the ignorance of the buyer who has purchased a (fake) painting which has no value and which, with respect to building and culture, only shows an embarrassing ignorance.

When the home becomes a sham package

Nevertheless, the industry and the building supplies dealers manufacturing and selling these fakes are doing good business. They offer almost all of the components which constitute a home. Advertised as Bavarian in Bavaria and as Saxon in Saxony they are apparently flying off the shelves. There is no real distinction between them and the mockups which can be found at theme parks lining entire blocks. This is how many homes in single family home areas dress up: with cheap carnival outfits. Because these fakes are sold very cheaply and the retailers bait the customers with special offers, the sale of fake doors, windows, or wall finishing is brisk. The market has found its ignorant customers. No wonder the result is the disappearance of regional distinctions and the suburban streets in the north, south, east, and west of the nation all look alike.

But how did the pleasant distinctions which existed until modernism, come to be? It was actually the climatic and economic conditions in addition to the existing materials of the respective regions that resulted in different building styles depending on the area. Today, architects speak of *genius loci* and refer to all the conditions that are inherent to a given place. This includes not only the quantifiable foundations, but also the cultural values which a region has developed with time. They are certainly closely related to the tangible factors — a fact which has also influenced the arts and crafts, poetry, music or painting of the particular place.

In this respect, there is nothing to be said against buildings which are designed and built based on a given tradition. However, the value of handmade items quickly becomes apparent. They usually cost several times more, and their investment only makes sense when you factor in their durability as an economic factor. They certainly also represent an emotional value which of course not everyone will share.

After all, our living conditions in modern times have changed, and with them, the impact that location and region have.

Typology, construction, and material

Certainly it makes sense to build a home so that the advantages of industrially produced products can be taken advantage of. This is basically related to tradition as well. After all, we are speaking of a building style which

began in the last century with modernism. The first landmarks from these times still appear to be appropriate today. When we look at historic photos of the Stuttgart *Weißenhofsiedlung* (Weissenhof settlement, image on page 13, left) we are surprised by the antediluvian aspect of the cars parking in the streets, rather than by the modern look of the houses. Most likely the photographer had placed them on purpose to set an example of the close link between technological advances and the new-style architecture.

The tiresome discussion about whether a house should follow historic models or whether modernism provides the correct architectural answer misses the point. Because both styles are historically validated. Hence it is more appropriate to discuss the typology of a building, the structures related to it which are the most suitable, and the requirements the future house should fulfill. It seems that the only really important aspect is that the final product be the result of the given conditions and not pretend to be something else — except when the client wishes to have a building for bragging purposes.

Genuine houses

Apart from the two tried and tested models, the traditional and the modern home, there is a third one: the experiment. We usually find it in places where environmental issues are present. In these cases the gamut ranges from high-tech construction to the most simple building styles, which could be called "barefoot architecture." Actually, experiments have always been part of building. One example is the Dymaxion House (image on page 14, left) by Buckminster Fuller which has played a major role in shaping the history of industrially produced and high-tech-oriented buildings. Architects also experimented with building types that don't show their experimental nature. While Paul Schmitthenner belonged among the preferred

architects at the beginning of the Third Reich due to his traditional stance, during the 1920s he had developed the so-called FaWe-Haus, a timber-framed construction which anticipated the modern prefabricated home with its low cost. Then there is the Bavinger House from 1955 (image on page 13, right) by the American architect Bruce Goff. It consists of a built sculpture which incorporates stone from the immediate area, including used items such as a drill string which in large part determined the form of the building. These three examples are impressive due to their inherent building method. One could also express it as follows: they are genuine.

In this regard they contain an aesthetic sustainability which should be inherent in any architecture that is intended to last.

We certainly have applied a simplified and invalid classification as to architectural theory of building styles or architectural types. However, we see how different the appearance of buildings can be and that every type provides very good examples. Their beauty is inherent in their harmonious solution. All of the components correspond to a superordinate idea and do not follow any romantic or formal principles. The concept of harmony is the reason we regard a house as beautiful. We are touching on a question which has concerned architects and clients for centuries and to which there is ultimately no final answer. However, there are a few basic rules which have conditioned architecture since antiquity. One of the first people who tried to define good architecture was the Roman architecture author Vitruv (Marcus Vitruvius Pollio) who, in the first century BCE, wrote the "Ten Books about Architecture." Any student of architecture absorbs these three parameters which make up his concept and which have to be balanced among each other: "Firmitas, utilitas, venustas," they proclaim. This is usually translated as "firmness, usefulness, and beauty," but there is a longstanding discussion as to the correct translation. Several hundred years later during the Renaissance, the author, artist, architect, and writer Leon Battista Alberti

refers to Vitruv in his ten-volume "Architectural Theory." Thanks to him, we have a formula which is well-suited even today to formulate the concepts of beauty or harmony. He says that if you can neither add to nor take away from an object or a building without it suffering a deficiency, it can be called beautiful. If you like architecture and you ask yourself the not-quite-simple question of whether something is good or bad architecture, you might appreciate Vitruv's trinity as well as Alberti's obvious formula to help you make a reasonable judgment.

Building is not a private matter

Architecture, like other forms of art, has an advantage in that there can never be one single solution to a task, but more often than not, an entire bundle of very different solutions can be called beautiful. This explains how buildings that are regarded as excellent by experts seem to have little if anything in common. They are like strangers to each other. For many would-be builders this aspect is not immediately obvious. After all, they are the ones who are paying for "their" building and its planning and construction. So it makes sense that he who pays calls the shots. However, if you build, you don't just build for yourself — you always build in the context of the street, the square, or the landscape. The builder contributes his share to the quality of the public space which belongs to all of us, and which has its quality determined by the common architectural sense. So building is not only a private matter but also a *res publica*. The architect Max Bächer wrote, "If you build, you make an interior and an exterior." He addressed the responsibility of those who want to build their own home, wherever that may be.

So it seems reasonable that our administrations provide rules and regulation which architects have to adhere to when making designs. This is not always an easy task, because the concepts about architecture can be very different from each other, while being perhaps very good ones. However, you should expect experienced and successful firms to be able to adjust to a given situation and its particular features.

The comprehensive design

People often ask the question of why their towns, neighborhoods, and streets are not as beautiful as those they have seen here and there when traveling. Usually they refer to historic city areas. We architects provide the answer by referring to the building codes which have always determined architecture, and we face astonishment. In many cases the houses at the *Piazza del Campo* (image page 14, right) in Siena are mentioned, with their harmony governed by a strict regulation of the number of floors, materials, and window sizes. The secret of beautiful cityscapes is based on an overarching design concept which nevertheless provides room for individual aesthetic expression. After all, the home is also a piece of the homeland, with qualities that might be characterized more by its surroundings than the context of its location.

The aforementioned responsibility toward the public space is also applicable to building in the countryside, since any intervention results in a major impact. Such situations, though, tend to be pretty rare, even if images of freestanding single family homes on the edge of a forest or on a cliff are a popular and successful motif. Most people in Central Europe who can afford their own home will tend to realize their project at the periphery of larger cities and communities. However, land in these areas is expensive and the supply is limited. If you grew up in a single family home during the 1950s and '60s, you will gasp at today's prices of towel-sized lots which cost many times the amount the previous generation had to pay. This of course has resulted in limitations for the planners.

The search for the appropriate architect

Even though we have not touched on the topics of functionality, heating, or the size of individual rooms, the issue of the conditions that determine the outer architecture and the complexity of it becomes clear. The fact that this part of planning is not always performed too well is obvious when looking at suburban neighborhoods with open eyes. Apparently some architects have trouble finding the right answer for a given question. A delicate topic! Moreso considering that we have not yet arrived at the issues concerning the interior layout of the house — the style of living and personal needs and preferences such as sleeping, kitchen and dining, or hygiene — which need to be considered.

All of this shows that you should choose an appropriate architect very carefully. In Germany, the search seems to be easy only at first glance, because of the oversupply of architecture firms. Apparently the profession still attracts many people despite its limited possibilites of economic development, since there is a consistently high demand for university degrees. So, in theory, you just have to walk around the corner.

However, with such a large selection the choice can become a chore. It is, after all, about different qualities. Good planning requires time and, as we know, steady nerves — on both sides. Hence it is important that the entire process, from the first design sketches to the last detail, can occur in a climate of mutual confidence. First, because there is a lot of money involved, and second, the perfect layout of a floor plan requires the knowledge of certain intimate aspects of the owner's lifestyle.

Incidentally, the cost involved in a new home often causes the future owners to be thrifty and the criterion of low architect fees is very much on top of their list when selecting the architect firm. However, this attitude may prove to be a considerable disadvantage and cause additional costs which have not been taken into account beforehand. Since the fees for architects are very low when compared to other professions the firms are not inclined to work out numerous design options. In addition, economic maximization requires even more intensive planning. So you are starting at the wrong end when you apply financial thumbscrews to the planners during the first negotiations.

A brief study of architecture

A much more elaborate part of the exercise for the potential owner-client consists of acquiring knowledge in order to choose the appropriate firm with confidence. This is also a challenging and exciting task. All you have to do is enter the world of architecture. Architecture in magazines and newspapers, architecture on the web, architecture when taking walks and while traveling. Your first assessment is often based on your own taste which can usually be enhanced, so it is a good idea to work yourself through the texts, drawings, and images as if it were a journey of discovery. This, by the way, is how architects stay on top of developments. Don't hesitate to ring the doorbell at a home that you particularly like. Most homeowners are proud to talk about their experiences. Ask about the architects and whether their service was satisfactory. Since you are always wiser after the building process and only then realize what might have been planned and executed in a better way, it makes sense to ask about details which did not turn out all that well. You should allow sufficient time for this step, since it involves nothing less than a brief study of architecture. After all, you want to enjoy your home for many years. And what good is a decision taken in haste?

In many cases one will receive the advice to deal only with experienced architecture firms. The length of professional experience is in fact an irreplaceable factor for solving the complex issues. On the other hand, routine can be a disadvantage and the expected dedication may not be up to par. Hence the dedication and enthusiasm of young architects weighs in favor of choosing them. Many excellent single family home designs come from young companies, and many famous architects started their career with the construction of their first house, typically a single family home. Even though architects play a key role with regard to planning, they cannot provide all of the required design services, so it is important to carefully choose the engineers who deal with the technological issues, that is, heating, sanitary and electrical installations, or the support structure of the future building. It also makes sense to involve an energy-efficiency expert as the strict regulations concerning energy consumption require certain special physical and technical knowledge which cannot be provided by other professionals. Calling in additional experts greatly depends on the size and complexity of the project. This entire set of topics is not to be taken lightly, as the necessary technical issues can certainly influence the look of the home.

The path to a viable design

Once you have completed getting your architecture self-education on this level, you might be tempted to make your own design. This is basically no problem. However, every beginner runs the risk of getting lost in inconsequential issues because of his personal predilections. Love causes blindness here as well because you cannot relinquish certain forms. Everybody who learns design at universities and colleges has undergone this experience. The path to a viable design is long and usually takes several semesters. Only very few students reach a level of expertise while studying. If you consider the fact that only a small fraction of architects can secure contracts via bidding, you realize that the discipline of designing is not that simple. The cliche that architects draw a design on a napkin at an Italian restaurant while having some spaghetti alle vongole and a glass of Brunello is unfortunately not correct. The planning is not perfect at all after jotting down the first ideas. So the architect instead lays out the planning strategy in several stages, starting with a basic sketch and progressing to detailed architectural designs and floor plans. The first sketch, corresponding to the stage of "initial design," comprises less than ten percent of the total effort and performance. Building is a long-term process and it is common to make changes and improvements to the already-detailed plans while building. Even though the designing takes center stage, it is only a small part of the real work.

Cost calculations and scheduling, making bills of quantities (BOQ) and setting up contracts as well as site management requires a much higher time expenditure.

Since the job involves a significant warranty risk, the project is further supported not by amateurish designing but via a precise verbalization of the ideas related to the future home. Perhaps you want to write your own script which describes the daily routine of your household. Good design firms know exatly how much space will be needed for specific ideas of the client. Precise areas are therefore not necessary and may even be counterproductive. Usability and the feeling of a room cannot be determined by an exact area or a certain height. You most likely don't know the size of the room you are sitting in right now.

The personal wish list

It helps to voice your ideas as to ambience and atmospheres: do you want a bright home, or should it have its cozy dark corners? In the case of a slope facing north, do you value the view, or do you want to follow the typical pattern to have the rooms face south? What kinds of materials do you consider to be pleasant, what kind of tactile qualities do you like, should surfaces be soft or hard, matte or shiny? What things do you want to set down inside the entrance, and do those require a large or a small storage element? Do you prefer an open or a closed kitchen, with direct access from the outside? Do you like to cook and to entertain guests? How do you sleep, together or separated? Built-in cupboards or freestanding furniture? Music or a preference for silence? Which fabrics' smell do you like, and which ones can't you stand?

Apart from these wishes (which often lead to a program that's excessive) the cost should be calculated with precision. House A cannot be compared with house B. You cannot really trust the costs listed in magazines as they often compare apples with oranges, so comparing prices per square meter or square foot is not sufficient. Building costs can vary significantly depending on the region and, of course, based on the type of lot and the ground conditions. Even if this particular point is often neglected during the first meetings with the architect, because not everybody mentions this topic when starting out in a cooperative relationship, the available financial resources should be mentioned early on. It is also advisable to be flexible as to the space and area well into the last planning stage, since the exact costs are often only available just before the start of construction, and in many cases only after the start.

Thinking one step ahead

It would be a rather one-dimensional attitude to look only at the cost of building. After a few years, it is the expenses which make up the cost of a property. For this reason the investors in large projects, for instance, the client who is the state or government, choose a facility management plan. This includes the handling of maintenance and repairs. What is applicable on a large scale also applies to small projects. It makes a lot of sense to think about the long-term maintenance costs of the building when studying the first sketches. This is closely related to the durability of the materials. Experts estimate the lifetime of structural elements like steel, concrete walls, supports, and beams to be at least 100 years while technical installations or windows have to be renewed after 25 years. The area of home technology seems to have an enormous potential for development, which creates a situation where older equipment appears to be obsolete, both due to the aging process and deterioration as well as to the improvements in this sector.

This aspect immediately leads into the environmental and energy-related discussion which has become very prominent in publications of new buildings. You will see that the primary concern is not the energy needed for heating. It is the sum of all of the components that provides the assessment of a building's sustainability: Can the building be repaired easily? Does it need a lot of maintenance? What is the cost of replacing certain parts, and how durable are they?

So it is not enough to consider heating, facade insulation, or the design of windows. Although such optimized buildings save a lot of heating energy, the summer months show the reverse effect of the building heating up. From the environmental point of view, one would have to consider not only the conditions during the usage of the building but also the entire complex including the materials, how they are derived or manufactured, and even how they are ultimately disposed of. There are now several guidelines provided by different organizations and it is well worth it to look into this somewhat contentious topic.

Architecture is an art in time

Finally, here is some advice for the first steps: there are only a few architects who still draw by hand. Most companies have computers with programs which not only provide exact floor plans, but also sections and views. If you have the required skills you can visualize the future home. These images look almost like photos. The house is shown with a level of detail which really should not be achievable at this stage of pre-planning. There are

many details such as gaps, surfaces, and materials which have not yet been determined and which still require a lengthy planning process. Whether the house will be red or blue, have window frames of wood or metal, a facade consisting of plaster, brick, or wood siding — all of this can and must change. If you don't keep an open mind and you instead say: "This is how my house is going to look, and no other way," you don't do yourself or architecture a favor. Furthermore, that type of perspective is only a part of the total as viewed from an arbitrary angle, an angle which you might not even have in reality. Architecture is an art in time, and that is where it touches music. Only when walking through do you experience all of the rooms. And only when you have viewed everything and walked through all of the rooms and hallways and have seen the building up close and from a distance, only then is architecture comprehended. First you understand the design and layout. For this reason it is a good idea to understand the composition of the rooms early on using models. This is not about the beauty of the model. The models used by architects can always be altered or added to during the design stage. If their scale is large enough, even a layperson can check the future impact of the rooms and simulate a movement with your eye, which can be a lot of fun. After all, home architecture is different from buildings that are built considering only the technical and economic aspects: it is more than the mere building itself, so that we may enjoy our constructed environment and find ourselves in it.

Notes to the reader:

Some of the technical data headings that appear at the start of the house projects include "Baukosten gesamt Kostengruppe" information. For example:

Baukosten gesamt Kostengruppe
300 + 400 HOAI [Regulations on Architects' and Engineers' Fees]

This is a "group of costs" which has no exact equivalent in English, and is based on the national German industrial standards set by DIN, the German Institute for Standardization. The two numbers refer to the costs of building construction (300, in the above example) and technical equipment (400, in the above example), respectively.

"kWh/(m²a)" is kilowatt hours per square meter per year. For example:

Primary energy consumption
61 kWh/m²a
Heating energy consumption
51 kWh/m²a

Challenging lots, restrictions, and conditions

18

Building in the countryside

32

Hillside lots, complicated substructures — great views

72

Small homes, economical solutions

100

132

Introverted or one-way orientation

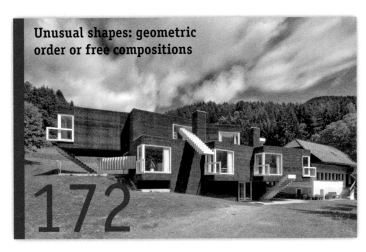

Unusual shapes: geometric order or free compositions

172

Conversions, attachments, fitting into grown environment

222

Separable floor plans for granny flats, guests, office space

238

Home in Niederkassel

Döring Dahmen Joeressen Architekten

Lot type	Type of construction	Building cost per m² of living area and effective area
along a pathway	Massive construction (steel concrete and sand-lime elements), composite heat insulation system with mineral plaster, felted; aluminum windows with sun screen blades; floor material first floor: dark-gray cement; top floor and staircase: oak parquet; floor heating system on all levels; ceiling-high wooden doors with steel frames painted white	1,747 Euro
Lot size		
521 m2		
Covered area		
235.72 m2		
Living area		
270 m2		
Effective area		
114.80 m2		
Gross volume		
1,568.57 m3		
Number of residents	**Baukosten gesamt**	
4	**Kostengruppe**	
Start of construction	**300 + 400 HOAI**	
February 2009	672,000 Euro, gross	
Completion		
December 2009		

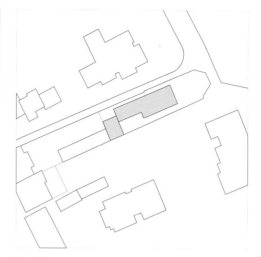

Site plan

On narrow ground

The lot used to be a garage yard and presented a tremendous challenge. It lies in the middle of the traditional village environment of Alt-Niederkassel on a pathway, almost 50 meters long but only 1 meter wide. This house for a family with two children reacts to this, with a long and narrow footprint. While the rear wall of the garage is standing on the lot boundary, the entrance, at about the center of the long side, is only two steps away from the sidewalk.

The interior corridor, lined with white built-in cupboards, allows one to experience the house in its entire length. A fireplace wall divides the open floor plan into living and kitchen/dining area. The air space above this section provides height and an unexpected spatial tension to this narrow home. At the opposite end is an office and a utility room as a transition to the garage. Since the width of the house can be less here, there is still room for a protected terrace.

The top floor with its rooms for children and parents follows a classical orientation. The hallway features built-in shelves and cupboards and the bathrooms are contiguous as a slim row. A large dressing room follows the main bedroom, with a view of the dining area.

The first floor features a dark gray cement finish while the top floor is fitted with white pigmented oak parquet. Floors and wall surfaces of the bathrooms are uniformly horizontally tiled. The white built-in cupboards are made from Corian and MDF boards.

The exterior materials are limited to gravel and lawn surfaces; terraces are fitted with large-format concrete slabs. The gray tone matches the profiles of the aluminum windows which contrast with the otherwise entirely white building. The old brick wall toward the sidewalk makes for a nice contrast, ending at the mailbox. A concrete slab at the southern side blocks the view to a neighboring school.

The projecting roof marks the entrance, which lies two steps back from the sidewalk.

The dimensions of the narrow and long lot have been successfully transferred to the home's organization.

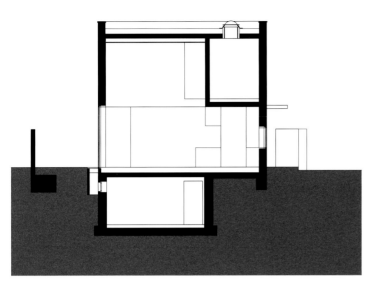

Section   scale 1:200

The depth in front of the office and the utility room can be less, which provides space for a roofed terrace.

The eating and dining area at the end of the house has its own terrace. The view is into the two-story kitchen.

The dining area is two floors in height. If you want to peek inside a pot on the stove, you can do it from the narrow window of the dressing room above.

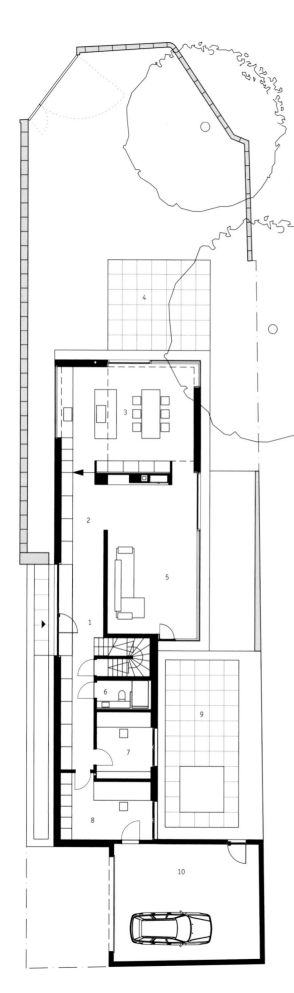

First floor   scale 1:200

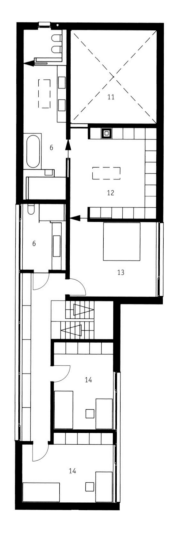

Second floor   scale 1:200

1   entry
2   wardrobe
3   cooking/eating
4   terrace
5   living
6   bathroom
7   office
8   technology/utility room
9   outdoor seat
10 garage
11 air space
12 dressing room
13 parents
14 child

Home in Stuttgart

Bottega + Ehrhardt Architekten

Lot type	Type of construction	Heating energy
freestanding	basement: precast concrete	consumption
Lot size	components; floors: wood;	51 kWh/m²a
317 m²	outer walls: plywood with	
Covered area	5 crosswise layers with	
79 m²	insulating material and	
Living area	cellulose filling	
198 m²	**Materials**	
Effective area	facade: Eternit; ceilings:	
63 m²	solid wood peg ceilings,	
Gross volume	painted white; interior	
965 m³	walls: wood frame walls,	
Number of residents	Fermacell planking, paint-	
5	ed white; floors: parquet in	
Start of construction	living area, white oak	
September 2010	**Primary energy**	
Completion	**consumption**	
July 2011	61 kWh/m²a	

Site plan

An alternative draft

Some lots and floor plans require that the architects pursue a utilization of space as if it were a forensic case. In this instance it was a trapezoid lot with its neighbors pressing in from all sides and which only allowed for a small floor plan. Only two full floors were permitted, something which was able to be circumvented by slightly digging in the first floor to get an additional level. The entrance as well could be reinterpreted. It lies protected under an outcrop as a protruding alcove. A bend of the lot boundary was utilized for a roof terrace recess.

The first floor features a ceiling height of 2.90 meters and leads into the street-side kitchen and from there to the living area with a fireplace. Take three steps down and you get to the curve in the floor plan, where the wardrobe pedestal indicates the entrance into the private quarters. The angular outer wall is completely glazed toward the garden with large sliding doors, and the dining room receives light from the west.

A staircase at the closed outer wall leads upwards where the home opens with one panoramic window toward the south. The rearmost of the three children's rooms can be divided with a sliding door, and belongs to the daughter who studies out of town; this allows for the window front toward the garden to largely remain unobstructed. Behind the bathroom, lighted by a satinized window glazing, the corridor opens into a play area by cleverly incorporating the facade areas; however, room and bathroom do not feature an inconvenient "anthroposophical" corner.

This pattern continues under the roof, with the distinction that the deeper bathroom receives additional light from the facade. A retreat for reading and working is formed in front of the roof terrace behind the parents' bedroom.

The building consists of crossed solid wood elements and only the area of the large window panes shows a few round steel supports. It stands on a concrete basement. Cellulose has been fitted for insulation and a ventilated, riveted, and dark-grey Eternit siding forms the outer skin.

The adverse conditions of the lot resulted in an extraordinary home.

The entrance is below an alcove-like protrusion; the glazed atelier provides light for the staircase and the deep corridors.

The interior surprises with exciting rooms; the bathroom on the second floor receives diffuse light via a satinized pane.

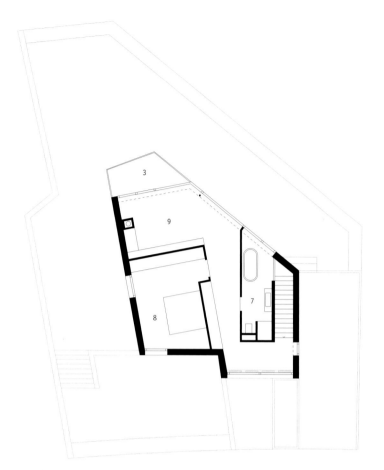

Third floor   scale 1:200

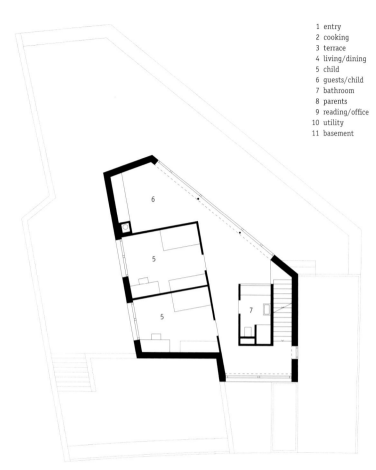

Second floor   scale 1:200

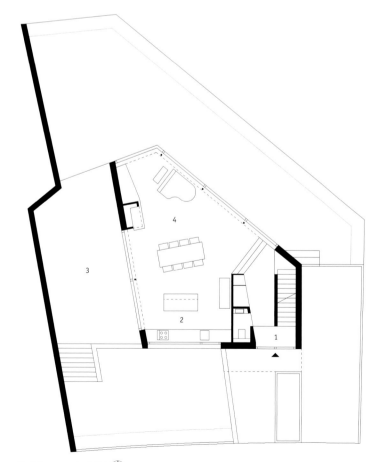

First floor   scale 1:200

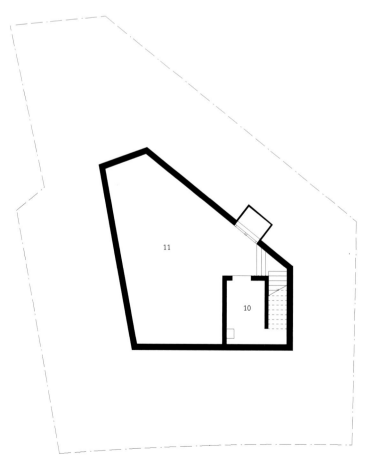

Basement   scale 1:200

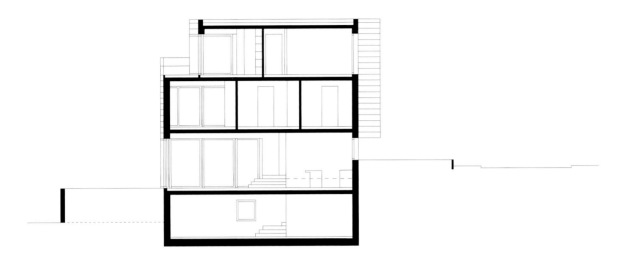

Section   scale 1:200

The living and dining area lies a
few steps lower, and therefore
features a generous height.

Lot size
1,145 m²
Covered area
398 m² plus pool of 64 m²
Living area
306 m² plus terrace of
110m² plus pool of 64 m²
Effective area
373 m² without terrace
and pool
Gross volume
1,900 m³
Number of residents
4
Start of construction
2009
Completion
2010

Type of construction and materials
massive construction with exterior bearing structure; interior insulation with drywall facing the rooms; walls and railing elements of colored concrete, large-format shuttering; ceilings and roof of steel concrete, insulated roof, seamless suspended ceiling partially with acoustic treatment; roof with liquid plastic sealing on concrete; aluminum sliding windows; floors of basement: colored granolithic concrete; floors

of first floor: cherry wood floor boards
Primary energy consumption
102,50 kWh/m²a
Heating energy consumption
81 kWh/m²a

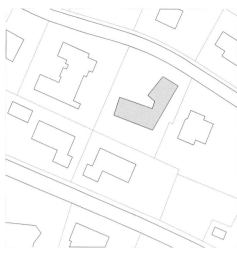

Site plan

A strong back

A large home that had to find support on a difficult moraine slope, had to limit its height due to a higher observation platform, and even had to get along with its orientation — however, this was not an emergency solution, but rather a majestic setting over Lake Zurich.

The only unusual thing is perhaps the access via the garage. However, due to the location, it will be rather uncommon for anyone to take the steep steps with a bike or even on foot; they'll use the car instead. The cars are parked under the top floor protruding toward the street on the northern side, and the same level features the windowless auxiliary rooms. A second access for guests is located next to the kitchen. Toward the valley is a special room used for hobbies and as a library. The center is occupied by a shelf block for books, made by a carpenter, and a flat screen TV monitor.

The floor over it contains the living and sleeping quarters around a piazza with a great view, which is lined by a solid concrete balustrade reminiscent of the 1960s. Where the two building wings meet, the cobblestone seating place runs toward a Zen garden elevated by a step containing gravel and bonsai trees. The two children's rooms face north, protected from the street by the private exterior room, accompanied by bathrooms and dressing rooms at the back or the slope. The climax is definitely the living area, changing between introverted interior view and a wide and sweeping view which is reached by the afternoon sun reflected by the lake. Toward the east, just behind the kitchen block, all you find is one obligatory window — because the owners were expressly not interested in the morning light.

All of the home's openings are oriented toward the lake. The pool provides a little anticipation.

The entrance is located below the eye-catching protrusion for the garage.

The living and bedroom area on the top floor folds around an additional terrace deck, out of sight, which runs toward a Zen garden.

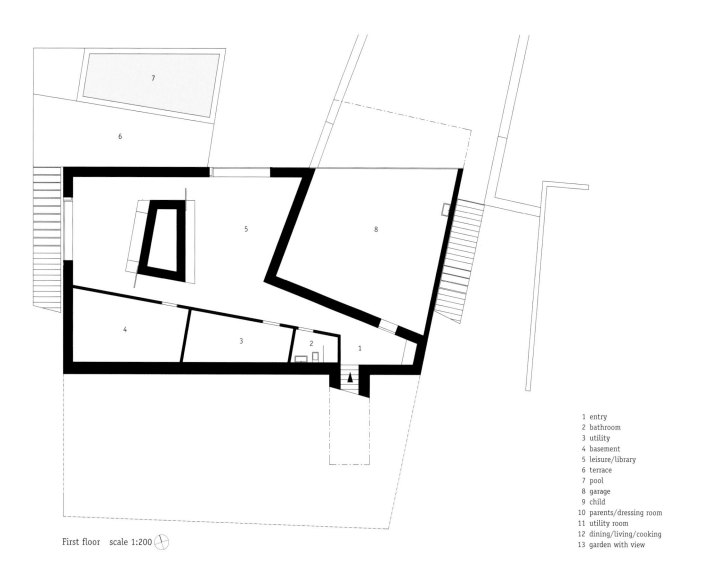

First floor   scale 1:200

1 entry
2 bathroom
3 utility
4 basement
5 leisure/library
6 terrace
7 pool
8 garage
9 child
10 parents/dressing room
11 utility room
12 dining/living/cooking
13 garden with view

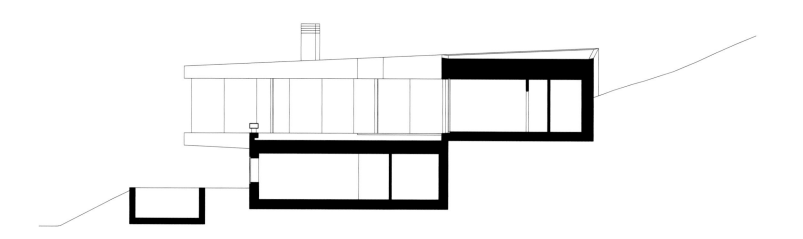

Section   scale 1:200

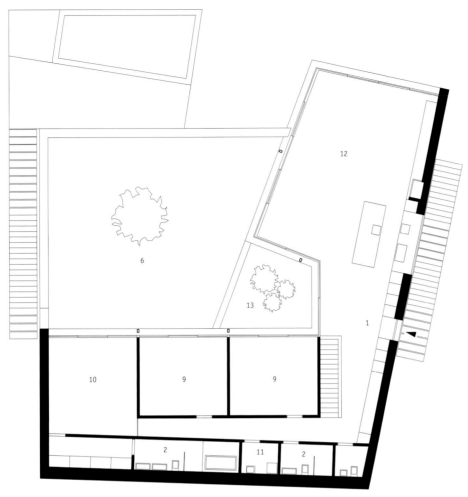

Top floor   scale 1:200

With such an attractive view the kitchen should not be a shuttered galley. Like an island it stands in the center of the room and receives additional daylight via a lateral band of windows.

Home in Aalen
Liebel Architekten

Lot type	**Type of construction**
Hang	steel concrete, massive
Lot size	construction
1,034 m²	**Materials**
Covered area	plastered facade, wood
160.5 m²	facade (garage and sauna),
Living area	interior plaster, wooden
201 m²	floors
Effective area	**Primary energy con-**
93 m²	**sumption**
Gross volume	58,9 kWh/m²a
1,116 m³	**Heating energy**
Number of residents	**consumption**
4	46,2 kWh/m²a
Start of construction	
February 2009	
Completion	
April 2010	

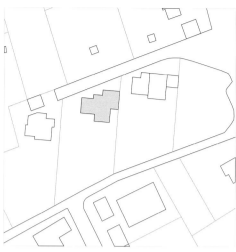

Site plan

Scouting game

A home that does not hide its structure from the outside. The garden view, elaborately glazed toward the south, lays out the interior structure and allows one to recognize all of its qualities. The home is somewhat secretive toward the street, where one single slit of glass opens up the facade while the entrance door is protected by the garage wall below the protruding top floor. Windows are placed only whenever the view is worthwhile, toward the green escarpment; rather than evenly-spaced all-around openings, the glass walls and ceilings meet to form solid cubes.

The unusual half floor offset follows the topography. A dip on the lot on a steep north-facing slope which was regarded as difficult to build on was absorbed by the architecture, and resulted in an attractive room which naturally connects to the garden. These different levels offer different ways of resting without clearly defined boundaries. The split-level solution provides a playful transition between the functional areas without additional corridors.

The entrance features a wardrobe element designed by the architects which marks the boundary with the living area. First you reach the kitchen and dining area, which should be the central location for a home that values

cooking and entertaining guests. The steps next to the staircase, which continue on the terrace, also invite the guests to sit down casually. The lower-lying living area leads to the basement and to an office facing the garden, with the upper edge of the desk in line with the height of the lawn: a rather special atmosphere which provides inspiration and distraction.

Going upstairs, the staircase from the entrance level leads first into the main bedroom with a dressing room en suite, then the stairs continue toward the other side (above the guest lavatory) which results in a flat ceiling in the living room and a clever spatial division at the very top. This area is the kingdom of the kids with a wide corridor for play, well laid-out rooms, and a common terrace, as well as the family bathroom. The garden is always within view.

A depression and a north-facing slope led to a tiered floor plan layout which is visible on the facade.

The result is not an emergency solution but rather, well-structured rooms at different levels.

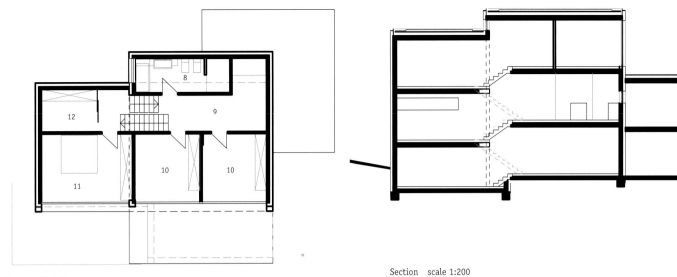

Section   scale 1:200

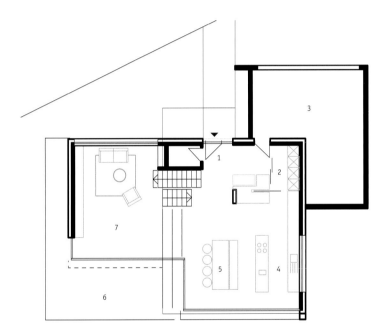

Top floor   scale 1:200

First floor   scale 1:200

1   entry
2   pantry
3   garage
4   cooking
5   dining
6   terrace
7   living
8   bathroom
9   hallway for play

10   child
11   parents
12   dressing room
13   utility room
14   storage
15   office
16   basement
17   technical

The seating steps between the
dining and living areas continue
toward the terrace.

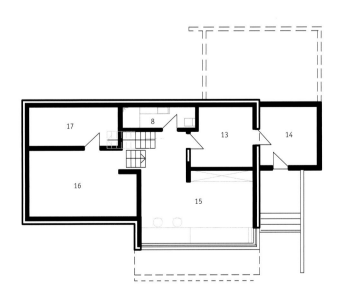

Basement   scale 1:200

Home in Niederpöcking
Muck Petzet Architekten

Lot type	**Type of construction**
freestanding	massive construction
Lot size	**Materials**
1,357 m²	brickwork, wood
Covered area	**Baukosten gesamt**
166 m²	**Kostengruppe**
Living area	**300 + 400 HOAI**
273 m²	454,000 Euro, gross
Effective area	**Building cost per m² of living**
47 m²	**area and effective area**[a]
Gross volume	effective area 1,420 Euro;
1,044 m³	living area 1,663 Euro
Number of residents	**Primary energy**
3	**consumption**
Start of construction	58.3 kWh/m²a
May 2009	**Heating energy**
Completion	**consumption**
May 2011	47.3 kWh/m²a

Site plan

Nothing beats Denmark

A black house is not exactly common when you build in Upper Bavaria. In this case the client is from Denmark, so the design can be read as a memory of the Scandinavian homeland.

The heterogenous building in the area did not provide an opportunity for connection. So the house is regarded as part of the garden, and the black color of the beech tree trunks, the shadows of the neighboring forest, the dark earth, and the dark brown of the facade match each other. Placed on the lot as much toward the north as possible, it forms an angle which opens toward the garden. The relationship of the rooms and the building to the exterior or determines its shape. The garden terrace with its protruding roof and a freestanding loggia is connected to a glass panel wall. At the entrance side, the roof frees itself from the alignments of the folded building shape and forms a high projecting roof. The open garage is incorporated into the house with a direct lateral access. A terrace lies on top of it, screened from the street by a wall which slopes down to the height of the balustrade.

The facades are different from each other and optimized with respect to the corresponding orientation. The outer walls are well insulated with mineral fibers and plastered on their northern and western sides, while wood is used for cladding the southern and eastern areas. The vertical chair rails of the wooden facades are pulled over the top-floor windows as a balustrade.

The first floor is defined by flowing transitions between the entrance hall, kitchen/dining areas, and the slightly lower living room. A piece of furniture next to the stairs which can be utilized from both sides divides the functions. The other side of the house leads to a separate guest room. A staircase connects the hall with the top floor where the bedrooms are located, along with an open office area which can later be divided into additional rooms. The ceiling-high windows facing the garden can be opened 180°. This way the hallway can be turned into a loggia during summer, and the white ceiling beams remain visible and emphasize the particular characteristics of the room. The lower floor also contains a large hobby room and there is space for a future sauna.

The first floor consists entirely of black slate slabs, the upper floor features larch floor boards.

The home complies with KfW-70 regulations (energy efficiency standards for houses in Germany); heating is done via air heat pumps and a fireplace.

The view from the street makes the home appear to be unusual, solitary, and hermetic.

The dark wooden facade explains itself toward the garden side: it integrates harmoniously with nature, trees, the earth, and the shaded forest.

The vertical chair rail of
the facade blends into the
balustrade of the balcony.

Second floor   scale 1:200

First floor   scale 1:200

1   entry
2   cooking
3   dining
4   living
5   terrace
6   garage
7   guest
8   wardrobe
9   bathroom
10 child
11 dressing room
12 parents
13 office
14 sauna
15 technical
16 leisure/guests

Basement   scale 1:200

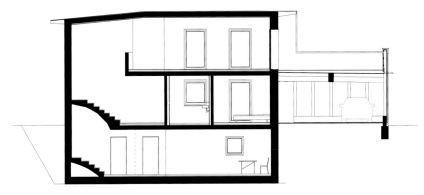

Section   scale 1:200

The shape of the interior staircase inside of the angular edge of the building makes for a soft transition between the floors.

The staircase leads into an open office area which can later be divided into additional rooms.

The high, large windows connect the living area with the garden.

Two single-family homes in Bochum
Dreibund Architekten

Lot type
freestanding
Lot size
645 m² each
Covered area
1a: 133 m² 1b: 141 m²
Effective area
1a: 165 m² 1b: 178 m²
Gross volume
673 m³ each
Start of construction
February 2009
Completion
December 2009
Type of construction
floor slab: thermal floor
slab (geothermal); wall:
vertical coring bricks,

plastered; wooden windows
(double and triple glazing);
ceiling: solid concrete
ceiling; utilities: hot water
supply system, hot water
storage, geothermal system,
solar system, floor heating
Materials
Glass, insulating bricks,
fine mineral plaster, wood
and stone floors
**Baukosten gesamt
Kostengruppe
300 + 400 HOAI**
640,000 Euro gross for
both houses, without lot

**Primary energy
consumption**
1a: 27 kWh/m²a;
1b: 57.5 kWh/m²a
**Heating energy
consumption**
1a: 25.7 kWh/m²a;
1b: 59.7 kWh/m²a

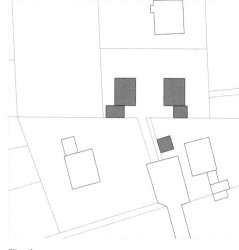

Site plan

Mixed double

These two low-energy homes stand next to each other, almost identical. The owner of one of them had contacted the architects because he had seen earlier designs of the firm and had immediately identified with them. The architects tend toward open floor plans; kitchen, dining, and living blend into each other, private quarters are upstairs, and the homes look rather reserved from the street — that concept seemed feasible here as well.

The client, a young professor at Ruhr University at Bochum, had already bought the undeveloped and totally overgrown lot some time earlier. The building regulations allowed for two homes on the park-like property. Even though a second client-owner was found soon, he at first had entirely contrarian ideas as to living style and building. Rather surprisingly it became apparent that the existing concept could be customized for both families.

At first sight the differences between the floor plans are not apparent, however, they turned out to become two distinctively different homes. Due to the absence of dividing fences the result is a generous common estate. The homes do not have basements and one of them utilizes the garage as a storage space. In addition the architects had to fit storage spaces and technical infrastructure (heat pump, ventilation system and such) in an inconspicuous way.

Both homes feature a front patio at their entrances which features a spatial barrier toward the living area. One of the houses has an office to the right of the entrance, and the other one fits the main bedroom in almost the same area. The space next to the staircase is used as a utility room in one case, while the other house interprets it as a library alcove. Both solutions retained the twofold access around this functional block.

The top floors give away their distinct divisions, just barely, behind their bands of windows. One house features three children's rooms, a main bedroom with dressing room, and two bathrooms, as well as a piano next to the gallery; the other fits two children's rooms, divided into bedroom and playroom, with a bathroom.

The architecture of both homes is characterized by a solid design. High-insulation brick, fine mineral plaster, wooden windows with covered sun deflectors, and floors of solid wood or natural stone are used. The architects did not get involved with thermoskin, however.

Without dividing fences, a large
common area results for both
homes, and you know who is
looking into your place.

A notch in the ceiling allowed for a gallery on the top floor, and provides a communicative generosity which is not possible for the apartment.

Just as in the "find the differences between these two pictures" game, you can locate the differences between the two houses. However, the differences of the facade follow a common concept.

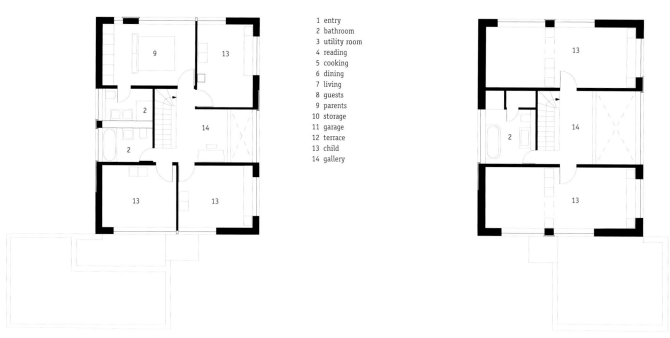

1 entry
2 bathroom
3 utility room
4 reading
5 cooking
6 dining
7 living
8 guests
9 parents
10 storage
11 garage
12 terrace
13 child
14 gallery

Second floor   scale 1:200

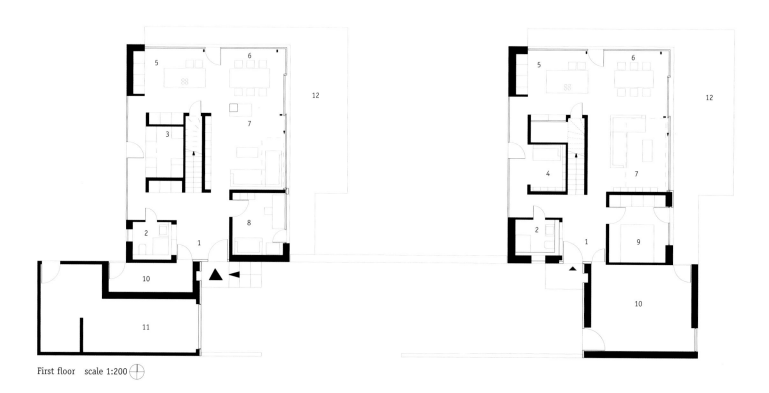

First floor   scale 1:200

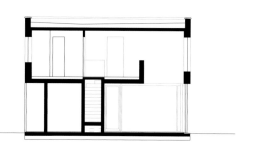

Section   scale 1:200

The left house has a book shelf lining the staircase and the fireplace.

The concept of the almost identical floor plans could be continued with small alterations to react to additional designs.

Home in Aschau

Gassner & Zarecky Architekten und Ingenieure

Lot type	**Completion**	**Primary energy**
meadow	December 2008, outdoor	**consumption**
Lot size	installation September 2009	41.73 kWh/m²a
1,134 m²	**Type of construction**	**Heating energy**
Covered area	timber frame construction,	**consumption**
main building 120 m²;	low energy standard, no	42.47 kWh/m²a
auxiliary building 78 m²	basement, groundwater	
Living area	heat pump, floor heating	
180 m²	system, larch wood siding,	
Effective area	southern sun screen with	
58 m²	doubled facade that can	
Gross volume	be retracted	
main building 1,060 m³;	**Building cost per m² of**	
auxiliary building 278 m³	**living area and effective**	
Number of residents	**area**	
4	1,900 Euro	
Start of construction		
November 2007		

Site plan

The inkling of regionality

In Upper Bavaria it is often rather difficult to build a home which does not exude the smell (figuratively!) of a stable. In this project, a regionally-styled and modern architecture makes a convincing case — without fake folklore, and also lacking any avant-garde pretension. Building density, proportions, and design constraints were laid out in the construction plan, but the regulations allowed for a flexible positioning of the building on the lot. The design did convince the community, which awarded it with its facade award in 2009.

A porch with a garage, workshop, and additional carport is situated in front of the house, and leads to the private area via a roofed portal. The atrium between the buildings forms a room for introverted family life, and the wooden floor terrace is further delimited by a pool and a storage box with a southern orientation. Hence the entrance does not lead from this roofed terrace, but some distance away at the northern narrow side of the house. This obvious structure continues on the inside.

The low-energy home, made from wood, lies inside of the flood zone of the Prien River, and has no basement, so there is an utility room on the first floor (for three groundwater heat pumps) and a large storage room; they also fulfill the function of structuring the space within its otherwise open floor plan layout. The living area is one step lower, and there is a connection for a wood stove. The windows are located so that you can see the town's church, the chain of hills to the west, and the Kamp rock wall as a backdrop. A second terrace facing east is convenient for having breakfast with the morning sun.

The top floor contains the bedrooms for parents and children as well as another narrow office corner and an additional relaxation room toward the rear.

Even without any folklore-derived ornaments the wooden home nevertheless shows sympathy for the traditional building style of the region.

The dining space with its terrace is screened from the street by a small workshop.

Due to the wide balustrade and the
wooden ceiling, the top corridor
gets a gallery-like upgrade.

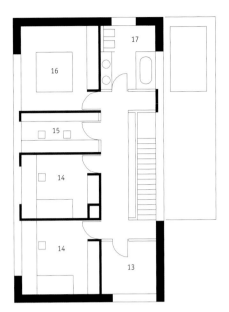

Top floor   scale 1:200

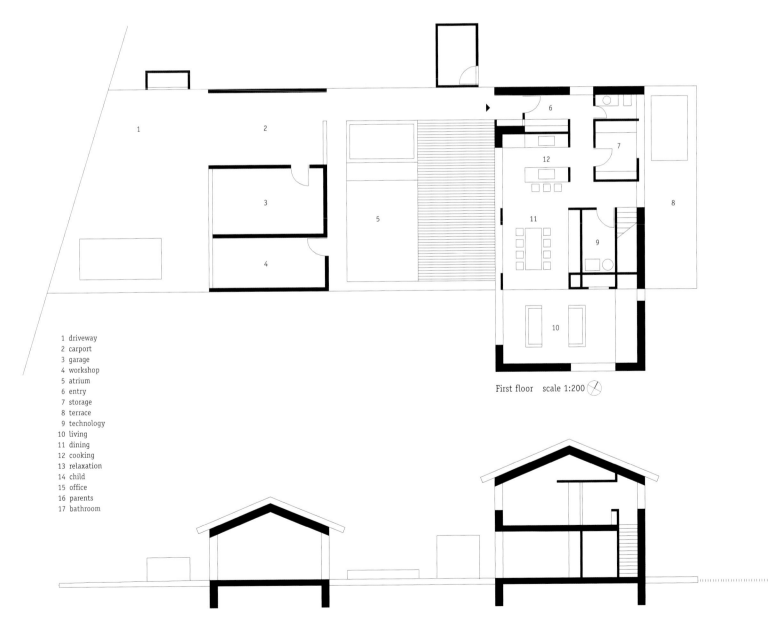

1 driveway
2 carport
3 garage
4 workshop
5 atrium
6 entry
7 storage
8 terrace
9 technology
10 living
11 dining
12 cooking
13 relaxation
14 child
15 office
16 parents
17 bathroom

First floor   scale 1:200

Section   scale 1:200

Home in Ennetmoos (Switzerland)

KEN Architekten

Lot type	**Type of construction and materials**	glass windows; outer surfaces with rocks from the excavation
slope		
Lot size	walls in the ground, floor, ceilings, roof: concrete;	**Heating energy consumption**
990 m²	outer and structural walls:	38 kWh/m²a
Covered area	brick; ventilated facade:	
130 m²	mineral insulation, air	
Living area	column, coarse spruce	
230 m²	tongue-and-groove siding;	
Effective area	siding treated with oil	
275 m²	varnish with metal pig-	
Gross volume	ment; ventilated roof; roof	
1.096 m³	covering: folded copper	
Number of residents	sheet; white interior	
4	plaster applied with brush;	
Start of construction	floors: oiled red oak par-	
September 2006	quet; bathrooms: flamed	
Completion	granite; wooden stepped	
May 2007		

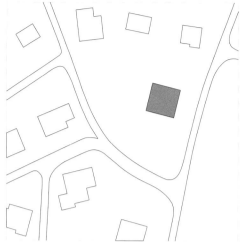

Site plan

Abstract approximation

The design of this house at the foothills of the Alps is based on the rocky ground of the location and the rural architecture of the region. The solid masonry building is clad with coarse spruce panels, and somehow reminds one of the stables in this area with their brickwork and board walls.

However, the look of the facade, which appears as two shells that don't quite fit placed over each other, has another context: the staggered pile of the wooden siding is supposed to look like the rocks around where the house has been anchored. In order to achieve this, the boards have been treated with special metal pigments mixed with linseed oil and fish scales in order to look like colored stone. In direct sunlight and from afar, the object looks like the rocks sticking out from the pasture; as one gets nearer, and with diffuse light, one recognizes the real material, and the interpretation of the traditional building style becomes primary.

While the exterior features only the surface relief of the wood's motif, the interior transposes it spatially. The rocks with their ridges, nooks, and crannies are integrated orthogonally into the functionality of a household for four people. The square layout features a central core consisting of staircase, guest lavatory, storage room, and kitchen counter; the living functions spread around it. The top floor contains three bedrooms for parents and children. Next to them is a common bathroom.

Two air spaces reaching from the first floor up to below the roof combine with the stairwell to form a Z-shaped break. This results in a hall-like opening at the entrance and above the living room, and provides a communicative zoning to the compact interior, all the more so in that the air spaces are not dark shafts but they integrate the real rocky landscape into the dialog using opposite facing windows. The ventilated facade forms deep embrasures toward the exterior and interior which emphasize the cave-like character of the home. A guest room and study are located on the lower floor, opposite the basement which reaches into the hillside.

The staggered wood siding over the solid structure references the agricultural buildings of the region.

The windows of varying height frame the view of the landscape.

The color treatment of the spruce boards is intended to appear similar to the rocks jutting out of the meadows.

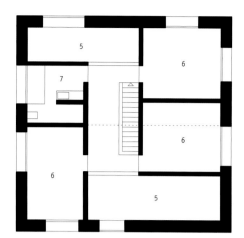

Top floor   scale 1:200

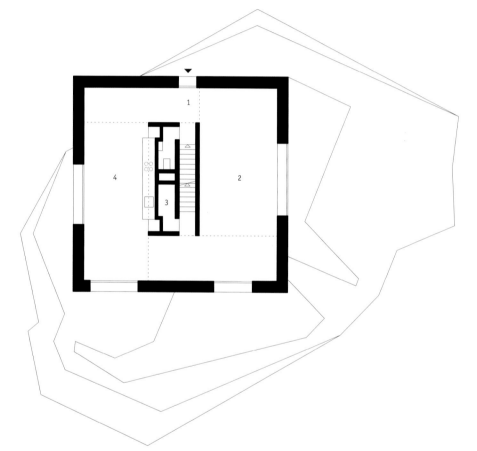

1 entry
2 living
3 storage
4 cooking/dining
5 air space
6 sleeping
7 bathroom
8 guests
9 office
10 basement
11 technical

First floor   scale 1:200

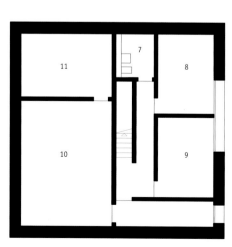

Basement   scale 1:200

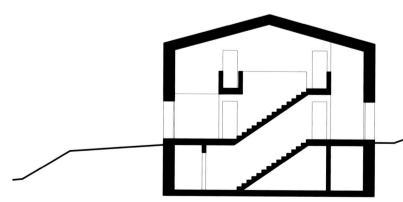

Section   scale 1:200

The first floor features a central core consisting of staircase, guest lavatory, storage room, and a kitchen counter, which can be walked around from all sides.

The special component is the experience of the dimensions. The two floors are connected in a hall-like fashion via the entrance and the living room.

Villa at Lake Zug (Switzerland)

Graber & Steiger Architekten

Lot type	Type of construction and
park-like lot with lakefront	**materials**
Lot size	pillar foundation; base-
2,475 m²	ment (in groundwater
Covered area	area): steel concrete; first
310 m²	floor and upper floor: steel
Living area	concrete shell construction
330 m²	and insulated brick; facade
Effective area	siding with Wittmund
450 m² (including garage,	clinker; wood and metal
basement floor)	windows, outside with
Gross volume	anodized aluminum; roof
1.755 m³	greenery; interior rooms:
Number of residents	painted white plaster;
4	floors: smoked oak
Start of construction	
2008	
Completion	
2009	

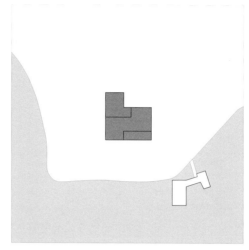

Site plan

Seaside rendezvous

The large park-like property located directly on Lake Zug, which offers a breathtaking view of the the mountains and the city, required a sensitive continuation of the grown surroundings. The architects chose Wittmund peat-baked bricks for the facade of the home which is repositioned from the street. These baked bricks with their lively changing colors provide a connection with the landscape during all of the seasons and light conditions, and its scale and haptic style causes the two-floor building with its strong structuring to blend with the location. In addition the robust and maintenance-free material of the two-layer exterior walls and the alternative energy carriers provide a contribution to sustainability.

This thinking in terms of life cycles includes a later use of the house. Presently, four residents share the 330 square meters of living area (in addition to the 450 square meters of effective area). Part of the layout consists of an office area with two rooms and a library, which are connected via their own staircase. This eastern section of the home can easily be partitioned off, containing bathrooms and an additional room, and be accessed via a separate entrance.

For now, the family enjoys the generous space of the villa which communicates with the landscape thanks to its spacious roof terraces, open-air lounges, recesses, and protrusions. The interior organization continues the interaction between areas and rooms. Ceiling-high wall elements allow a different definition of the interior if desired, from a flowing continuum to an intimate chamber, creating a comfortable atmosphere.

The house is accessed from the north within a protective niche next to the garage. Once inside, you are greeted by a light space behind the staircase which opens upwards into a sculptural gallery. The block of the guest lavatory separates the kitchen on the open level, and a fireplace column seems to mark the boundary to the dining area. The living area next to the office with its large glass fronts faces south. The level above it forms a cluster of parents', children's, and guest bedrooms with their respective bathrooms, cupboards, and dressing niches, as well as the light space. The surrounding gallery corridors are more than traffic lanes; instead they are are visual and motion spaces which lead to the terrace, as a courtesy.

The white neutrality of the flowing interior provides a sensitivity to nature, changing with the seasons.

Roof terraces, open-air lounges, and carefully arranged openings put the qualities of the location into the spotlight.

Imported from the north: the lively changing look of the Wittmund peat-baked brickwork provides a harmonious proximity to the landscape under any light conditions.

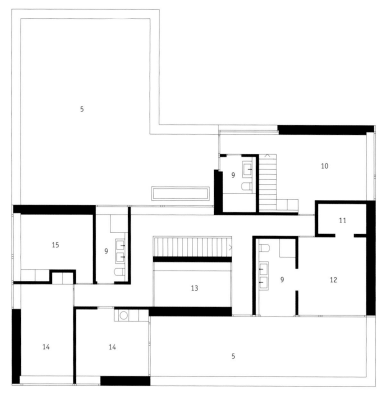

Top floor   scale 1:200

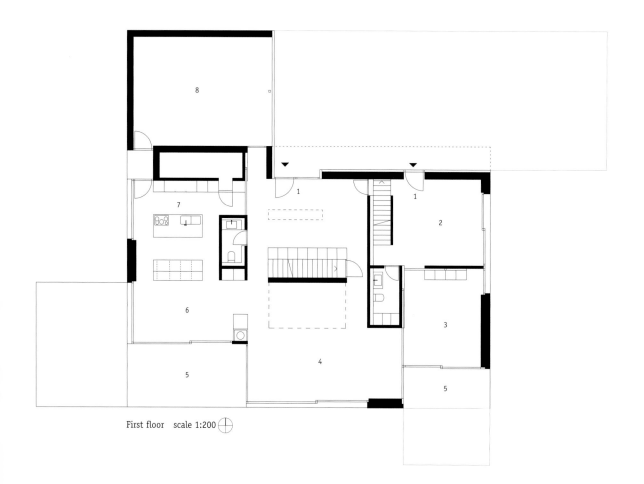

First floor   scale 1:200

1 entry
2 office
3 library
4 living
5 terrace
6 dining
7 cooking
8 garage
9 bathroom
10 room
11 dressing room
12 bedroom
13 air space
14 child
15 guests

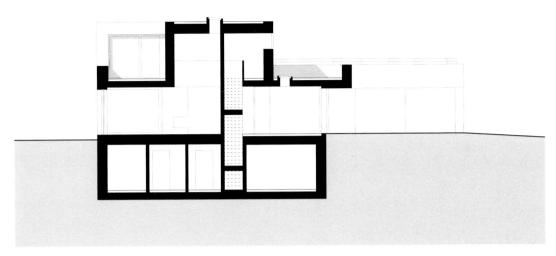

Section   scale 1:200

White walls and floors of dark
smoked oak allow spaces to feature
pieces of art.

The two-story atrium is the meeting
point of all the pathways and
functions. The floor plan with two
staircases has been prepared so that
one section of the house can be
divided off easily.

Lot type	Type of construction, materials	Primary energy consumption
rural	steel concrete foundation,	121 kWh/m²a
Lot size	wood frame construction,	**Heating energy**
85,905 m²	corrugated, gray; interior	**consumption**
Covered area	walls: steel concrete and	28 kWh/m²a
285 m²	bricks; prefabricated MDF	
Living area	boards, cement screed;	
137 m²	walls treated with beeswax	
Effective area	**Total construction cost**	
149 m²	630,000 CHF	
Gross volume	**Construction cost**	
605 m³	**living area**	
Number of residents	4,600 CHF	
2	**Construction cost**	
Start of construction	**effective area**	
July 2009	4,230 CHF	
Completion		
May 2010		

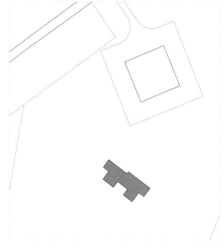

Site plan

Over level

The essence of the house consists of its building material and its facade of corrugated fiber cement, and nevertheless it appears to be neither an industrial structure nor a collection of materials. Quite the contrary. With its position over the surrounding meadows it reminds one of the lightness of pavilions as they became popular during the 1950s — but with contemporary precision. Everything happens on this platform: there is the concrete foundation which seems to want to take as little area as possible from the densely-vegetated landscape, as it supports the single-level home with a stable close to it which is also clad with corrugated Eternit boards.

You can walk all the way around the house on the elevated platform, if you dare to climb up the staircase which is precariously approaching it without handrails. From this point the recessed access under the protruding flat roof leads to the entrance door at about the center. The other side also features recesses for three protected terraces.

The gray corrugated facade boards are guided inwards while the support walls of concrete are clad with the boards. The predilection for the charm of untreated material continues with the cement screed treated with linseed oil, while the drywall surfaces were treated with beeswax. Additional built-in furniture consists of lacquered MDF boards, and the kitchen features stainless steel. The architects utilized very little color and instead relied on the views over the natural landscape toward the southwest and the southeast, provided by the generously-glazed outer walls.

The floor plan is well-organized and foresees the possibility of dividing to create a second children's room, or utilizing the guest areas as a granny flat for the parents sometime in the future. For this reason the home level has been laid out in two separate compartments, one for bedrooms with bathroom, and the other for guests and utilities. The open living area meanders in front of these functional blocks with its center terrace creating a bright break between the kitchen/dining and the living areas.

A living island inside of the cornfield. Like an aircraft carrier, the home rests above the wavy vegetation.

The industrial and mostly gray building materials clearly contrast with nature.

1 entry
2 bathroom
3 bedroom
4 storage
5 terrace
6 cooking/
   dining
7 living
8 technical
9 guests

First floor   scale 1:200 ⊗

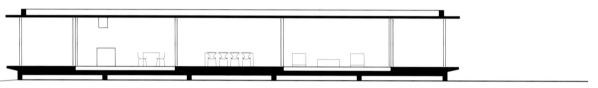

Section   scale 1:200

The floor plan is divided into functional zones and opens toward terraces on all sides. These stages allow you to keep the landscape in view at all times.

Living as raw material: the stark materials continue into the interior. The residents make themselves comfortable, spontaneously and unassumingly.

Villa in Hamburg
Lohmann Architekten

Lot type freestanding **Lot size** approx. 2,200 m² **Covered area** 522.42 m² **Living area** 687.13 m² **Effective area** 189.84 m² **Gross volume** 4035.03 m³ **Number of residents** 3 **Start of construction** 2008 **Completion** spring of 2009	**Type of construction** massive construction; basement: waterproof concrete; walls: sand-lime brickwork; roof: lattice girder floors with concrete **Materials** facade: ETICS and steel/ aluminum windows; ex- posed concrete; roof clad- ding: flat roof; roof terraces with wood floor covering; building services: dehumid- ification and ventilation system with heat recovery for pool, living area venti- lation with heat recovery, gas condensing boiler	heating system, floor heating, rainwater recovery, exclusive lighting concept **Baukosten gesamt** **Kostengruppe** **300 + 400 HOAI** 1,160,000 Euro **Building cost per m²** **living area and effective** **area** 1,330 Euro **Primary energy** **consumption** 64 kWh/m²a

Site plan

Landscape living

White and straightforward villas are known to the general public as "Bauhaus style." But these aesthetic parameters developed by Gropius and his colleagues can be applied widely because of the fact that concrete has become harder, machine-applied plaster has become smoother, and the window profiles have become slimmer or even unnecessary due to glued glass panes. The interplay between the building and its openings can now be taken advantage of without any risk. Of course the technical installations are hidden without neglecting the building physics — something one could only dream of during the 1920s. In this case a generous villa was created from the white cubes (lime-sand masonry with insulation system) that are reminiscent of Bauhaus.

The lot lies in the second row and a small brook marks its eastern boundary. The entrance is made up of an exposed concrete wall with a gate, and marks the limit between public and private spaces. Exterior buildings and the structure of the home are intentionally matched. The water pool and cobblestone anticipate the dominating east-west orientation and terminate with the interior pool which has the same width as the outer basin. The entrance is flanked by an exposed concrete wall (with the family's coat of arms) and leads to the interior, to a central axis, which is followed by the foyer, kitchen counter, and dining area. A rather unusual frameless glass wall separates the swimming pool at its continuation. Additional light enters via two large skylights over the foyer and the dining table.

The western side comprises auxiliary rooms, pantry, and a guest room within a more narrow functional area. Also, a more private staircase leads to the upper bedrooms, while a billiard/pool room, a lowered living space illuminated from two sides, and a garden loggia surround the building toward the east.

This motif of stacked cubes continues on the top floor. Access is provided via a generous wardrobe as well as a more official platform stairway. Here we find an au-pair apartment, and an additional office opposite it with bathrooms and dressing rooms. Both of the children's rooms meet symmetrically at the center of the house and are placed on the building so that two gaps illuminate the first floor. The main bedroom with dressing room and main bathroom takes up the entire width of the house toward the north.

White plaster inside as well as outside, exposed concrete, and large anthracite-colored steel and aluminum windows constitute the neutral background for a sterling living ambience.

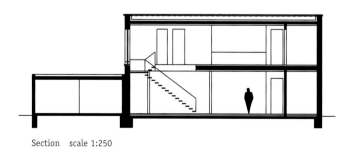

Section   scale 1:250

A large home on narrow ground, its structured building continuously incorporates open spaces.

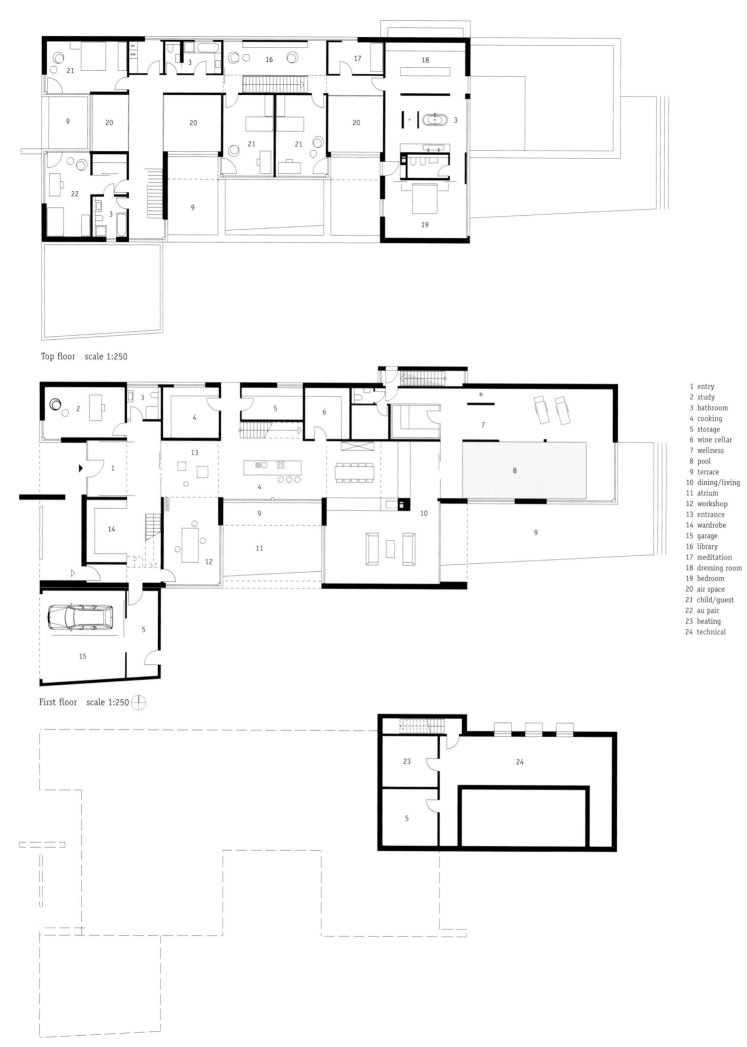

Top floor   scale 1:250

First floor   scale 1:250

Basement   scale 1:250

1 entry
2 study
3 bathroom
4 cooking
5 storage
6 wine cellar
7 wellness
8 pool
9 terrace
10 dining/living
11 atrium
12 workshop
13 entrance
14 wardrobe
15 garage
16 library
17 meditation
18 dressing room
19 bedroom
20 air space
21 child/guest
22 au pair
23 heating
24 technical

The open floor plan, enhanced and structured by the steps and skylights, allows for plenty of space to host guests.

The surprise of the seamless solution to fit the pool area to the dining area: they're separated by only a glass pane.

Home in the Puster Valley (Italy)

Bergmeisterwolf Architekten

Lot type slope	**Type of construction** solid construction; 30 cm	mm, depending on layer). Modeling of surface based
Lot size 920 m²	bricks; composite thermal insulation system (ETICS)	on the look of concrete; painted plaster surface
Covered area 206 m²	with thickness of 16 cm; concrete ceilings.	with silicate paint.
Living area 240 m²	**Materials** ETICS base: fixation of a	**Primary energy consumption** −1.82 kWh/m²a
Effective area 447.96 m²	bonding base with a notched trowel to provide	**Heating energy consumption** 9.02 kWh/m²a
Gross volume 2,153.41 m³	a chemical and mechanical adhesion between the	
Number of residents 4	insulation and the final layer. Two-layer application	
Start of construction 2009	of a modified mineral rough finish (hydrophobic	
Completion 2010	and algicide) of 7–10 mm with precise thickness (7	

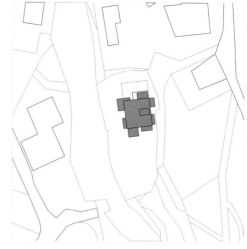

Site plan

Habitat in the Puster Valley

At first sight the house is reminiscent of the famous building designed by Moshe Safdi for the 1967 World Fair in Montreal. In the case of this "habitat" in the Puster Valley, it was not about a serial production based on a flexible modular system, but rather about a new kind of living quality which can be appreciated from the outside: the individual rooms flow into each other but they do not remain without purpose nor are they only defined by the furniture. Rather, they obtain their distinctive atmospheres through matching sizes, proportions, and window openings. The intersection of the individual units sticking out of the basic cubic facade results in an obvious zone structure without interior walls and doors.

This was achieved based on the design layout of the house. The two main levels, which rise up over two lengthwise rectangular basement floors, conform a cube-shaped shell with individual volumes being added to it or cut out from it. The result are protected loggias and the large alcove which dominates the exterior. They are a typical building feature for South Tyrol, in this case integrated in an abstract manner. The garden and landscape are mirrored in the glass walls and the shiny black frames made from aluminum sandwich panels. They contrast with the brickwork foundation section which has been covered with several layers of mineral plaster. The effect looks very much like a concrete surface.

Approaching by car, you drive into the underground garage on the second basement level, and by foot you reach the house from the valley side, one level higher. This is where the wellness area with its pool and guest room, hidden halfway inside the earth, is located, illuminated by an interior patio, just like the laundry room below. The living level as such, which is accessed via an elevator or an angular platform stairwell, opens up as a braceless continuum where the kitchen, dining area, library, and sitting area reach centrifugally into said alcove. This results in a private moment; depending on the choice of location, you are also more or less connected to the other areas. Lavatory and pantry consist of an inserted, inconspicuous cabinet element.

On the third floor the protrusions shift. The compartments contain a generous area for the parents, hygiene installations, bedroom, and wardrobe; and the two children's rooms are veritable apartments with their own bathrooms and loggia.

The highly insulated house is energy self-sufficient via geothermal probes and photovoltaics.

A home where you can look from the inside toward the outside and back inside again. The view from the dining area to the kitchen is shown here.

The facade with its dormers on all sides anticipates an unusual floor plan.

The protruding glass alcoves are framed by black aluminum sandwich boards. Several layers of mineral plaster have been applied onto the insulation of the brick walls, looking almost like concrete.

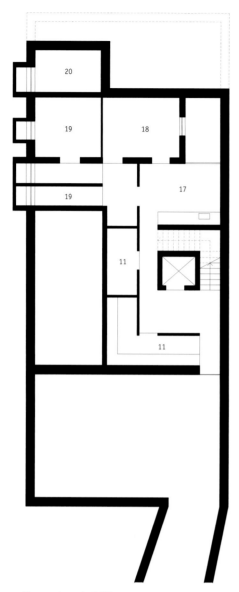

Basement   scale 1:200

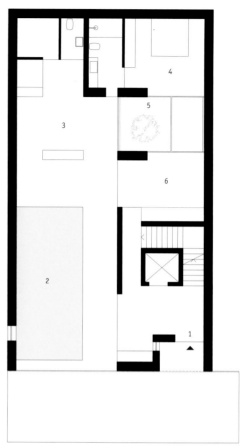

First floor   scale 1:200

1 entry
2 pool
3 wellness
4 guest
5 interior patio
6 hobby
7 living
8 library
9 dining
10 cooking
11 storage
12 terrace
13 bathroom
14 parents
15 dressing room
16 child
17 utility room
18 wine cellar
19 technical
20 silo

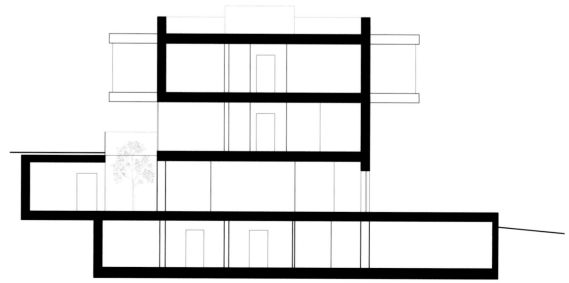

Section   scale 1:200

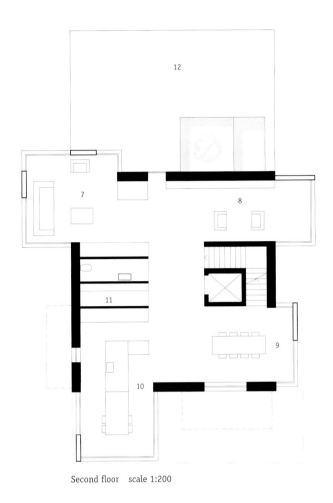

Second floor   scale 1:200

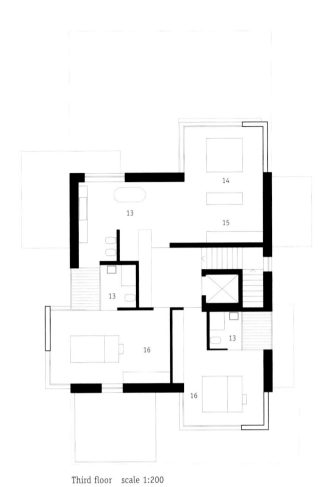

Third floor   scale 1:200

Each room is a special case, but on
the living room level they are all
coming together. The surfaces of
the floor above are pegged into
each other like a stacking game.

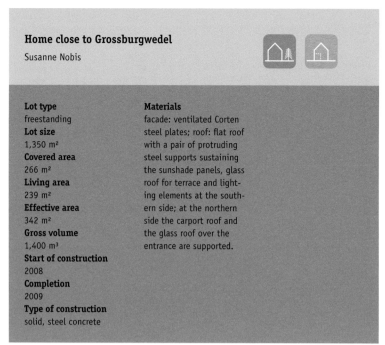

Home close to Grossburgwedel

Susanne Nobis

Lot type
freestanding
Lot size
1,350 m²
Covered area
266 m²
Living area
239 m²
Effective area
342 m²
Gross volume
1,400 m³
Start of construction
2008
Completion
2009
Type of construction
solid, steel concrete

Materials
facade: ventilated Corten steel plates; roof: flat roof with a pair of protruding steel supports sustaining the sunshade panels, glass roof for terrace and lighting elements at the southern side; at the northern side the carport roof and the glass roof over the entrance are supported.

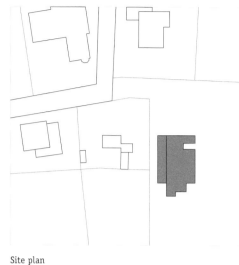

Site plan

Land art

A house that confronts the landscape like an artistic artifact! The lot lies at the edge of the city of Grossburgwedel. Large meadows and fields are located to the east and south. An old oak boulevard with twenty pairs of trees, facing diagonally from the house into the landscape, catches the eye.

The architecture had to work with these almost poetic circumstances. The house was supposed to have a single level, lying under the treetops and corresponding with the dark oaks. The high groundwater level suggested not digging into the ground, but instead creating ground-level storage areas behind the carport instead of a basement. The result is a composition which consists of long offset glass walls forming a shell. Viewed from the inside, the space-dividing bulkheads outside of the building's footprint dissolve into stelae, and farther south they terminate in low walls which sink into the lawn of the park-like property. The house merges with the wide, flowing landscape. The decision to clad the facade with Corten steel plates under-

scores the idea of fitting in with the tree scenery and the colors of nature, while avoiding any hiding of the cultural intervention of the building.

The floor plan continues the generous interaction with the landscape. The center contains the living area, which is expanded with choirs for the library and the office areas. It remains open toward the main access running from north to south; it is used as a gallery, and from it art flows into the rooms. A broad roof glazing provides the appropriate lighting for the exhibits. Ceiling-high glass panes offer sweeping views to all sides, not as an endless film but rather framed by the dark profiles of the facade and the closed wall elements, as if continually finding a new balance between interior and exterior.

The outer ends contain the bedrooms and office rooms, with sun shade panels playing with the light of the steel supports protruding from the cube.

At night the illuminated steel bulkheads behind the dark oak trees are even more mysterious.

With its terraces facing south, the body of the building dissolves into stelae — as if Richard Serra were the director. Protective sun panels connect the soaring Corten sheets.

A home which steps into the park-like garden landscape without occupying it. The seams under the oxidized steel sheets make it seem as if it were a transitory touch.

First floor   scale 1:200

1 entry
2 office
3 gallery
4 library
5 living
6 dining
7 cooking
8 terrace
9 bedroom
10 bathroom
11 dressing room
12 storage
13 utility room
14 carport

The Corten steel facade sheets absorb the colors of nature and also provide a marked material contrast.

As if the house wants to slowly disappear into the garden the axes of the construction terminate as low walls in the grass.

The seamless glazing reaching above the ceiling of the room offers maximum proximity to nature.

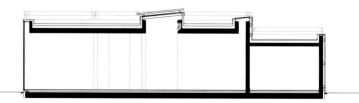

Section   scale 1:200

View from the dining niche.

An inspiring workplace in nature, offering eye contact with the living area.

A corridor axis illuminated from above runs through the house like an art gallery course, which expands to both sides into the living and dining areas.

Home at Lake Scharmützel

Doris Schäffler

Lot type	**Start of construction**
freestanding	March 2009
Lot size	**Completion**
3,500 m²	April 2010
Covered area	**Type of construction**
238 m² with terrace	concrete strip foundations,
Living area	no basement; wood panel
102 m² (without terraces);	construction; outer clad-
189 m² (with terraces)	ding: Siberian larch; interi-
Effective area	or (walls, ceilings, doors):
5.5 m²	triple layer pine boards,
Gross volume	pine floor
area A (without terraces):	
390 m³; area B (roofed	
terraces): 194 m³	
Number of residents	
4	

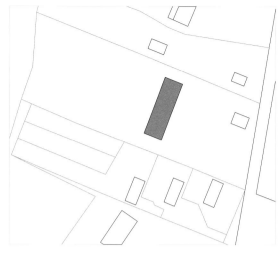

Site plan

Vacation camp

A small vacation home which respectfully sets the scene for the luxurious landscape. The lakefront lot features black alder trees, and the house creates an appealing contrast to the lofty green branches. The natural vegetation has largely been left intact.

From the entrance side, the wood-clad transversal transom appears like a public gallery pavilion. A discontinuity at the facade clad with Siberian larch allows for a view across the dining area toward the private areas and the lake. It works like the viewfinder of a small camera. Both fronts are accompanied by long and narrow terraces with the flat roof extending like a band over them. During summer it deflects heat when the sun is standing high while during winter it allows for it to enter the large glass panes at a low angle.

The interior rooms are relatively low and except for the central area for kitchen, dining, and living, they are executed as reduced, cabin-like boxes. At one of the ends is the main bedroom with its bathroom, and in front of it are the cabins of the children's rooms with their wardrobes. If required, one or two bed racks can be fitted to the walls so that friends can stay overnight. The other side behind the kitchen features another bathroom and an office/guest room as well as a utility room for the gas heater.

The facilities are reduced to essential items, as the main attraction is the landscape which the family wants to enjoy during weekends while outdoors. Light is mainly provided via downlights so that no light fixtures disrupt the room. Pine floor boards painted white are used for the floors, walls, and built-in cupboards which constitute the closed shell of the room. The rhythm of the ceiling-high, partially sliding glass windows shows the landscape like a picture frame. In front of it, radiators are set into the floor. In addition there is a wood stove which is sufficient to heat the home during the transitional seasons.

Functional tight quarters. The bunks are arranged so they utilize little space, like on a yacht.

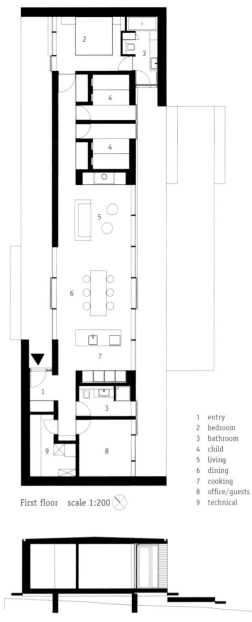

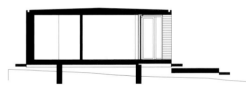

First floor   scale 1:200 ⊗

1   entry
2   bedroom
3   bathroom
4   child
5   living
6   dining
7   cooking
8   office/guests
9   technical

Section   scale 1:200

While on vacation you want to live differently. This home sitting in the landscape provides a central light-filled living room and small cabins as bedrooms.

The entrance, like the viewfinder of a camera, indicates the highlight of the seascape toward the back.

Home in Lana (Italy)

Höller & Klotzner Architekten

Lot type	Type of construction	finish; outer wall cladding
slope	steel concrete support	with Z-shaped aluminum
Lot size	structure of floor and roof	panels, powder-coated
1,180 m²	ceiling inluding northern	**Primary energy**
Covered area	facade, U-shaped, mounted	**consumption**
4 m²	on steel supports; addi-	18 kWh/m²a
Effective area	tional reinforcing cylindri-	**Heating energy**
134 m²	cal tower, with exterior	**consumption**
Gross volume	and interior steel pipes	23 kWh/m²a
1,440 m³	with concrete core; entire	
Number of residents	outer cladding with pow-	
2	der-coated aluminum	
Start of construction	panels; glass foam interior	
2007	insulation; dry-built interi-	
Completion	or; basement, garage box	
2009	and parking deck: steel	
	concrete walls and ceil-	
	ings, exposed concrete	

Site plan

Simply out of this world

How do you build in a landscape with sweeping views over a vineyard, where any activity can be a mistake? This is a constant challenge for architects in Southern Tyrol. They try to keep the building low and absorb the topography via sweeping shapes, and they base their designs on traditional building methods from the area including the concrete aggregate.

In the present case the architect has found a different solution for his own home. It does not fit in at all, it does not reflect South Tyrolian rusticity, but rather it is clad with black panels like an industrial building. However, it keeps a respectful distance from the slightly sloping terrain which runs almost undisturbed below the living level supported by round columns. With its dark color it takes on a contrarian position while affirming its stance, and shows the combination of function, material, precision, and aesthetics as a reference. An elegy of perfection, even if it were empty this house would justify its existence. It seems to float among the vineyards as a shiny black object. A roof overhang and turning panels protect the surrounding ceiling-high glazing of the living level, which is accessed via an exterior staircase.

Below this deck is the garage block, barely touching it, with the slim cylinder of a spiral staircase connecting the levels between the garden and the roof terrace. The wine cellar remains invisible on the level facing the sloping hill. Except for the study with its row of bookshelves the interior features the ascetic emptiness and strict concept of an architect's household — as if nothing should distract from the breathtaking view. A terrace lines the entire width of the home with a glass balustrade, which continues the living room indefinitely. The view over the Etsch Valley does not allow for furniture, at least for now. Even the kitchen block is glazed.

The furnishing, consisting of white built-in cupboards, provides a bright order above the dark parquet. The craftsmanship of the uniformly matte white surfaces, walls, and fittings is superb and characterized by sharp joints and seams. The ceiling-high doors feature hidden bands. They latch at exactly 90° without the door handle touching the wall. Anything else would be entirely inappropriate.

Respectful yet detached, the black sheet metal shell floats above the vineyards.

Like a camera it focuses the dreamlike landscape; nothing should block the view.

Aside from the shaft of the spiral staircase and the garage block, only a few necessary steel columns touch the ground.

Toward the valley, the roof overhang functions as a sun protector. The opening of the facades at the flanks can be regulated with moving blade panels.

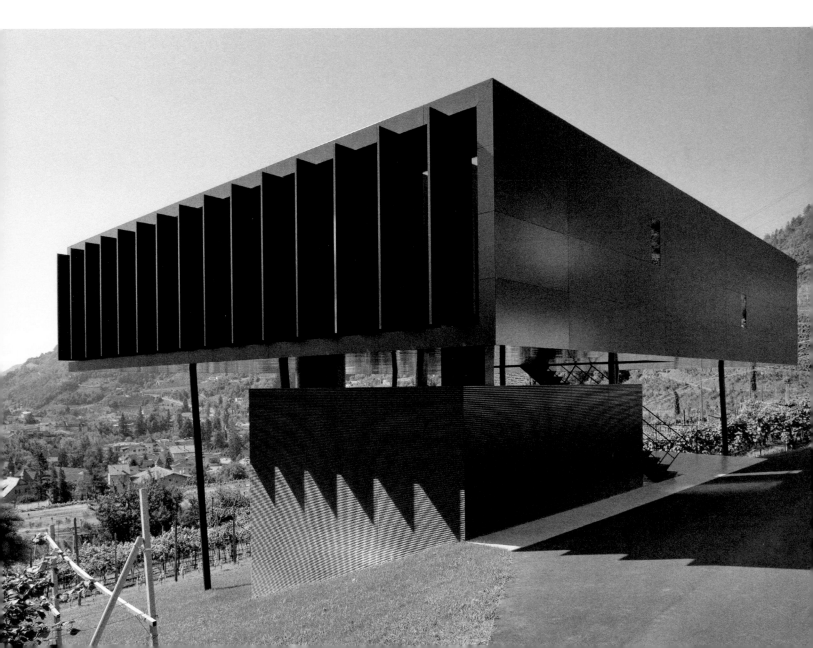

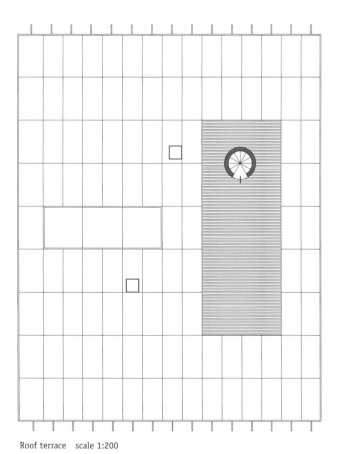

Roof terrace   scale 1:200

Floor plan level 1   scale 1:200

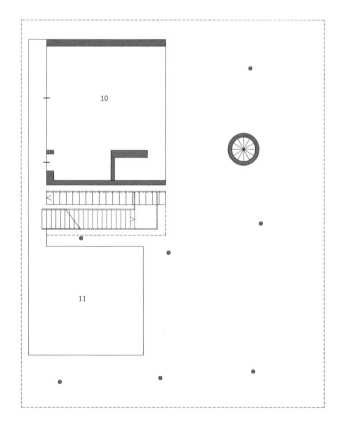

Floor plan level 0   scale 1:200 ⊗

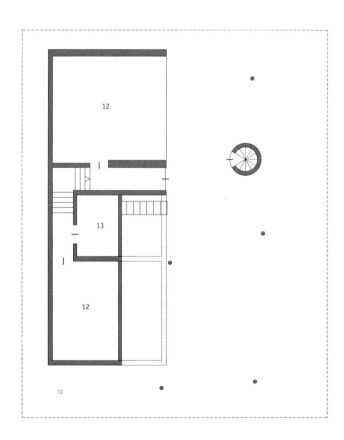

Floor plan   scale 1:200

1	entry	8	terrace
2	bathroom	9	library
3	bedroom	10	garage
4	office	11	parking
5	dining		space
6	cooking	12	(wine) cellar
7	living	13	technical

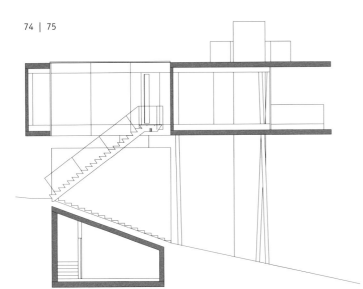

Section   scale 1:200

A spiral staircase passes through all of the levels, from the garden to the roof terrace.

The living level is accessed via a straight stairway. The entrance is kept in view via a glass wall.

Dark parquet and white surfaces with almost entirely hidden built-in cabinets define the emptiness. There are only a few pieces of furniture.

The kitchen laboratory requires clean work as well as discipline.

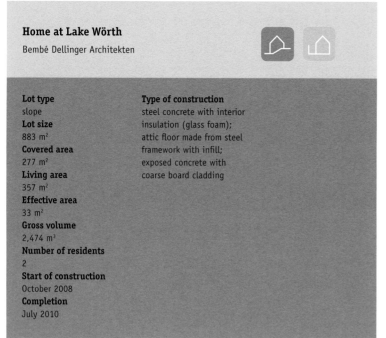

Home at Lake Wörth
Bembé Dellinger Architekten

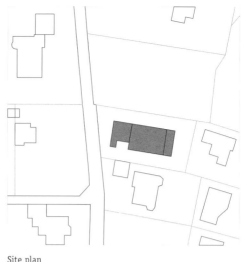

Lot type	Type of construction
slope	steel concrete with interior
Lot size	insulation (glass foam);
883 m²	attic floor made from steel
Covered area	framework with infill;
277 m²	exposed concrete with
Living area	coarse board cladding
357 m²	
Effective area	
33 m²	
Gross volume	
2,474 m³	
Number of residents	
2	
Start of construction	
October 2008	
Completion	
July 2010	

Site plan

Views and vistas

When the clients purchased the property there was still a small house standing on the narrow sloping terrain. You could only enjoy the view of Lake Wörth after stepping up to the top floor. This basically described the concept of the new home: the living spaces should be facing east and the fantastic view of the lake was a primary consideration.

The best view is from the office of the homeowner; like a captain on the upper deck he looks into the landscape while at the same time partaking of the living areas via ceiling-high glazing. The penetration of the levels, including the terraces marked by concrete balustrades, characterizes the spatial experience of the house. It sits there as an angular block, however, its even footprint is continuously opened via recesses. The course-like lay-out begins on the intermediate level at the entrance. From here a clear view of the kitchen, dining, and living area is provided via a generous frameless glazing. An opening toward the right indicates that things continue below on the garden level. The spacious study of the owner is located here and illuminated from above.

A flat ramp is spatially worked out for the kitchen countertop, separated by a wedge-like step. The rear wall from fumed oak reaches the upper level and results in a lively and warm background. The living area is defined by a staircase and a flanking chimney which seems to float over the fireplace, however, it is not separated. This results in an open, flowing room which is not casual and arbitrary but rather it provides architectural clues where other uses are possible ... even if that simply means a deep block step which announces the staircase bearing.

On the garden level you reach the private bedrooms and a sculpturally seg-mented bathroom with a sauna. Here as well, exposed concrete is visible on the inside as if to remind one of the solid foundation of the home. The floor repeats the fumed oak of the tall kitchen wall unit.

A bathroom with living room qualities. When the glass sliding door is open, the garden terrace becomes part of it.

The concrete entrance announces the essential features of the home.

Concrete bands define the building. They reach over the entrance as a projecting roof ... (photo below)

... or they fold as balustrades around balconies and terraces with views toward the bottom (extreme right)

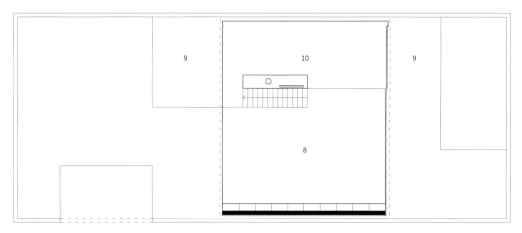

Top floor   scale 1:200

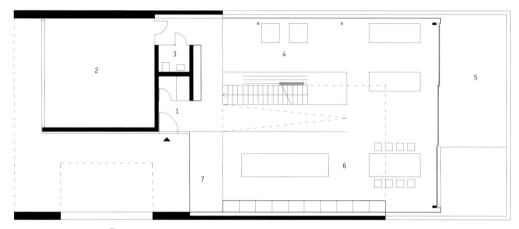

First floor   scale 1:200

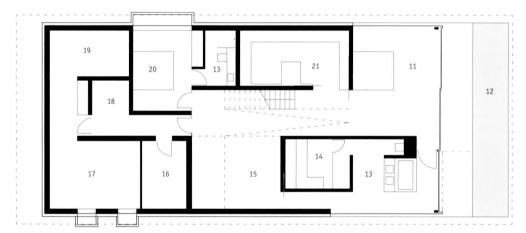

Basement   scale 1:200

1 entry
2 garage
3 lavatory
4 living
5 terrace
6 dining/cooking
7 air space
8 kitchen air space
9 roof terrace
10 office gallery
11 bedroom
12 pool
13 bathroom
14 sauna
15 leisure/hobby
16 wine cellar
17 storage
18 utility room
19 technical
20 guests
21 dressing room

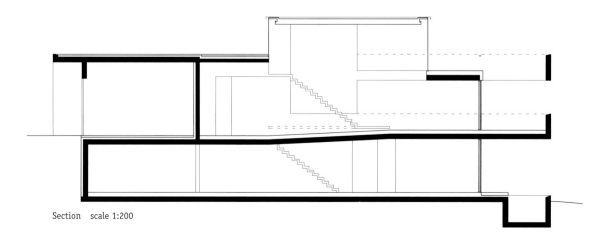

Section   scale 1:200

The home is accessed from an intermediate level. A high hall opens up, dominated by the kitchen counter.

The high kitchen is set in front of an elegant wall made from fumed oak.

Home in Stuttgart

Fuchs, Wacker Architekten

Lot type
slope facing south, view
cannot be developed, long
driveway to the house
Lot size
1,575 m²
Living area
290 m²
Effective area
17 m²
Gross volume
1,245 m³
Number of residents
2
Start of construction
August 2009
Completion
December 2010

Type of construction
steel concrete/brick (solid)
Materials
facade: ETICS, paint plaster; anodized aluminum
windows; metal panel
facade; pergola: exposed
concrete; doors covered
with synthetic leather
**Primary energy
consumption**
46.1 kWh/m²a

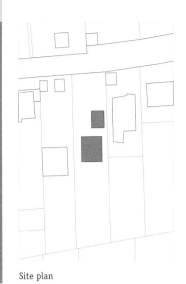

Site plan

Facade with draft

The large yet narrow southward-sloping lot was a challenge for this present
design. It offers a fantastic view in the Schönberg neighborhood, however, it
has to be accessed via its own curved driveway. First you reach a large garage
with three parking spaces; a solid pergola made from exposed concrete connects this preceding unit, which is cut into the slope, with the home.

The facade material, consisting of dark horizontal aluminum blades which
hide the hinged gate of the garage, leads to the entrance pedestal of the
house which features the same anodized blades. They also clad the almost
invisible entrance door. Above it the facade gleams with a smooth white
coat of plaster, interrupted by dark aluminum window elements.

Except for the window of the office, all of the apertures were utilized to
provide a sculptural depth to the outer walls, featuring horizontal and vertical cuts and additional balconies. A wall niche (in the kitchen), a protruding bulkhead-like wall (in the living room), and the plastered exposed concrete stairwell shape the building in its three dimensions. The gill-shaped
glass panes in front of the bathroom are also quite fitting.

The floor plan provides for the ground level to be the actual living area. The
wardrobe, which can be accessed from both sides, divides the open zone
between kitchen/dining and the lowered living quarters. Utility rooms such
as storage, access to the garden level, and the guest lavatory are hidden
behind doors covered with synthetic leather without visible fittings. The
lower level contains a spacious fitness course with sauna, which opens to
the garden at ground level. An opening in the ceiling next to the staircase
in the living room causes curiosity as to the upper level. Apart from the
separate bedroom section and an office, a fireplace room provides a secluded space.

All of the fixtures and fittings were designed by the architects. The ceiling-high doors are frameless and feature covered fittings. The living quarters feature fumed oak floor boards. The built-in furniture consists of zebrano veneer or white lacquered sandwich boards.

A solid pergola covers the pathway from
the garage, set into the hillside toward
the home.

The living room suite is defined by a step. The broad staircase recess connects the top floor with the living area.

The building is clearly defined. Apertures, balcony, terrace, and staircase provided the occasion for sculptural drama.

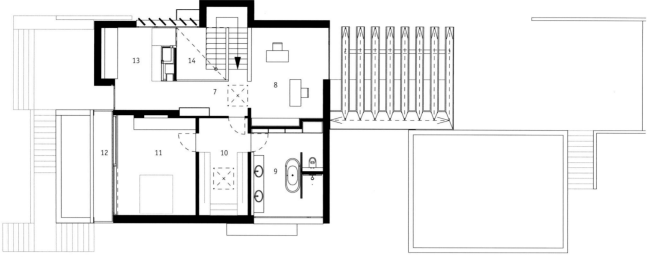

Top floor   scale 1:200

First floor   scale 1:200

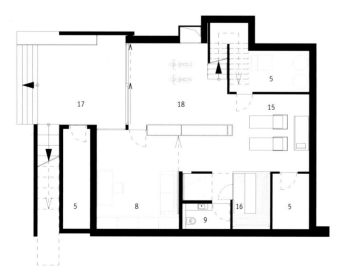

Basement   scale 1:200

 1 entry
 2 cooking
 3 dining
 4 living
 5 storage
 6 garage
 7 gallery
 8 office
 9 bathroom
10 dressing room
11 parents
12 balcony
13 fireplace
14 air space
15 relaxation
16 sauna
17 roofed terrace
18 fitness

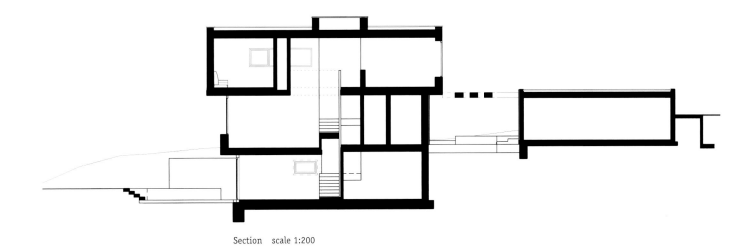

Section   scale 1:200

The kitchen area lies behind the dividing
wardrobe cabinet. It can be used from
both sides.

Home in Dornbirn (Austria)

Hein-Troy Architekten

Lot type	Completion	Heating energy
slope	2009	consumption
Lot size	**Type of construction,**	56 kWh/m²a
679.4 m²	**materials**	
Covered area	exposed concrete in base	
102.8 m²	and carport area; prefabri-	
Living area	cated wood panel con-	
134.5 m²	struction with cellulose	
Effective area	insulation and ventilated	
140.5 m²	facade. roof: extensive	
Gross heated floor area	greenery; facade:	
217.2 m²	bush-hammered exposed	
Gross volume	concrete, ventilated bat-	
787.0 m³	ten, local coarse white fir,	
Number of residents	untreated; windows: local	
2	larch; interior construc-	
Start of construction	tion: local planed white	
2008	fir, untreated	

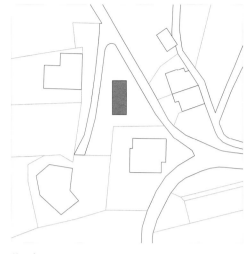

Site plan

Point of attack

It appears to be the reward for all the effort and expense: the view over the Rhine Valley is sensational. However, a few hurdles had to be overcome in order to enjoy it from the house. The property features an inconvenient triangular layout, it is very steep, and the access via a small street was restricted. This also contributed to the decision for a prefabricated wood frame construction which could be erected in one day. The foundation pedestal and the carport are made from concrete with a bush-hammered surface. A basement reaches into the depths of the hillside, but, except for a few light apertures, the house is entirely oriented toward the west.

For this reason it was unrealistic to try to achieve the energy standards of a passive home. Instead of choosing ventilation, the clients opted for high-quality cellulose insulation with a geothermal heat pump and a thermal solar system. The roof features extensive greenery to fulfill its role as a fifth facade within the hillside location with plenty of views. The outer walls are clad with coarse white fir boards while the windows are made from larch wood.

The simple floor plan for two residents (for now) is self-explanatory and can be functionally interpreted. From the upper entrance level you reach the open living quarters with kitchen and dining area. Here a large wood-clad balcony protrudes from the facade like a drawer. The bedroom and bathroom, with natural lighting, connect to the kitchen. This eliminates the need for a corridor and allows for a self-contained retreat whenever the lower level is reserved for the children or for guests.

The way downstairs follows a staircase suspended from bars from the wardrobe next to the entrance. You reach a corridor which opens up to a central open room with a large window facing the valley. Two same-sized rooms are located at both sides. The corridor ends in front of a bathroom on one side and at a small laundry on the other.

A visible foundation pedestal provides support on the sloping hillside.

It reaches into the depths of the construction below a concrete carport with a basement room.

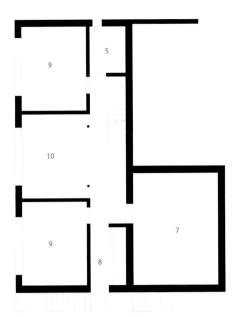

Basement   scale 1:200

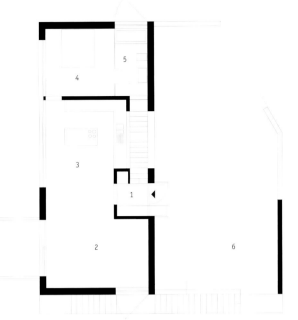

First floor   scale 1:200

1 entry
2 living
3 cooking
4 bedroom
5 bathroom
6 carport
7 basement
8 laundry
9 bedroom
10 multipurpose area

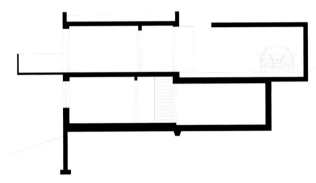

Section   scale 1:200

From the kitchen you enjoy the view of the Rhine Valley, while at the same time you can catch a glimpse of the entrance via a slit in the wall.

A staircase suspended from bars leads to the private quarters below.

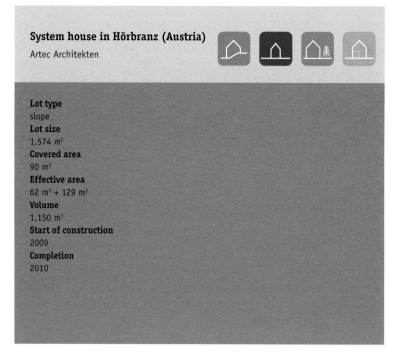

System house in Hörbranz (Austria)

Artec Architekten

Lot type
slope
Lot size
1,574 m²
Covered area
90 m²
Effective area
62 m² + 129 m²
Volume
1,150 m³
Start of construction
2009
Completion
2010

Site plan

Game of dice

The design of the home, towering over the surroundings with its three floors, is characterized by a steep hillside lot with a view over Lake Constance with a forest and a stream toward the back. The floor plan of the modular building made from prefabricated concrete elements describes a modified square with an edge length of 840 centimeters. This results in three modules of 280 centimeters which can be discerned at the facade either as closed or glazed areas.

Even though this is a geometrically reduced minimal home utilizing simple building methods, it was created by slightly altering some parameters, resulting in a spatially sophisticated house: the base of the staircase bearings is lengthened to the outside on three levels, while the top floor consists of an air space. The facade at first follows the expansion, and toward the north a glazed diagonal closes the shortened outer square.

The core-insulated outer walls are made with a load-dissipating interior and thin exterior shell. The facade is characterized by building-high elements with building-high frames. The floors consist of concrete ceilings or feature screed which is polished and impregnated. The window profiles consist of

aluminum on the outside, and the interior features wide larch wood boards. The staircase handrails are executed as furniture. While the interior fitting consists of larch wood, shiny black and white mirrored surfaces dominate the bathrooms.

The building is designed both as a standard as well as a semi-prefabricated home which is adapted to the desires of the corresponding clients and the conditions of the lot. A second entrance leads over the terrace which reaches into the landscape. From here, you access the bedrooms on the top floor with the adjoining bathrooms, kitchen, living and dining room after passing through the high entrance hallway. The rooms behind the oblique glass front are rather unique: from here you enjoy the view via a transparent balustrade or a ceiling-high glass front over the triangular intermediate space — even from the bathroom.

The access to the carport lies under the laterally protruding balcony bridge. The location on a sloping hill provided for an additional segregated level.

The construction based on prefabricated elements is visible on the facade, however, the evenly stacked cube design is interrupted because of a shifted layout.

Low concrete stairs lead to the entrance on the middle level.

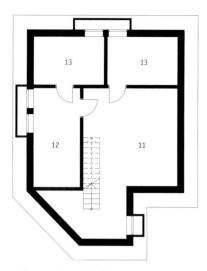

Basement   scale 1:200

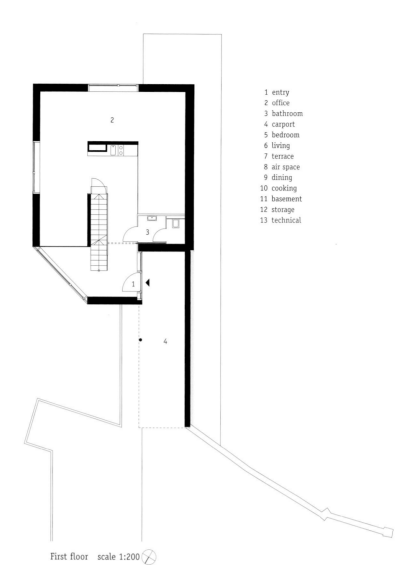

1 entry
2 office
3 bathroom
4 carport
5 bedroom
6 living
7 terrace
8 air space
9 dining
10 cooking
11 basement
12 storage
13 technical

Handrails and embrasures are made
from larch wood and designed like
furniture. The deep window sills can
be used for storage.

First floor   scale 1:200

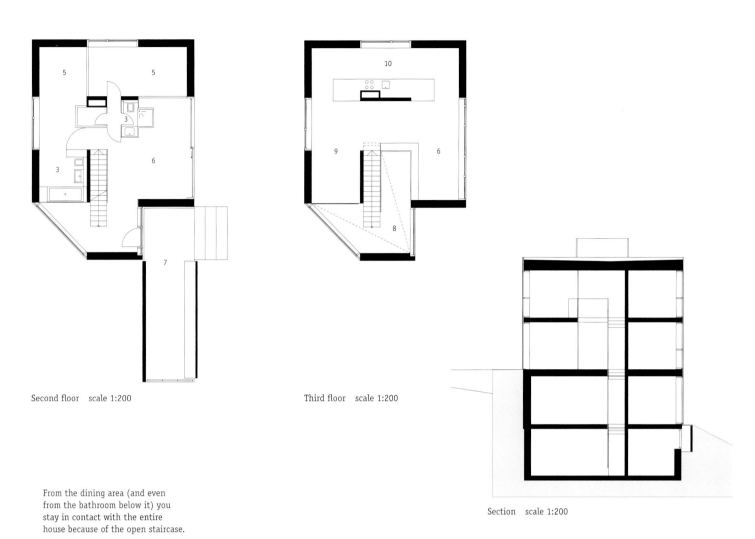

Second floor   scale 1:200

Third floor   scale 1:200

Section   scale 1:200

From the dining area (and even
from the bathroom below it) you
stay in contact with the entire
house because of the open staircase.

Home in Richterswil (Switzerland)
Jeuch Architekten

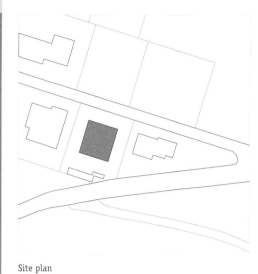

Lot type	Type of construction
slope	solid construction (steel
Lot size	concrete and brick) with
784.1 m²	plastered exterior heat
Covered area	insulation
194.8 m²	
Living area	
263.5 m²	
Effective area	
339.0 m²	
Gross volume	
1,216.3 m³	
Number of residents	
4	
Start of construction	
2008	
Completion	
2009	

Site plan

A lot for playrooms

The home at Lake Zurich is well-located, with its view toward the east and the shore, as well as toward the southeast to take advantage of the sun's course. The facade of the solid construction with its outer dark-plastered insulation emphasizes the horizontal stacking of the levels while the meandering transition of walls and ceilings traces the different functions.

The house built into the hillside is accessed from the valley, with the entrance located between the hobby room and the double garage. From here a staircase leads toward an intermediate level which reaches even deeper into the terrain. For the private quarters, consisting of three bedrooms and two offices, to be well illuminated an intimate atrium has been cut into the western side and opens toward the exterior with a loggia, which serves to access the lot upwards and downwards via stairs. A welcome side effect was that this recess allowed for downsizing the cubature. A small balcony follows the facade toward the street while the ceiling-high glazing reaches above the oblique main bathroom, resulting in a neutral front.

The culmination is the living level on the top floor. Here a balcony lines the kitchen/dining area, while the living area following the fireplace is oriented toward the mountain toward the south. Only a few white steel columns support the roof. At the rear of the house you reach the garden level where an additional loggia is located, with a wooden gangplank leading outside. The protected seat also illuminates the lower-lying atrium next to a core consisting of staircase, fireplace, and lavatory which can be walked around entirely. This results in the living cube interlocking with the lot on all of the levels, while large plant troughs and a utility room provide privacy. A garden fireplace is set into a niche: architectural elements wherever you look.

The second floor features an atrium (photo, opposite) with a walkway on the living level above it leading around it from the garden and the loggia toward the kitchen.

Every level features distinctive solutions in order to enjoy the views and the steep garden lot from protected open spaces.

The band consisting of walls and ceilings seems to mirror the labyrinthine interior on the facade.

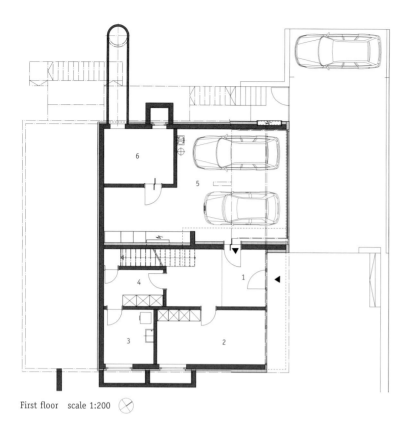

First floor   scale 1:200

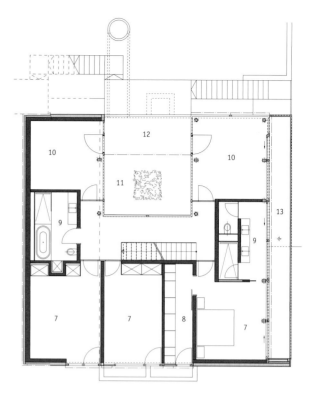

Second floor   scale 1:200

The top floor is arranged around a core
consisting of staircase, guest lavatory,
and fireplace.

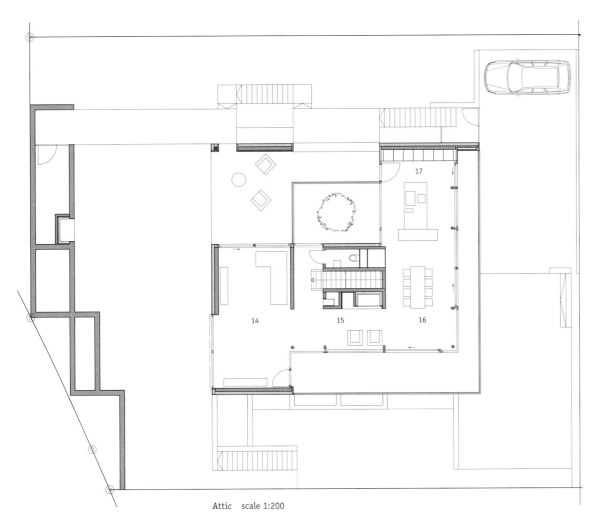

Attic   scale 1:200

1	entry	10	office
2	leisure/hobby	11	atrium
3	technical	12	loggia
4	storage	13	balcony
5	garage	14	living
6	technical	15	fireplace
7	bedroom	16	dining
8	dressing room	17	cooking
9	bathroom		

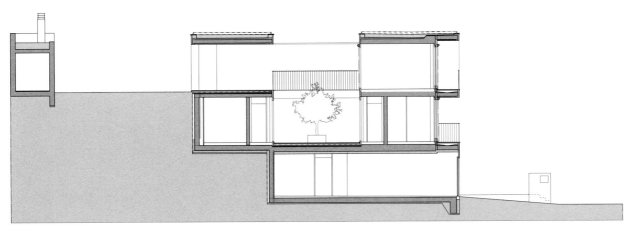

Section   scale 1:200

Home in Salins/Sion (Switzerland)

anako'architecture, Olivier Cheseaux

Lot type	Type of construction,
slope, vineyard	materials
Lot size	floor, walls: concrete; roof:
2,624 m²	concrete with greenery
Covered area	**Total building cost**
230 m²	800,000 CHF
Living area	**Building cost per m²**
230 m²	**living area and effective**
Effective area	**area**
220 m²	3,650 CHF/m²
Gross volume	
1,200 m³	
Number of residents	
4	
Start of construction	
2009	
Completion	
2009	

Site plan

Mountain building

There are different possibilities for setting a house onto a sloping hillside: the inclination can be absorbed by each floor, the building can be placed on columns over the terrain with a dramatic protrusion, or, as is the case here — high above the Rhône Valley with a view of the Valais Alps — consign the home to the sloping topography. The key to the solution was to find a balance between the view and the introverted seclusion.

The sloping lot faces northwest and the panorama offers not only pure landscapes but also an industrial area and an airport. The architects proposed staggered levels which, following the surrounding vineyards, look like three open drawers on top of each other while providing terraces with greenery on the respective roof of the building block below. The balustrades block the view to the less attractive surroundings.

The concrete cascade is low and the building is camouflaged; despite the difficult location it provides the residents with a distinct and extroverted

view of the landscape with its changing lighting. While most of the building receives light from the north, the top floor is illuminated via a light strip on the roof which runs along the entire width of the home. It looks like the continuation of the access which consists of a "stairway to heaven" at the flank of the building. A wide play area is formed next to the street behind the enclosure and the entrance hall. The only rooms pushing into the mountain are the basement, workshop, and a small bathroom. On top of them are the children's and guest rooms with a sweeping view toward the valley, accessed via a long corridor fitted with cabinets. At the very top you climb toward the dining area and the living area, which is separated from an open kitchen block and features a fireplace cut into the rear wall.

There are only a few colorful accents punctuating the bright concrete shell. The ceilings show the imprints of the formwork panels with seamless large round lights, while the floor consists of gray screed and white walls, and glass balustrades exhibit sober materiality: a living stage which wants to be conquered.

Both ... and: the location not only provides an attractive panorama. You can also retreat behind the massive balustrades and enjoy the view of the sky.

The roof of each lower unit provides the terrace for the one on top.

The three building units cut deeply into the vineyard. Still uninhabited, they are stacked into the hillside like an erratic sculpture.

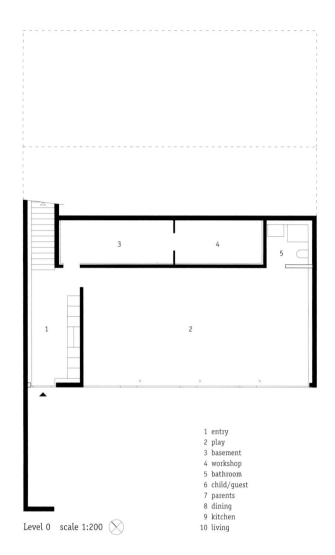

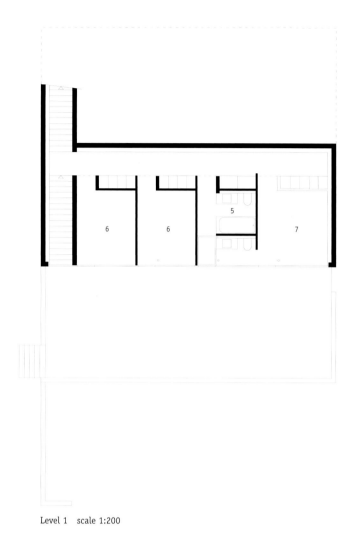

1 entry
2 play
3 basement
4 workshop
5 bathroom
6 child/guest
7 parents
8 dining
9 kitchen
10 living

Level 0   scale 1:200

Level 1   scale 1:200

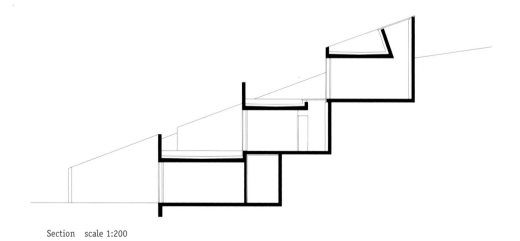

Section   scale 1:200

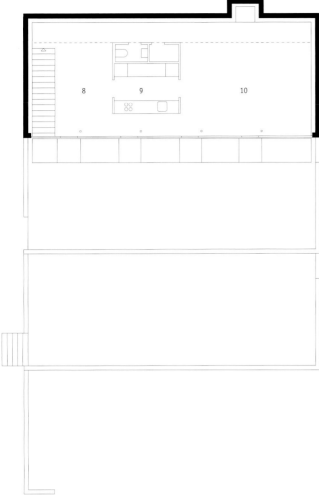

Level 2   scale 1:200

The living level is on the top section; in addition, light enters via the glass roof. A playroom has been fitted on the lower level in front of the basement. The interior finish matches the exterior shell.

Home in Hamburg
LA'KET Architekten

Lot type	**Type of construction**	**Baukosten gesamt**
slight slope	basement: waterproof	**Kostengruppe**
Lot size	concrete; first floor, top	**300 + 400 HOAI**
791 m²	floor: lime-sand bricks,	Gross: 390,000 Euro
Covered area	stucco plaster, plasterboard	**Building cost per m² of**
95 m²	walls; exposed concrete	**living area and effective**
Living area	ceilings; floors first and	**area**
147 m²	upper floor: linoleum; first	living area: 2,650 Euro;
Effective area	floor, staircases: white oiled	effective area 2,000 Euro
195 m²	oak, brushed; facade: brick	**Primary energy**
Gross volume	with mineral plaster, upright	**consumption**
785 m³	bricks; parapet of Aluco-	70.2 kWh/m²a
Number of residents	bond; wooden windows with	**Heating energy**
4	column and beam structure;	**consumption**
Start of construction	custom-made glass support	58.9 kWh/m²a
March 2009	for extremely high weights,	
Completion	triple glazing, energy	
April 2010	generation via probe and	
	heat pump	

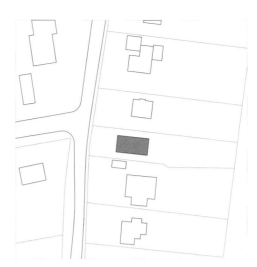

Site plan

The order of things

Surrounding this small compact home is a residential area which grew over the years. Among the large variety of building styles some whitewashed houses from the 1960s and 1970s stand out nicely and the new construction incorporates their discreet elegance and haptic features.

The clever staggering of the volume and the slightly sloping location allowed for three levels instead of the single floor dictated by the building code. The building remains low toward the street, and the only visible item is the living room window with the terrace of the receding top floor continuing above its smooth aluminum-clad ledges. The almost entirely windowless flanks reflect as broken surfaces in the grazing light. The irregularly slanted whitewashed bricks are glued onto rigid foam insulation. The rear side of the house facing the lower-lying, park-like garden opens like a portal under the massive frame of the construction which continues the structure of the lateral sides. A narrow balcony in front of the high living room's panoramic window divides the frontal view. The generously glazed lower level features a wooden terrace cut into the lot, providing a slight floating grace to the top floor.

The access to the home is located on the northern side. The first floor is the center level. A functional core consisting of staircase, bathroom, and kitchen divides the dining area from the living room. Ceiling-high white sliding doors on both sides allow variable divisions to be performed here, for example, steering the arriving guests toward the wardrobe, to sitting down, or toward the other levels.

Stepping down you reach two bedrooms for the parents and guests with a dressing room en suite and bathroom; behind it, in the depths of the hillside, lies the basement. A staircase leads up to the two children's rooms which share the terrace facing the street. An additional lavatory could be fitted over the run of stairs. All of the functions are clearly located within the tight footprint, which does not conform to the standard typology of a single family home. It actually is an object, a piece of equipment that arranges living.

The location on a hillside slope allowed for three levels facing the garden. The whitewashed brick facade emulates the look of the homes in the neighborhood.

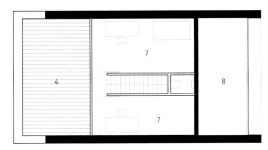

1 entry
2 bathroom
3 dining
4 terrace
5 cooking
6 living
7 child
8 air space
9 basement
10 bedroom
11 dressing room
12 utility room

Top floor   scale 1:200

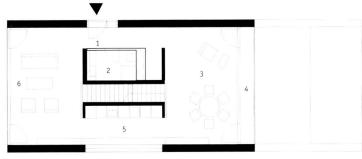

First floor   scale 1:200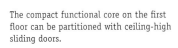

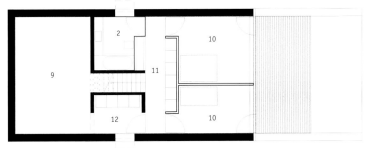

Basement   scale 1:200

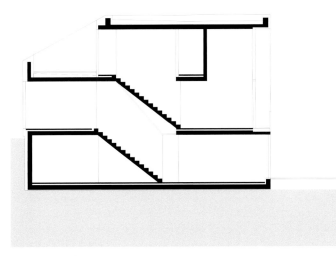

Section   scale 1:200

The compact functional core on the first floor can be partitioned with ceiling-high sliding doors.

The living space of the small house reaches up to the roof, from where you have an unobstructed view of the neighboring nature reserve.

Vacation home in the Oderbruch

Heide & von Beckerath Architekten

Lot type	Type of construction	Building costs per m² of
freestanding	wood frame construction	living area and effective
Lot size	with ventilated wooden	area
2,600 m²	siding, prefabricated walls,	2,070 Euro
Covered area	roof built on location.	
108 m²	Tongue and groove spruce	
Living area	siding, coarse outer clad-	
115 m²	ding painted twice with	
Gross volume	Swedish sludge paint.	
568 m³	Interior walls cladded with	
Number of residents	OSB boards and drywall	
4	panels, wooden ceiling and	
Start of construction	roof cladded with plaster-	
August 2008	board. Roof covering from	
Completion	copper sheets, plain tiles.	
June 2009	**Total building costs**	
	238,061 Euro	

Site plan

On location

The shape of the house is unusual. It replaces a historical fish-processing building, although it is not made from bricks as its predecessor, and it is also shifted to the side due to a protected elm tree. The black paint on the tongue-and-groove spruce reminds one of traditional agricultural buildings and provides an austere look.

In order to receive building approval, the codes related to this area had to be revised, as it stands right behind the embankment and the Oder River begins further down. Such a location only allows for vacation homes. For the time being. It could also provide a nest for old age once the two kids are independent. So it didn't turn out to be a cabin, but rather, a comfortable home.

The wood frame construction is divided into three sections at the facade and the interior. Large sliding gates from coarse spruce boards provide se-

curity when the owners are away. Small windows with flush shutters provide light for the room and the auxiliary rooms.

The room layout is like that of the old farm houses where people lived under one roof with their extended family, farm hands, and cattle. The high living room foyer in the center, with a fireplace and seating bench, can be diagonally expanded via sliding doors. All of the living activities occur in one single room. Two gallery levels over the bedrooms are reached via two staircases to both sides, one of them remaining open toward the center.

The floors of the foyer are made from the bricks of the demolished building and reach to the terrace. This is the sort-of "official" part of the home. The remaining floor surfaces as well as the built-in fittings, cabinets, and sliding doors are made from oak boards.

From the outside the small dark home looks unassuming, like a small barn for agricultural gear.

The classic foyer division can be used in many ways. Light enters abundantly through the roof.

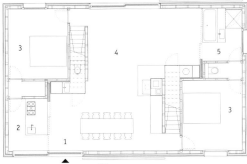

First floor   scale 1:200

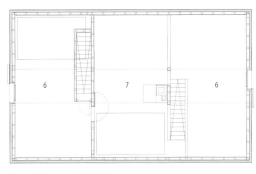

Second floor   scale 1:200

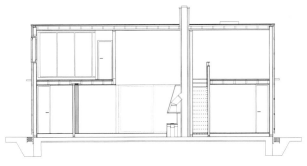

Section   scale 1:200

1   entry
2   cooking
3   bedroom
4   living/dining
5   bathroom
6   gallery
7   air space

It is still mostly used as a vacation home;
solid roller shutters secure the property.

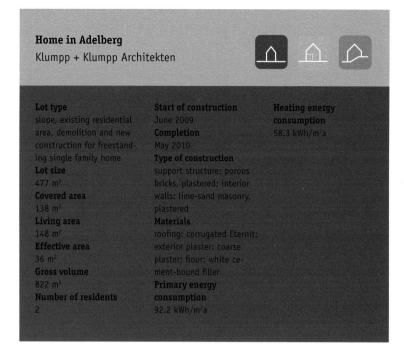

Lot type	Start of construction	Heating energy
slope, existing residential	June 2009	consumption
area, demolition and new	**Completion**	58.3 kWh/m²a
construction for freestand-	May 2010	
ing single family home	**Type of construction**	
Lot size	support structure: porous	
477 m²	bricks, plastered; interior	
Covered area	walls: lime-sand masonry,	
138 m²	plastered	
Living area	**Materials**	
148 m²	roofing: corrugated Eternit;	
Effective area	exterior plaster: coarse	
36 m²	plaster; floor: white ce-	
Gross volume	ment-bound filler	
822 m³	**Primary energy**	
Number of residents	**consumption**	
2	92.2 kWh/m²a	

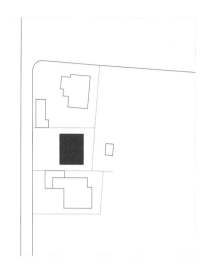

Site plan

Keeping the house in perspective

The small home is located on a slight slope which is characterized by a heterogenous building style of single family homes. So there was really no incentive to emulate any of the wildly divergent architecture. However, the countryside flair with humble agricultural auxiliary buildings, and barns with their typology and colors, provided ideas to incorporate into the design. The clients allowed the architects to go "all the way"; they did not want a uniform and "well-behaved" house.

A long flat staircase leads from the street to the entrance. From here you reach half a level down to the guest floor which can also be used as a granny flat. The basement and heating system are toward the hillside. A platform staircase leads through a high stairwell hall to the upper living level. The center contains a sizable living room, reaching almost to the roof, with a fireplace, flanked by two areas: the continuation of the staircase leads to the kitchen while the opposite side leads via a portal-like area to two low bedrooms with bathroom.

The living and dining areas are lined by broad wall niches for shelves, leaving more room for seating furniture. This room reaches from the southern valley side with the large glass fronts to the loggia patio in the north. The small windows of the bedrooms, however, emphasize privacy.

The house was built with monolithic brickwork as a solid structure without insulation systems. The porous brick is plastered on the interior side while the outer facade features a coarse finish. It has a changing and satin-like appearance due to various layers of paint which emulate the weathered wood sheds in the neighborhood. Both have a connection to the earth and the landscape, and are more unassuming than the various individual single home efforts in the neighborhood.

Both floors feature floor heating. A fuel cell converts natural gas into heat and electricity for the home.

The architecture does not exactly cozy up to the countryside surroundings, but its size, cubature, and color show sympathy for the neighborhood.

The guest level is in the basement and could also be rented out as an apartment. The roofed terrace faces the street.

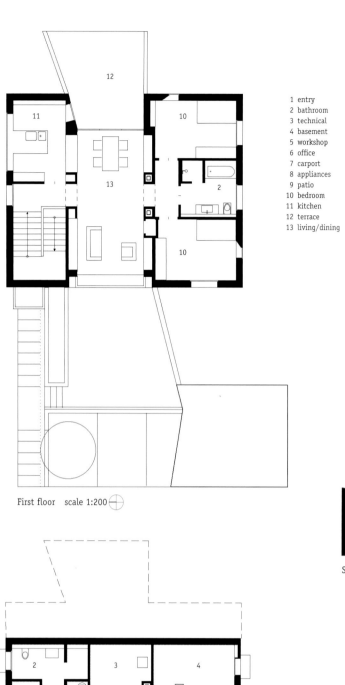

First floor   scale 1:200 ⊕

1 entry
2 bathroom
3 technical
4 basement
5 workshop
6 office
7 carport
8 appliances
9 patio
10 bedroom
11 kitchen
12 terrace
13 living/dining

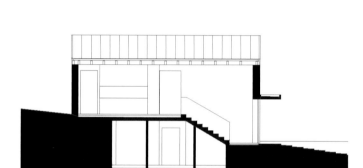

Section   scale 1:200

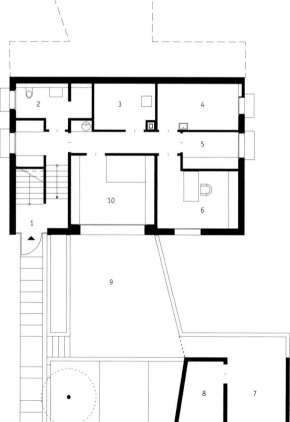

Basement   scale 1:200

All of the paths meet at the upper level in the living room. The portal-like passages divide the access and the bedroom.

The garden terrace faces toward the back (photo, right) and you can view the street through the glass cabinet-like window (below).

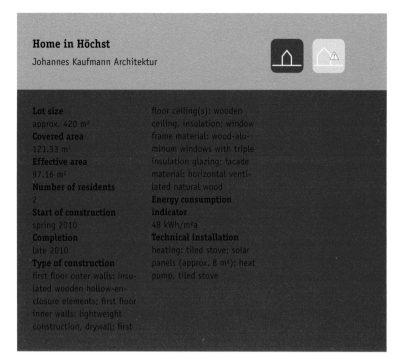

Home in Höchst
Johannes Kaufmann Architektur

Lot size
approx. 420 m²
Covered area
121.33 m²
Effective area
97.16 m²
Number of residents
2
Start of construction
spring 2010
Completion
late 2010
Type of construction
first floor outer walls: insulated wooden hollow-en-
closure elements; first floor
inner walls: lightweight
construction, drywall; first

floor ceiling(s): wooden
ceiling, insulation; window
frame material: wood-alu-
minum windows with triple
insulation glazing; facade
material: horizontal ventilated natural wood
**Energy consumption
indicator**
48 kWh/m²a
Technical installation
heating: tiled stove; solar
panels (approx. 8 m²); heat
pump, tiled stove

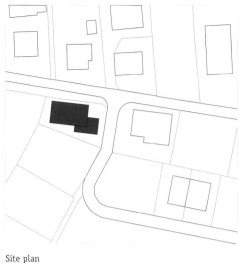

Site plan

Simple solution for a difficult lot

The planning and execution of this house correspond to a particularity of the Vorarlberg region. A well-known wood construction company, which mainly builds single family homes designed by freelance architects, took on the role of the general contractor, including cost planning and details. The architectural company Johannes Kaufmann did the plans.

The house is located in Höchst at the edge of a neighborhood, on a lot which is difficult for building due to the small size and its position at the edge, but which has a beautiful view. By taking advantage of the applicable building regulations, the single-floor construction, and its interior functions, the narrow parcel could be designed appropriately.

A covered carport with a flanking garage for trailer and bicycles results in a protected entrance at one side. Toward the other side, a closed storage and utility room (for the air heat pump) emphasizes the corner of the house. The roof features a solar energy system.

Past the wardrobe you reach a large open space with kitchen, dining area, and living area which opens toward the landscape, while the ceiling-high triple glazed fronts allow for plenty of light for the rooms. A roofed terrace continues toward the garden side and the frontal carport. The living room is divided by custom-made furniture and a sizable fireplace, open on two sides. In the background is an office room and a passage leads to the private quarters for the residents and their guests. Only this dividing center wall is load-dissipating; all of the other walls are made as light-weight construction.

The facade is clad with horizontal wooden strips. The wood siding was painted with gray paint to simulate the inevitable weathering, so an even patina was present from the very beginning.

The carport separates a roofed open-air seat from the kitchen and also leads to the recessed entrance.

The facade is clad with horizontal, pre-weathered wood siding.

The long and narrow room expands from
the kitchen counter to the sofa corner;
the dining area is separated from it by a
large fireplace.

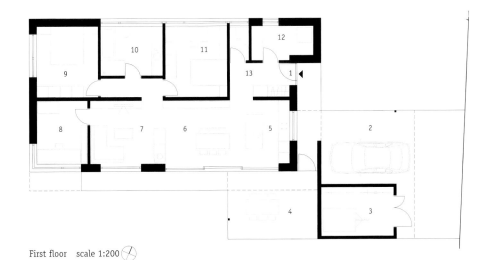

First floor   scale 1:200

1 entry
2 carport
3 garage
4 terrace
5 cooking
6 dining
7 living
8 office
9 bedroom
10 bathroom
11 guests
12 technical
13 wardrobe

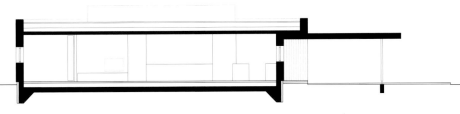

Section   scale 1:200

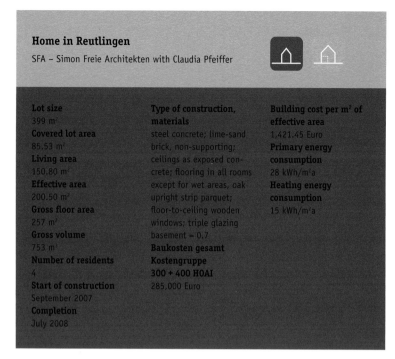

Home in Reutlingen

SFA – Simon Freie Architekten with Claudia Pfeiffer

Lot size	**Type of construction, materials**	**Building cost per m² of effective area**
399 m²	steel concrete; lime-sand	1,421.45 Euro
Covered lot area	brick, non-supporting;	**Primary energy**
85.53 m²	ceilings as exposed con-	**consumption**
Living area	crete; flooring in all rooms	28 kWh/m²a
150.80 m²	except for wet areas, oak	**Heating energy**
Effective area	upright strip parquet;	**consumption**
200.50 m²	floor-to-ceiling wooden	15 kWh/m²a
Gross floor area	windows; triple glazing	
257 m²	basement = 0.7	
Gross volume	**Baukosten gesamt**	
753 m³	**Kostengruppe**	
Number of residents	**300 + 400 HOAI**	
4	285,000 Euro	
Start of construction		
September 2007		
Completion		
July 2008		

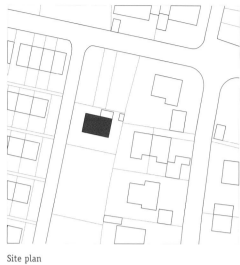

Site plan

Outside neutral, inside flexible

The design layout provided for a two-floor building with a flat roof. The resulting compact house on the 400-square-meter lot realized the mundane guidelines of the surrounding conditions in an ostensive and straightforward manner. The large ceiling-high windows which are divided only by the level's ceiling characterize the views.

If you were to eliminate the non-supporting drywalls and installations, only the kitchen and bathrooms as well as one supporting column on each level would remain within the surrounding walls. This allows for the home to be adjusted for a changing family structure.

The northern section of the first floor contains the entrance with the staircase, lavatory, storage/pantry, and kitchen. Toward the south lies an area which can be customized consisting of dining area, living room, and office.

Via sliding doors which retreat into the built-in cabinets, the area can be experienced either as an open level or as one room next to the other. Since the walls are not load-dissipating, this division between the hallway and the living area could be removed sometime later.

The corridor on the upper floor expands after the staircase to form a playroom area. Here as well, the spacious bedrooms of parents and children are separated only by a continuous division for storage. This allows for changing the floor plan easily once the grown-up children have left the home.

The lower floor allows for an additional fully functional room to be furnished, illuminated via an interior patio. The end of the corridor is ready to accommodate a bathroom.

The rather small and compact home is characterized by ceiling-high windows. They can be opened behind the balustrades, converting the rooms into loggias.

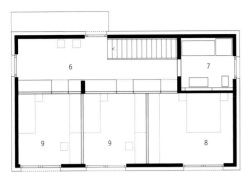

Top floor   scale 1:200

1 entry
2 bathroom
3 office
4 dining/living
5 cooking
6 play hallway
7 bathroom
8 parents
9 child
10 guest
11 storage
12 leisure/hobby
13 technical

First floor   scale 1:200

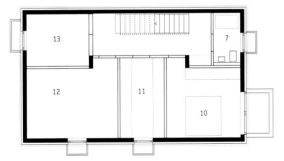

Basement   scale 1:200

Section   scale 1:200

Exposed concrete and oak parquet
neutralize the rooms.

The sliding doors allow for the first floor to
be used either as a large single room or as a
row of rooms. Except for the bathrooms and
two supporting columns, nothing stands in
the way of a simple conversion.

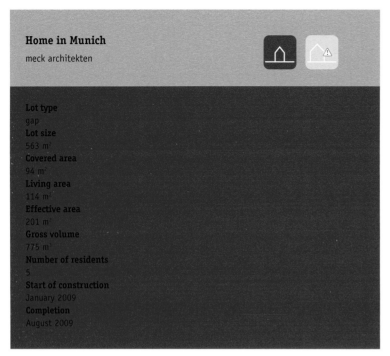

Home in Munich
meck architekten

Lot type
gap
Lot size
563 m²
Covered area
94 m²
Living area
114 m²
Effective area
201 m²
Gross volume
775 m³
Number of residents
5
Start of construction
January 2009
Completion
August 2009

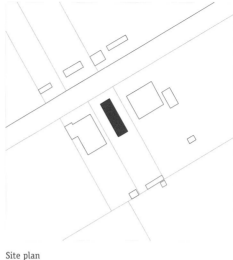

Site plan

Parking space

When two architecture journalists have their home built, one should not necessarily conclude that they would tend to do a better job at it. But you can assume that not only would they formulate their needs more clearly, they would also know how to choose their architects. And there is another issue: if architecture is important to you then the building itself is primary, and you ignore the (expensive) real estate saying of "location, location, location"!

This allowed the family with three children to acquire a narrow lot to the east of Munich which would not fit one of the large impressive homes of this neighborhood. A prefabricated wood frame home was the most feasible solution with regards to cost, building physics, and schedules, and the maximum outer width of 4.80 meters also favored this solution which nevertheless incorporates 20 cm of mineral fiber insulation. The outer wood boards are made from spruce of varying width and painted black; the interior is clad with white drywall. Only the sharp concrete staircase is solid.

Inevitably the floor plan must be organized in a linear manner. The family asked for an open common space and small private quarters for the five members. Hence the only fixed section of the first floor is a bathroom and the kitchen's installation wall. Next to it is an office facing the street, with a ceiling-high sliding door, while the slightly higher living and dining area is oriented toward the garden, as expected.

The children's rooms are lined up in the high upper floor and feature a seemingly endless book shelf along the broad corridor, which will probably help to prepare the children who play here for the demands of life. Initially each child would only get a kind of felt igloo as his or her own private space; however, these later were converted into real cubicles with their own bedroom or work space.

The parents also got their own bedroom gallery above the office space and bathroom. The section shows the different room heights of the parents' and children's quarters which develop from the first floor upwards.

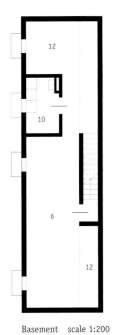

Basement   scale 1:200

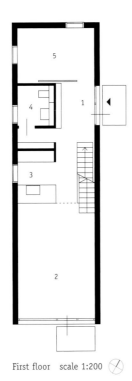

First floor   scale 1:200

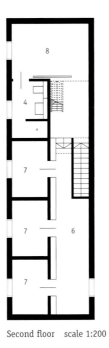

Second floor   scale 1:200

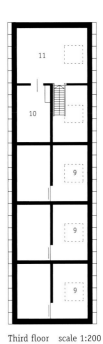

Third floor   scale 1:200

1 entry
2 living
3 kitchen
4 bathroom
5 office
6 play
7 child
8 parents
9 gallery
10 technical
11 library
12 storage

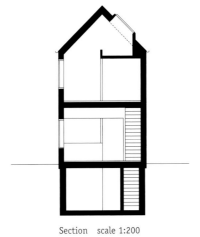

Section   scale 1:200

Even without indentical windows
the architecture has a rhythm.

The house on the narrow lot could
not be wider than the length of a
Porsche Cayenne.

Only band-like apertures are featured on the outer walls. Instead of the balcony, choosing the stroll to the garden is always worthwhile.

Alone and with company: each of the children (as well as the parents) has their gallery.

The common corridor for play is in front of the doors where the parents have set up their large library.

Kitchen and dining area, with a concrete staircase leading upwards. Even the cement screed is coarse: architecture forms the background.

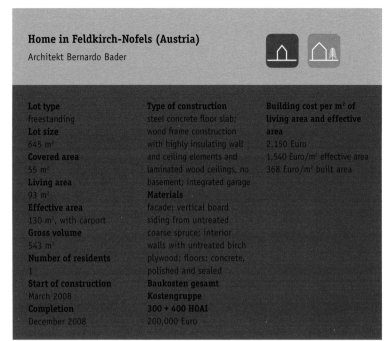

Home in Feldkirch-Nofels (Austria)

Architekt Bernardo Bader

Lot type	**Type of construction**	**Building cost per m² of**
freestanding	steel concrete floor slab;	**living area and effective**
Lot size	wood frame construction	**area**
645 m²	with highly insulating wall	2,150 Euro
Covered area	and ceiling elements and	1,540 Euro/m² effective area
55 m²	laminated wood ceilings, no	368 Euro/m² built area
Living area	basement; integrated garage	
93 m²	**Materials**	
Effective area	facade: vertical board	
130 m², with carport	siding from untreated	
Gross volume	coarse spruce; interior	
543 m³	walls with untreated birch	
Number of residents	plywood; floors: concrete,	
1	polished and sealed	
Start of construction	**Baukosten gesamt**	
March 2008	**Kostengruppe**	
Completion	**300 + 400 HOAI**	
December 2008	200,000 Euro	

Site plan

High-rise

When building, a tight budget is not a sign of poverty; rather, it's a requirement to determine the needs and conditions in detail and to react with a precise design. Here in the Rhine Valley the usual single family home neighborhoods spread in all directions, and this high wood home looks like an ascetic counter model. In order to affect the lot as little as possible, the owner chose to stack three floors on a base of only 56 square meters. A parking space had to be fitted into the first floor as well. Next to it a so-called summer room opens toward a wooden terrace and the garden. A compact staircase from sandwich boards with a pedestal leads upstairs to the shell clad with birch wood, first to two bedrooms or offices with bathroom, then to a living room of 40 square meters under the roof. So cooking, dining, and living occur in an area with a view. Hence the window sills reach very low, and you can sit inside of the deep embrasures facing west. The kitchen window opens to the inside and leaves space for flower and herb pots. This well-thought out order applies to all of the apertures — they don't follow a conventional layout but rather they are placed and sized as is optimal for the view and the illumination.

The exterior is clad with vertical coarse tongue-and-groove fir boards resulting in a planar look. Due to the careful planning and the entire prefabrication at the manufacturer, the time for setting up the construction was reduced to one and a half days. The plywood boards were lined up precisely and bolted. The only luxury consists of the window sills framed with copper sheeting. Heating is provided via a geothermal heat pump.

For the architect it proves how precise and playful the demand for affordable living can turn out to be.

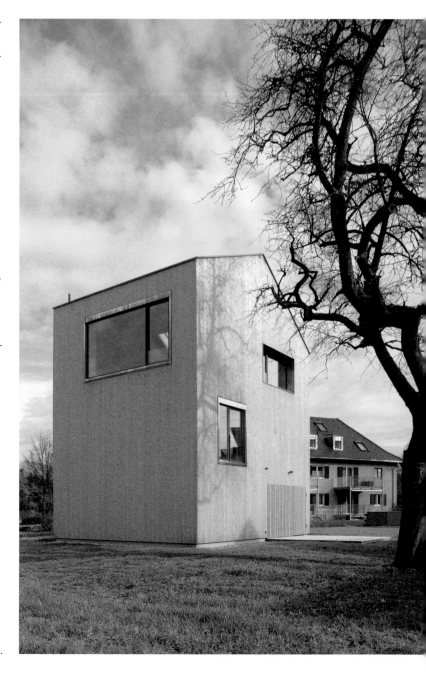

By stacking the small footprints the garden lot was left largely untouched.

Except for the shower cabin the
bathroom features untreated birch
plywood as well.

The living room is below the roof.
The main attraction here is the low
window inviting you to sit on the
broad sill.

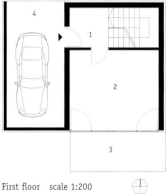

First floor   scale 1:200

Second floor   scale 1:200

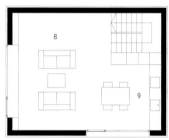

Third floor   scale 1:200

1   entry
2   studio/summer room
3   terrace
4   garage
5   bathroom
6   office
7   bedroom
8   living
9   kitchen/dining

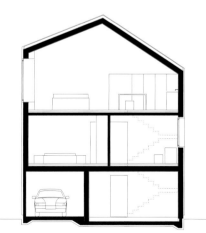

Section   scale 1:200

The wooden staircase is reduced to
its most basic geometry, and the
cuts were selected so as to discard
as little material as possible.

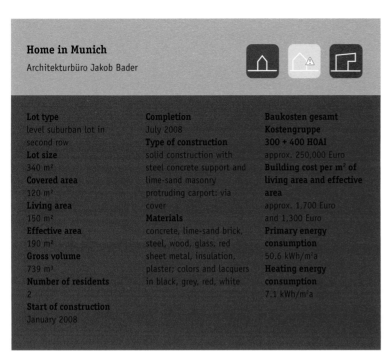

Lot type	Completion	Baukosten gesamt Kostengruppe
level suburban lot in second row	July 2008	300 + 400 HOAI
Lot size	**Type of construction**	approx. 250,000 Euro
340 m²	solid construction with	**Building cost per m² of living area and effective area**
Covered area	steel concrete support and lime-sand masonry	approx. 1,700 Euro
120 m²	protruding carport: via cover	and 1,300 Euro
Living area	**Materials**	**Primary energy consumption**
150 m²	concrete, lime-sand brick,	50.6 kWh/m²a
Effective area	steel, wood, glass, red	**Heating energy consumption**
190 m²	sheet metal, insulation,	7.1 kWh/m²a
Gross volume	plaster; colors and lacquers	
739 m³	in black, grey, red, white	
Number of residents		
2		
Start of construction		
January 2008		

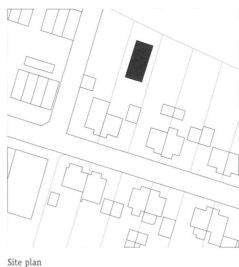

Site plan

Little red rooster

Actually the section — or the mostly-windowless lateral views — shows the design principle of the home in the clearest manner. The largely T-shaped concrete structure stands on a wide base at the center of the building; the upper floor protrudes toward the southern side and provides the two parking spaces below it, while the wedge facing north encompasses a glass facade on the first floor from three sides. There are no supports; rather, tie rods were required to provide the proper balance of static forces.

This, however, was not about challenging the planners in charge of the support structure, but about fitting the required living spaces on the lot and having as much free space as possible. The terrain in a second row is accessed from the south while the view toward the north leads into an exuberant wilderness which was left undeveloped because of the heating pipes crossing the property. One can pretend to be looking into a landscape illuminated by southern light, and reminiscent of English manors. The proportion between open and closed surfaces resulted from the optimal performance of the heat pump.

The dimensions of the home on the small lot could only be realized by skillfully interpreting the building code: the neighbor to the south agreed to share part of the building load on his property, while the lateral distance could be reduced to half due to the 16-meter privilege.

The square basement contains storage spaces and utilities such as the groundwater heat pump which can be controlled online. The entrances lie under the protruding section of the building: to the right is the first floor while the staircase to the top floor is to the left. The floor plans are symmetrical and the kitchen is located in front of the dining area and sofas, like an altar. On top of that you reach the bedroom, with a view of the sky due to the glass roof, which features a terrace hidden behind the flanks of the building. To the south is an office space which can be partitioned into two children's rooms.

The determining feature consists of the overall design, not its specific details. The red facade and the painted insulating plaster emit a signal: a shining cubature for a reasonable design.

1 entry
2 kitchen
3 dining/living
4 office
5 bathroom
6 bedroom
7 terrace
8 technical
9 storage

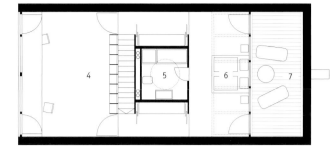

Top floor   scale 1:200

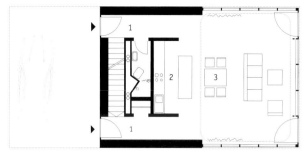

First floor   scale 1:200

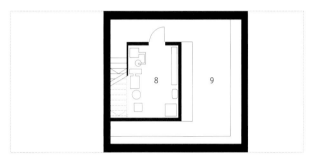

Basement   scale 1:200

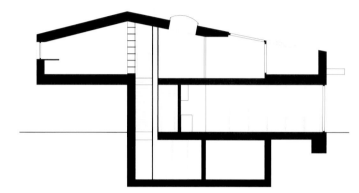

Section   scale 1:200

The protruding top floor saves lot area. The two entrances are behind the carport (photo, opposite left).

The living room, glazed on three sides with the kitchen behind it like an altar. The finish appears austere and robust; the emphasis is on the general idea, not on artificial details.

Lot type	Completion	Baukosten gesamt
forest lot	2010	Kostengruppe
Lot size	**Type of construction,**	**300 + 400 HOAI**
995 m²	**materials**	approx. 90,000 Euro
Covered area	the goal was to create a	
49 m²	home entirely from pine	**Building cost per m²**
Living area	wood, the primary building	**living area and effective**
62 m²	material; entirely made from	**area**
Effective area	wood — wood frame walls,	approx. 1,450 Euro
62 m²	exterior sides with dark-	
Gross volume	brown varnished pine	
218 m³	siding, interior entirely with	
Number of residents	painted white pine siding;	
3	rafter roof with insulation,	
Start of construction	strip foundations	
2010		

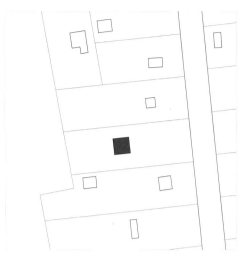

Site plan

Irony and deeper meaning

The architects had purchased a wooden home from 1926 on a wooded lot as a weekend home. Unfortunately it turned out to be so rotted that a renovation was out of the question. So they built it anew. The result, though, was not a basic bungalow but a forest cabin that combines functionality, love for detail, and craftsmanship with personal mythologies.

At first sight you would expect a traditional weekend home behind the horizontal dark-brown siding ending in arch-like edges. It must have been built ages ago. But then you notice the irony which characterizes the charming house. The bright deck over the entire broadside is highly unusual, just like the white passe-partout around the windows and the entrance door. The house seems to have rescued a few images from the recent history of building. The interior, clad with white tongue-and-groove boards, lies somewhere between a houseboat and an American East Coast home, and the shower cabin with small red tiles and their rounded edges reminds one of the

1960s. The kitchen made from spruce plywood seems to originate from a Swedish furniture retail chain.

But apart from this uninhibited treatment of the appointments, the home exhibits much spatial economy for a weekend home. The kitchen and bathroom are accessed from the lateral sides of the entrance. The only-4-meter-wide living room with dining area lies straight ahead. The deck features fully glazed sliding door elements. When you enter the kitchen you are not locked up either: a room-wide service hatch opens toward the dining table.

There are two ways to get upstairs: to a reading and guest gallery via a ladder, and, somewhat more comfortable and more discreet, via a narrow door and a steep stairwell to the sleeping bunks for parents and child. In between, the small house presents itself in its real size, reaching up under the roof.

The entrance side in particular provides clues as to the year of manufacture. The taxidermied animals leave no doubt: one has become lost in a magic forest.

The central living space with its two lateral galleries reaches under the roof. A wood stove is sufficient to heat the small house.

First floor   scale 1:200

Attic   scale 1:200

1 entry
2 kitchen
3 living
4 terrace
5 bathroom
6 bedroom
7 air space
8 gallery

Section   scale 1:200

An inconspicuous door leads to the
sleeping bunks upstairs, and the
reading gallery is accessed by
climbing a ladder.

The forest home replaces a rotten
hut which was not worth restoring.
The new design leaves hints as to
the former house, but also sets new
standards with its bright deck.

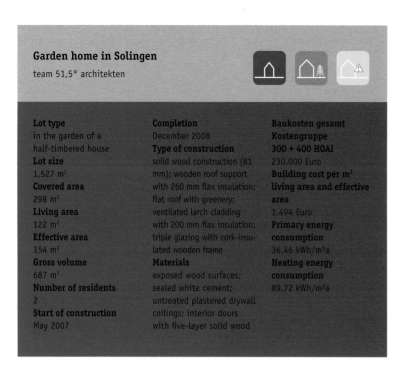
Lot type	**Completion**	**Baukosten gesamt**
in the garden of a	December 2008	**Kostengruppe**
half-timbered house	**Type of construction**	**300 + 400 HOAI**
Lot size	solid wood construction (81	230,000 Euro
1,527 m²	mm); wooden roof support	**Building cost per m²**
Covered area	with 260 mm flax insulation;	**living area and effective**
298 m²	flat roof with greenery;	**area**
Living area	ventilated larch cladding	1,494 Euro
122 m²	with 200 mm flax insulation;	**Primary energy**
Effective area	triple glazing with cork-insu-	**consumption**
154 m²	lated wooden frame	36.46 kWh/m²a
Gross volume	**Materials**	**Heating energy**
687 m³	exposed wood surfaces;	**consumption**
Number of residents	sealed white cement;	89.72 kWh/m²a
2	untreated plastered drywall	
Start of construction	ceilings; interior doors	
May 2007	with five-layer solid wood	

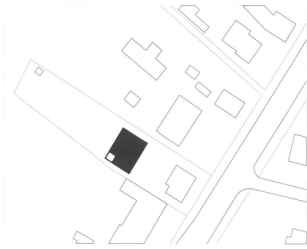

Site plan

Square, convenient, no barriers

A home that answers several questions regarding contemporary building: it is located in the second row of a deep lot and makes a contribution to urban densification, since as a low-energy house it makes effective use of renewable resources (solid wood elements with flax insulation and larch siding), and in particular it shows a functional floor plan for two older residents.

The concept of living space of the two clients who are close to retirement was shaped by the ideas of "dream homes" during the 1960s and experiences with a 200-year-old half-timber home and its garden where this flat-roofed bungalow was built. The space allocation is elaborate.

Unusual is how the small open functional rooms are set around the central dining area (also lighted from above), while being clearly oriented toward the garden. The tight compartments for living, bedrooms, and office do not have doors; they are located at the edges of the square house like the wings

of a windmill and only separated from the atrium of the dining area by narrow doorways. Only the kitchen, bathrooms, and a small room for guests feature doors. A storage room is located next to the entrance.

The layout of these boxes results in a floor plan with minimal barriers, and you can drive a wheelchair around without problems. The central room is lined with ceiling-high built-in shelves which interrupt the wood siding of the dividing walls. A utility room, fireplace, and a sauna are part of the affordable home's facilities.

The windows with their cork-insulated wooden frames are triple glazed, and energy is provided by a solar system on the roof with greenery as well as a wood pellet furnace for the floor heating. The fuel is stored inside a roof trough over the low sauna and the solar module: a retirement home which follows young modern concepts.

Urban densification in your own yard: the deep lot allowed for building a new retirement home.

Unusual: the wood pellets for the heating system are stored in a container on the roof of the bungalow.

The footprint is divided into niches and closed rooms.

The dining table is located at the center, with additional light entering via a window in the flat roof.

The house was built cost-effectively, but due to the ceiling-high wood and glass elements it does not appear to be frugal.

1 entry
2 bathroom
3 living
4 guest
5 bedroom
6 dining
7 technical
8 sauna
9 office
10 utility room
11 cooking
12 carport
13 storage

First floor   scale 1:200 ⊗

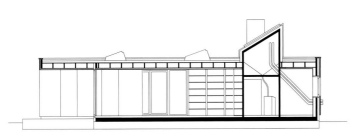

Section   scale 1:200

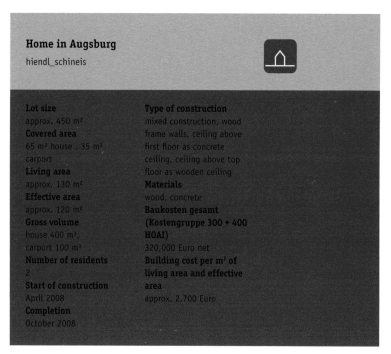

Home in Augsburg

hiendl_schineis

Lot size	**Type of construction**
approx. 450 m²	mixed construction, wood
Covered area	frame walls, ceiling above
65 m² house , 35 m²	first floor as concrete
carport	ceiling, ceiling above top
Living area	floor as wooden ceiling
approx. 130 m²	**Materials**
Effective area	wood, concrete
approx. 120 m²	**Baukosten gesamt**
Gross volume	**(Kostengruppe 300 + 400**
house 400 m³,	**HOAI)**
carport 100 m³	320,000 Euro net
Number of residents	**Building cost per m² of**
2	**living area and effective**
Start of construction	**area**
April 2008	approx. 2,700 Euro
Completion	
October 2008	

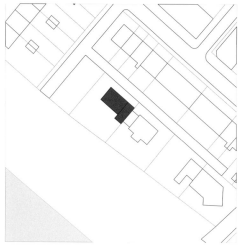

Site plan

Peaceful Lechfeld

The flat lot located in the Augsburg neighborhood of Lechhausen lies right at the river bank, and is accessed via a private street. The clients wanted a small home without a carport, with a footprint of only 60 square meters, two floors, and a flat roof: a simple, sharp-edged cube in mixed construction with its ceiling-high glass fronts opening up toward the garden. The closed facades are clad with vertical white-lacquered larch wood boards which are of varying width, and the enclosure picks up this pattern. The entire building is made without diffusion barriers and no solvent-containing materials were used. Even silicone was avoided wherever possible; all of the seams are done as shadow gaps.

The construction type is a mix of wood and concrete. The concrete basement supports wood frame walls which are insulated on the inside with Fermacell. On top of it lies another concrete ceiling while the roof over the top floor consists of glued laminated timber elements.

The bright look and feel is continued in the interior. The floors consist of white pigmented screed finished with white silicate paint, and the window profiles are also painted white. Rails for sliding doors are set into the light-colored concrete ceilings of the first floor and the large-format, white Lenotec elements on the top floor.

The layout of the home is organized very clearly and logically. The corridor below is separated from the open living/dining area below, parallel to the staircase at the exterior wall, and by the guest lavatory, wardrobe, and book shelves, while the library continues on the top floor, only interrupted by the corridor next to the stairwell. The kitchen counter organizes the remaining functions and terminates at a fireplace. A door for the short distance between storage space, car, and trash is located on the other side.

The top floor shows the luxury of living on a small area. Apart from the bedroom, enough space was provided for two office rooms (or a guest room) while a sauna is located past the bathroom. Toward the garden is a loggia which allows for a view of the surroundings. All of the built-in furniture is made from oak.

The home has a partial basement with a utility room for the heat pump that powers the floor heating system.

A bookshelf wall lines the staircase and a small gallery on top of it. The fireplace defines the transition between the kitchen/dining area and the living room.

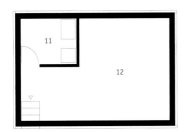

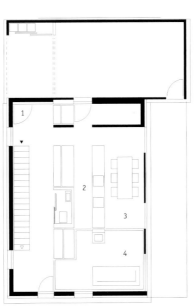

1 entry
2 kitchen
3 dining
4 living
5 guest
6 bedroom
7 bathroom
8 loggia
9 office
10 sauna
11 technical
12 storage

Basement   scale 1:200

First floor   scale 1:200

Top floor   scale 1:200

The small and compact home lies directly beside the river. Once the snow has melted you can see the poplars and willows at the bank.

Even the bathroom, protected by a loggia on the top floor, offers an uninterrupted view.

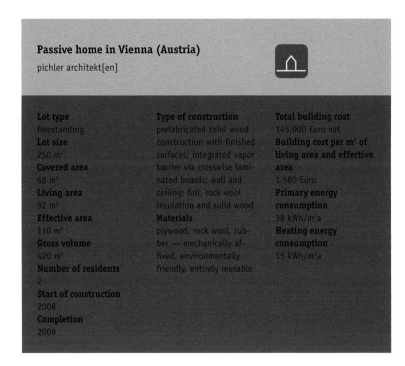

Passive home in Vienna (Austria)
pichler architekt[en]

Lot type	Type of construction	Total building cost
freestanding	prefabricated solid wood	145,000 Euro net
Lot size	construction with finished	**Building cost per m² of**
250 m²	surfaces; integrated vapor	**living area and effective**
Covered area	barrier via crosswise lami-	**area**
68 m²	nated boards; wall and	1,580 Euro
Living area	ceiling: foil, rock wool	**Primary energy**
92 m²	insulation and solid wood	**consumption**
Effective area	**Materials**	38 kWh/m²a
110 m²	plywood, rock wool, rub-	**Heating energy**
Gross volume	ber — mechanically af-	**consumption**
420 m³	fixed, environmentally	15 kWh/m²a
Number of residents	friendly, entirely reusable	
2		
Start of construction		
2008		
Completion		
2009		

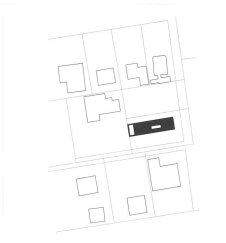

Site plan

The small black one

A passive home does not have to demonstrate an ascetic worldview any-more — there are now plenty of examples that do not exhibit their energy concept. In the case of this black house things were different. They includ-ed a very narrow lot, a minimal living area, and a manageable budget to-gether with an alternative design. This example shows that architects tend to build for themselves with much ingenuity, and forsaking common finish-ing details.

The construction itself is unusual. Rockwool mats of 18 cm thickness were affixed with anchors to the 9-cm-thick spruce plywood boards on the sup-porting exposed structure. The triple gluing of the three-layer wood ele-ments functions as a vapor retarder. Now the outer finish of the facade is followed by black synthetic rubber sections. The architect ironically calls this cladding a "diving suit" which also serves as a heat collector. A large section of the facade, however, is closed with triple-glazed windows.

The dimensions of the house are unusual: 16.35 x 4.20 meters. This, at 68 square meters of covered area, results in a living area of 92 square meters.

The spatial economy starts at the entrance and leads directly into the living area. The core is a block consisting of a bathroom and staircase, and right behind it you reach the open kitchen with the dining area. A large pantry is located at the closed narrow side. A long slit in the ceiling remains open next to the staircase, and provides volume to the compact rooms. Toward the top you enter the office and bedroom, which are only suggestively sepa-rated by built-in cabinet and shelf elements next to the staircase. A fixed glazed opening in the roof provides illumination and seems to interrupt the apparently hermetic circumvallation.

The utility room in the basement contains a groundwater heat pump since this area does not allow for a total reliance on the passive home standard during cold winter days. It services the floor heating system on the first floor, covered with black ceramic tiles, where a stove is located as well. The rising heat is sufficient for the top floor.

Apparently a wooden home. The support
structure is visible on the inside. The
layout of the areas can do almost entirely
without corridors.

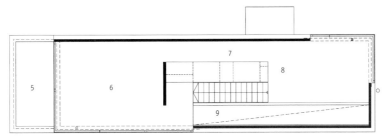

Top floor   scale 1:200

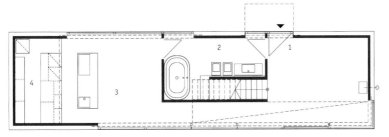

First floor   scale 1:200

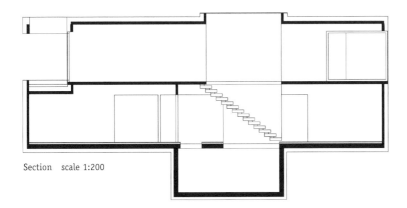

Section   scale 1:200

1   entry
2   bathroom
3   dining/cooking
4   pantry
5   terrace
6   bedroom
7   dressing room
8   office
9   air space

Because money had to be saved with regards to the total surface, a cut in the ceiling provides subjective size.

The insulating facade is clad with black sections of synthetic rubber.

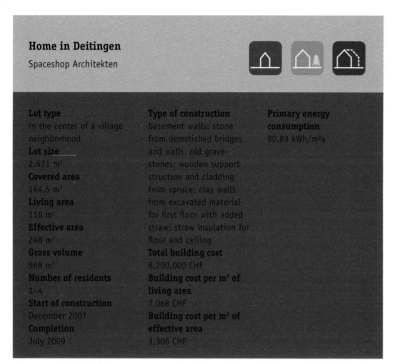

Home in Deitingen
Spaceshop Architekten

Lot type	Type of construction	Primary energy
in the center of a village	basement walls: stone	consumption
neighborhood	from demolished bridges	90.83 kWh/m²a
Lot size	and walls, old grave-	
2,671 m²	stones; wooden support	
Covered area	structure and cladding	
164.5 m²	from spruce; clay walls	
Living area	from excavated material	
116 m²	for first floor with added	
Effective area	straw; straw insulation for	
248 m²	floor and ceiling	
Gross volume	**Total building cost**	
968 m³	8,200,000 CHF	
Number of residents	**Building cost per m² of**	
1–4	**living area**	
Start of construction	7,068 CHF	
December 2007	**Building cost per m² of**	
Completion	**effective area**	
July 2009	3,306 CHF	

Site plan

Living naturally

When building a conventional freestanding single family home, one does not provide a sustainable contribution to the stabilization of the environment. The manufacture and transport of the materials, the running and maintenance of the home, perhaps the daily commute to the workplace all result in a negative energy balance compared to if the clients had stayed in their apartment in the city.

But there are other alternatives. This energy-self-sufficient home was built from renewable or recycled materials and is heated exclusively with renewable energy sources. The client, a master gardener, built the home next to the large farmhouse after his children moved out, and instructed his design team to consider all of the aspects related to autonomy, ecology, and health. The extraordinary consequence is the result of four different architecture firms.

The final home reacts to the terrain as a single-floor pavilion with a slightly staggered design, and this arrangement allows for a variety of ambiences and moods between the patio and the garden. It celebrates living in nature via an equilibrium between openness and private seclusion. The design consists of three volumes, of two offset L-shaped walls with their frontal sides glazed along the entire height. The entrance leads to the center with

a kitchen stove and dining area, and a garden room with a view of the old farmhouse is located following the narrow corridor. The more quiet area for the bedroom and bathroom faces the other side toward the stream. The basement is accessed via an exterior stairwell.

The main building material is clay — which was piled up, with mixed-in shredded straw, to 80-centimeter-thick straight walls — and some load-bearing wooden columns. The basement was built with unfinished gravestones which the owner had collected over the years, and stones left over from the demolition. The wood for the support structure comes from the nearby forest. Attention was paid to the fact that all of the materials had to come from areas no farther away than 10 kilometers. Even the craftsmen had only short distances to cover to get to the building site. The dimensions of the wood beams of the floor and roof construction resulted from the width of the insulating straw bales.

A spring provides running water and a sand filtering system takes care of the sewage. Heating is provided by a wood-burning furnace, and electricity is generated by photovoltaics. Living becomes a personal and essential ritual. The client enjoys it.

The floors in the basement consist of marl while the living level features spruce. The layout corresponds to an active living style.

Behind the former farmhouse the owner enjoys his small new pavilion for retreating into nature.

The simple construction method is entirely based on environmentally friendly parameters.

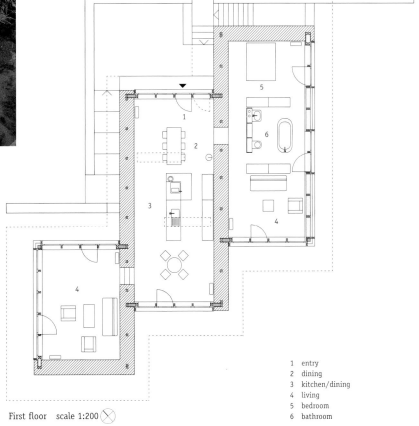

First floor   scale 1:200 ⊗

1   entry
2   dining
3   kitchen/dining
4   living
5   bedroom
6   bathroom

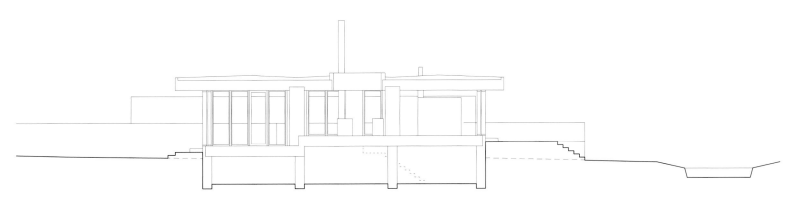

Section   scale 1:200

Home in Hesbaye (Belgium)

Atelier d'Architecture Alain Richard

Lot type	Type of construction, materials
freestanding	foundations made from
Lot size	in-situ concrete; supporting
300 m²	brickwork from clad and
Covered area	precast concrete elements;
180 m²	precast concrete elements
Living area	for ceiling; exposed con-
120 m²	crete facade; fiber cement
Effective area	shingles; wood
90 m²	**Building cost**
Gross volume	208,000 Euro
560 m³	**Building cost for house**
Number of residents	170,000 Euro
2	**For auxiliary buildings**
Planning	25,000 Euro
February to November 2007	**For furniture**
Duration of construction	13,000 Euro
April 2008 to April 2009	

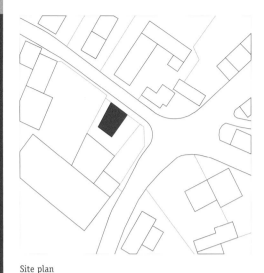

Site plan

Elementary particle

You would have to know the area, the small unassuming homes which have been refurbished and expanded over the course of time. The lots are somewhat carelessly fenced in, and poles with cables, electric, and telephone lines stand next to the patched streets. The family's parents owned a vegetable garden in the village, a part of which could be utilized for the lot.

It seemed obvious to build a house with a fairly simple cubature with a basic randomly perforated facade as a response to the heterogenous neighborhood. Formal cohesion is provided to the monopitched roof of the slightly angular house cube with gray fiber cement shingles which are affixed diagonally with a rhombic pattern. The shingle texture covers the facade without any specific pattern and provides a uniform background for the different window and door designs. Verge, ridge, and house edges are unassuming to emphasize the physicality of the cube.

The wooden gate of the garage, which continues as a high screen next to the house, makes a difference toward the street, a motif which repeats on the side as a home entrance. Past the garage you reach the basement which

extends to the garden. The main access is located on the other side, half a floor farther up over the staircase platform. Farther up lies the entrance to the garden level. Here lies a single room heated by a wood stove where, after passing the wardrobe and the laundry room, you can take a shower after working in the garden. Past the low kitchen you enter the living/dining area which reaches up to the roof, illuminated via a glazed sliding element in the corner. The tilting outer wall, the back of the seating corner, indicates a protective motif on the terrace.

The top floor contains a single bedroom and a bathroom. Next to it lies an office space which is open toward the lower living room as a gallery and heated by its wood stove. In case of extreme cold, electric radiators help out. All of the functions are organized in a compact way as if it were a cockpit; the frugality of the surroundings has found a charming and modern match.

The home fits into the unassuming environment without exhibiting its condition as a newcomer.

A central wood stove stands in the low kitchen; the higher living area provides size to the small house.

A terrace is located facing the garden.

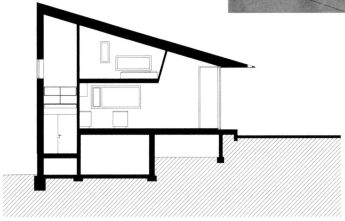

Section   scale 1:200

1 entry
2 kitchen
3 dining
4 living
5 terrace
6 laundry/shower
7 technical
8 bedroom
9 office
10 bathroom

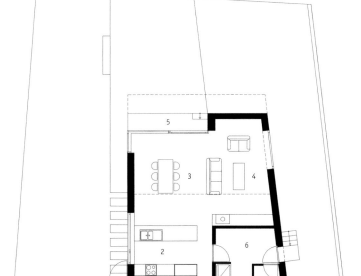

First floor   scale 1:200

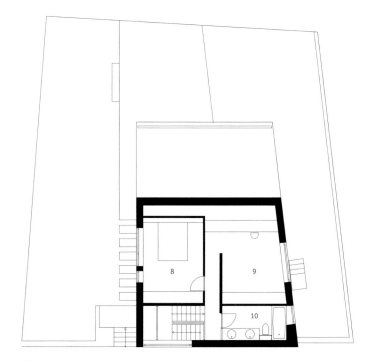

Top floor   scale 1:200

Hunting lodge in Tamers (Italy)
EM2 Architekten

Lot type
on a slightly sloping
hillside in the Fanes
Sennes Prags National
Park, South Tyrol, Italy
Lot size
1,700 m²
Covered area
87 m²
Net living area
108 m²
Gross volume
533 m³
Number of residents
4
Start of construction
2008
Completion
2009

**Type of construction,
materials**
wood (The hunting lodge
in Tamers consists of two
separate buildings. Traditional building concept;
openings in living and
dining room reduced to a
minimum.)
**Baukosten gesamt
Kostengruppe
300 + 400 HOAI**
600,000 Euro
**Building cost per m²
net living area**
5,555 Euro
**Primary energy
consumption**
47.71 kWh/m²a

**Heating energy
consumption**
12.96 kWh/m²a

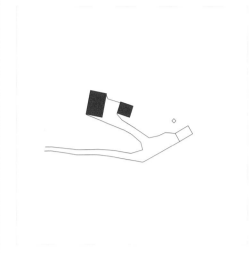

Site plan

Forest aroma

It is called a hunting lodge, and you might ask yourself whether you need one
for yourself. Actually the peaceful vacation home exhibits a wealth of ideas on
how to build a vacation cabin in the forest that is compatible with nature.

The building mass is reduced by being divided between two small houses.
The main building consists of two floors. The first floor is reserved for cooking and living. A brickwork oven stands firmly in the center of this house
made entirely from wood. The floor above contains the bathroom and two
sleeping bunks. Benches, cabinets, beds, and even the sofa are arranged as
box-like built-in furnishings, certainly the best solution when the vacation
home is used by various guests and visitors.

The second smaller building is intended to be a refuge. Its western side
consists of two gates so it can be almost entirely opened toward the main
building. The two buildings are definitely in some sort of dialog with each
other, the existing topography, and the surrounding trees, and the corresponding entrances of these slightly offset artifacts of different size create
a subtle tension.

The houses are built with the regional block building method. The edges of
the homes clearly allow the fitting of the logs to be seen ("Tyrolean castle"). This type of construction, the spatial typology, and the saddle roofs
are based on the tradition of the location. The apertures have been reduced
to a minimum and are limited to the living and dining areas, and can be
closed off with solid sliding doors on the outside when nobody is home. The
rooms camouflage themselves behind the highly insulated facade with window slits of the size of the squared timber. The interior features long lights
which are inserted into the planed larch boards. A floor heating system is
installed under the floor boards.

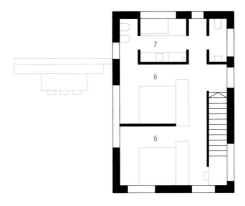

Top floor   scale 1:200

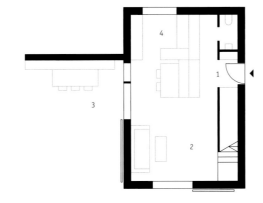
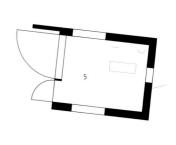

1 entry
2 living
3 terrace
4 kitchen
5 meditation
6 bedroom
7 bathroom

First floor   scale 1:200

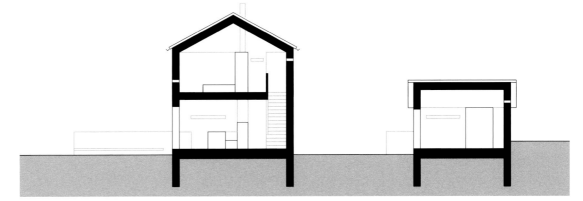

Apart from the small window slits, there are large openings which can be secured with sliding doors.

The hunting lodge was intended to be of small size, so a relaxing and meditation room was placed next to it (photo, opposite bottom).

A brickwork stove is the warm center of the home. The built-in furniture is convenient for changing residents.

Section   scale 1:200

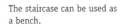

The staircase can be used as a bench.

Home in Leichlingen

köppen strauch, architekten

Lot type
freestanding
Lot size
1,500 m²
Covered area
300 m²
Living area
375 m²
Effective area
71 m²
Gross volume
1,900 m³
Number of residents
3
Start of construction
February 2008
Completion
June 2009

Type of construction
solid construction with
lime-sand bricks; lintels
over windows prefabricated;
geothermal heat pump with
solar installation and use of
rainwater; two-layer facade
construction with insulation
Materials
facade: peat-baked bricks;
roof: flat roof with extensive
greenery; windows: alumi-
num profiles, triple glazing;
lime plaster; wood floors:
solid oiled and waxed
wooden boards; natural
stone bathroom: limestone;
entrance area with zebrano

wall cladding; terrace cover:
black natural stone
**Primary energy
consumption**
82.1 kWh/m²a
**Heating energy
consumption**
62.46 kWh/m²a

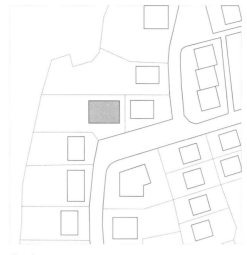

Site plan

Neutral and flexible use

Leichlingen is a small town at the northen corner of the Rhine-Bergische district. The lot lies above the city — in an area with a heterogenous mix of freestanding homes, but which features an attractive view of the lower-lying valley of the Wupper River. The compact and reduced shape of the building and the peat-baked brick facades are intended to mediate between these contradictory conditions. The reddish masonry emphasizes the solidity of the two-layer construction type of the home: the supporting walls consist of lime-sand bricks. Large closed areas remain between the window openings which are divided by the pattern of the bricks; a lively color effect on their irregular surface provides an interesting look.

From the street the house welcomes the visitor with a recessed patio, with its lateral wall flanks connecting to an inviting hall glazing with a height of two floors. The interior of the entrance is clad with zebrano wood. The main section of the home is located on the first floor which opens toward a terrace which surrounds the house, particularly toward the west. It expands, protected by a pergola at the corner, over an auxiliary room sticking up from the sloping lot like a bulwark.

The interior layout is free of barriers and flexibly organized as a multigenerational home. The top floor features a granny flat which can be used by the parents or the children. The orientation of the floor plans allows for maximum privacy while the tree-lined garden is readily accessible. The geometry and the proportions of the rooms are laid out so that later changes for new applications and uses are easily made.

The home had to be as environmentally friendly as possible. A geothermal heat pump, solar system, and usage of rainwater are part of the concept. The extensive greenery on the roof replaces sealed surfaces.

The surrounding terrace features a steel pergola as the seating area in front of the living room.

The garden slope is modeled by steps, and the seating space on the bulwark-like utility room provides an overview.

The house has a formal look toward the street due to its glazed entrance hall and the large closed wall surfaces.

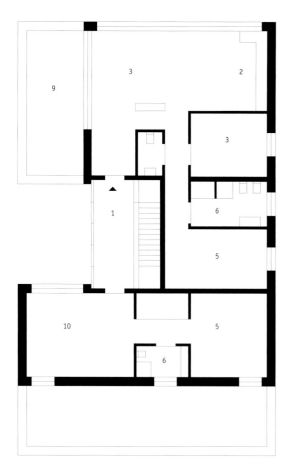

Second floor   scale 1:200

1 entry
2 kitchen
3 living
4 utility room
5 bedroom
6 bathroom
7 garage
8 office
9 terrace
10 studio

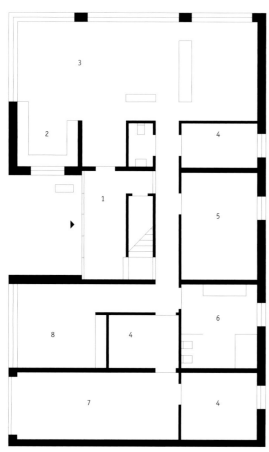

First floor   scale 1:200

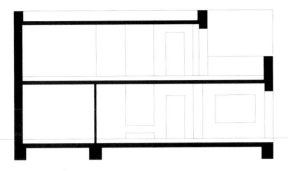

Section   scale 1:200

The interior rooms are laid out without
barriers. The structure of the rooms facilitates
later modifications for new usages.

Lot type	Type of construction,
freestanding	materials
Lot size	steel concrete, steel,
500 m²	facade: clad with
Covered area	semi-transparent polycar-
200 m²	bonate elements; floor:
Living area	first floor with sealed
300 m²	screed, top floor with
Effective area	parquet; leveled and
300 m²	painted walls
Number of residents	**Primary energy**
3	**consumption**
Start of construction	22 kWh/m²a
May 2010	
Completion	
December 2010	

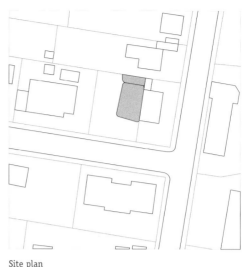

Site plan

Inside the living garden

A family with one child wanted to swap their inner city apartment for a move to the edge of town. This change was intended to provide all of the good things related to living in nature with a garden, not so much a romantic simulation of apparently slow-growth, wooden surroundings, but as a balance between modern architecture and green nature.

The central theme here is the 500-square-meter garden which looks like a huge walk-in terrarium with hills, trees, and a lawn continuing the living room, and a pond and its filtering system completing the green concept. A semitransparent fence consisting of 2.10-meter-high polycarbonate boards, the same material as the facades, prolongs the soft contour of the three-level home. On the outer walls of the top floor the insulation on the supporting concrete is covered with aluminum foil, which results in appealing light effects and reflections on the polycarbonate boards.

The first floor continues the green theme leaning against the entrance and wellness area at a hermetic angle. The living room is lowered and fitted with a green deep-pile carpet. A fireplace with a sill and media equipment divides the dining area from the built-in kitchen installations along the

curved outer wall. The motif of rounded edges connects the interior and exterior, and a light-colored outer curtain protects the ceiling-high glass front facing the garden.

On the top floor the main bedroom takes up the southwest curve, completed by a bathroom and dressing room. Three children's bedrooms or guest rooms follow, divided from the corridor by a cabinet wall.

Another highlight is accessed via a second staircase on the roof. A study/office lies under a cupola which leads to a roof garden. The section shows that the massive floor ceiling has been generously filled with earth so that trees and larger plants can grow. This "hilly office" landscape brings back the green area which has been lost due to the building at ground level.

The main topic of the design is the garden which continues the smooth, shiny contour of the house with its transparent fence.

Whatever was lost of the green areas due to the building process was recovered with the lush greenery on the roof.

The glazed living level can be protected with a light-colored curtain.

The rounded facade is clad with polycarbonate boards, and silver shimmer is enhanced with aluminum foil on the insulation.

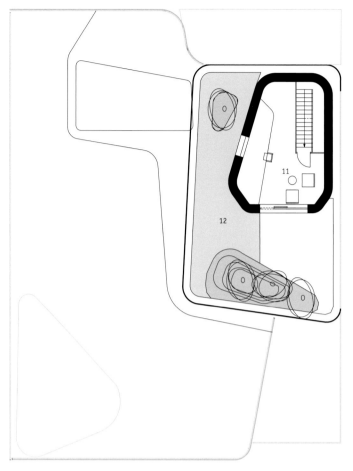

Attic   scale 1:200

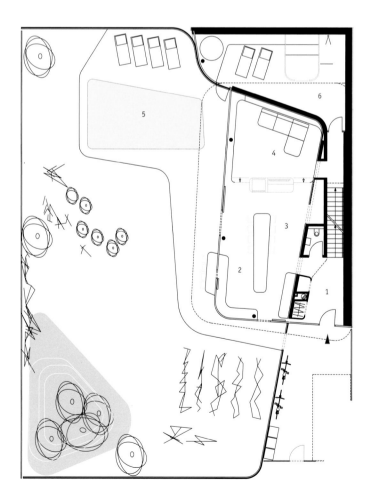

First floor   scale 1:200

1 entry
2 kitchen/dining
3 fireplace
4 living
5 pool
6 wellness
7 bathroom
8 parents
9 dressing room
10 child/guest
11 office
12 roof garden

Top floor   scale 1:200

Basement   scale 1:200

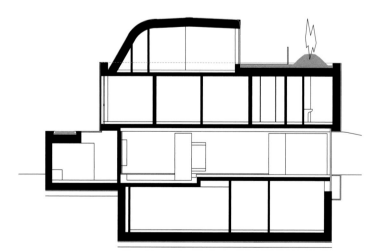

Section   scale 1:200

The office is located below the roof cupola and features an exit toward a roof garden.

The bright pop colors of the bedrooms match the style (photo, right).

A custom-made shelf with a fireplace and media equipment divides the kitchen, dining area, and the sofa corner. The soft contours are reminiscent of designs from the 1960s.

Dining area and kitchen. The rear side of the media-fireplace unit contains the bar.

A separate staircase leads to the study under the roof.

Home in Binningen (Switzerland)
Buchner Bründler Architekten

Lot size
1,130 m²
Covered area
210 m²
Effective area
290 m²
Number of residents
4
Start of construction
January 2008
Completion
February 2009
Type of construction
concrete outer visible
support structure; concrete
for kitchen, bathroom,
fireplace and seating, with
white pigments

Materials
outside: exposed
white-pigmented concrete;
bathroom: glass mosaic;
windows: larch wood

Site plan

Enclave

The home is located in a quiet residential area in Binningen, providing an almost hermetic, private retreat for a young family. Its roughly-finished concrete shell rests on a hill, slightly set into the ground, its type corresponding to that of a patio home creating an almost convent-like enclave. The property, surrounded by rows of single family homes, is accessed via a private driveway from the east and ends in front of a gate with the height of the perimeter wall of the windowless first floor.

Behind it a dark cobblestone patio opens up, containing the ceiling-high glazed hobby area and lined with utility rooms and garages. The entrance to the upper floor is located laterally at the outer wall, closed off by a massive wing.

The main architectural themes are supporting and spanning. The sculptural concrete clearly shows its support function as a column, beam, or wall. The patio is straddled by a wing of the upper floor resulting in a second, even more intimate open space which illuminates the deep structure like an atrium. The white concrete is exhibited in the interior as well, as in the kitchen elements, bathroom, fireplace, and seating.

The upper floor openly surrounds the atrium, which is lined by the kitchen. The L-shaped living room is open toward the southwest and a protruding pergola from solid concrete panels provides shade over the terrace. A top garden is also surrounded by a solid wall. Robinia and birch trees contrast with the austere and hard surfaces. Between the terrace and the outer wall is a swimming pool with a small patio at its end, serving also to illuminate the main bedroom.

The two chidren's rooms are oriented toward the south on the section straddling the patio. A narrow corridor provides access and closes off the roundabout of the atrium. Next to the staircase is another office room which reaches above the wall of the first floor. The furniture consists of white lacquered larch wood fixtures which fill niches and follow the suite of rooms. As continuations of the wood-paneled wall surfaces and lacquered window embrasures, the furniture items become spatially determining sculptures.

The protecting barriers continue on the top floor with the massive canopy of the terrace pergola.

There is no need for signs; the architecture clearly indicates where the private quarters begin.

Auxiliary rooms and garages line the atrium on the lower level, which is partially straddled by the top floor like a bridge.

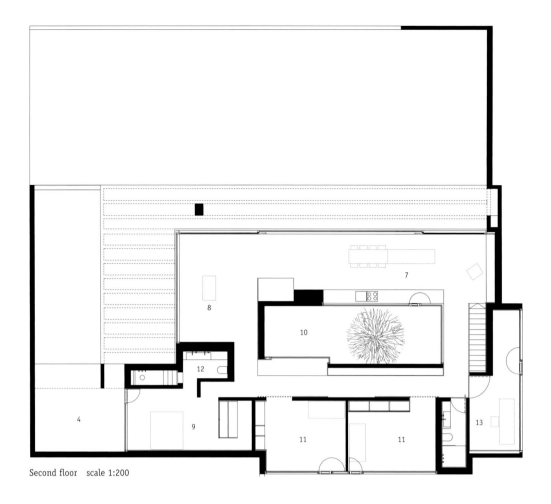

Second floor   scale 1:200

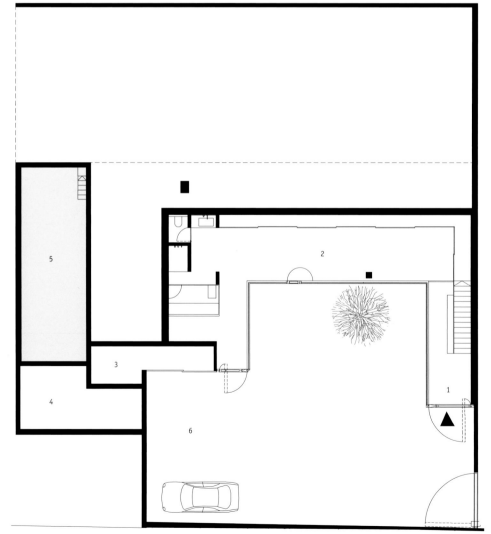

First floor   scale 1:200

1 entry
2 hobby/wellness
3 technical
4 atrium
5 pool
6 garage
7 kitchen/dining
8 living
9 parents
10 interior patio
11 child
12 bathroom
13 guest

The kitchen as a navigation bridge. From here you can see the terrace and the gate. The built-in furniture conforms to the immobile architectural elements.

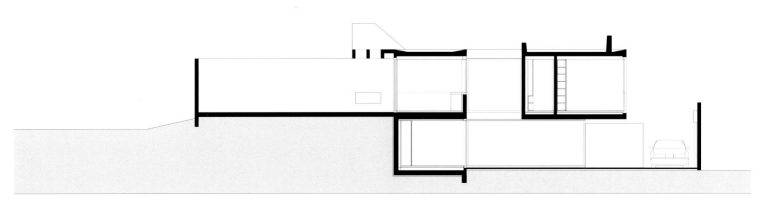

Section   scale 1:200

Home in Nürtingen

Zelle_03 Manuela Fernández Langenegger

Lot type	Type of construction, materials
freestanding	solid concrete construction
Lot size	combines with wood for
634 m²	the upper floor; three
Covered area	materials dominate: con-
approx. 160 m²	crete, larch, glass
Living area	
approx. 186 m²	
Number of residents	
3	
Start of construction	
January 2009	
Completion	
October 2009	

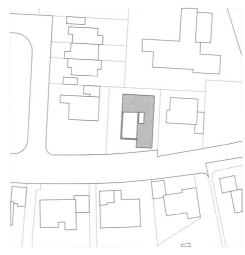

Site plan

Part of the ground

It took the architect three years to get the building permit for her home. The concept of an environmentally friendly low-energy home cleverly balances local building codes and personal ideas and helped to finally get the green light.

The lot is part of a larger property owned by the family and rises some 1.70 meters to the street toward the south. As the height of the lower edge and the crest of the room were predetermined, the ground could have been leveled to only allow for a two-floor house. The view would have been less attractive. The alternative solution was to accept the lot with its wonderful tall trees and to nest the architecture within it. The first floor became a partial basement and the generous depression at the south does not result in a subterranean feeling, rather, the intimate view from the protected atrium toward the treetops can be enjoyed from here.

After a few low steps you reach the entrance, and inside the bright foyer, the view follows over the terrace into the garden and proves the crafty negotia-

tion with the topography. The L-shaped building's first floor circumscribes the atrium with the shorter leg fitting utility rooms while the larger wing contains the kitchen/dining area and living room, separated only by a staircase.

The staircase rests on a low cabinet which is crossed via the angular top steps. It is the sculptural part of the design concept which, together with the built-in furniture, conforms the characteristic spatial features. Free-flowing rooms with several bench-like seating accommodations allow for space without being crowded with household items. The staircase leads to the top floor, arriving at a large playroom corridor with the bedrooms for parents, children, and guests, flanked by bathrooms.

The basement is made from concrete with the ceiling not being covered with screed; on top of it is a wooden construction. The facades as well are clad with vertical larch boards. The triple-glazed windows are united to form large surfaces. Architecture in this case clearly shows how it can surround the residents with a friendly and coherent concept.

The street side with the inconspicuous entrance next to the carport hides the clever solution for the basement.

Rather than leveling the lot and building a taller home with a less attractive view, the architects provided an introverted garden solution with the excavation of the basement.

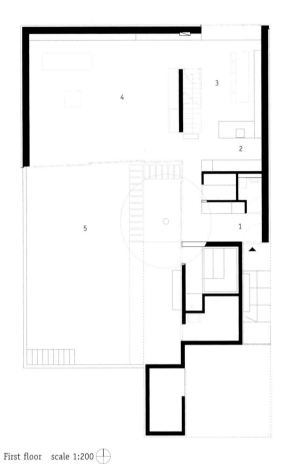

First floor   scale 1:200

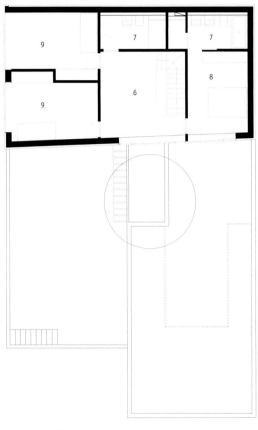

Top floor   scale 1:200

1   entry
2   kitchen
3   dining
4   living
5   atrium
6   play hallway
7   bathroom
8   parents
9   child/guest

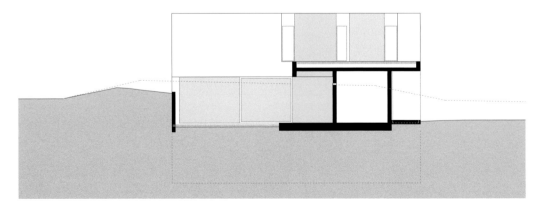

Section   scale 1:200

The floor plan shows how the custom-made furniture continues the
architectural design.

For example, a low cabinet forms the base
of the staircase between the living and
dining area.

Home with jewelry workshop in Wißgoldingen

Kaestle Ocker Roeder Architekten

Lot type	**Type of construction, materials**	height up to 3.8 m, partly on four rails, flush-mount
slope		
Lot size	strip concrete foundations on ductile poured posts, depth up to 40 m, ceiling-high wall supports in the entrance floor, solid in-situ concrete ceilings protruding up to 6.5 m; wall/ceiling: clay-gypsum plaster, smoothed surface, mineral paint; facade in the living area: frameless large sliding windows from aluminum/stainless steel,	**Primary energy consumption**
1,320 m²		75 kWh/m²a
Covered area		
615 m²		
Effective area		
541 m²		
Gross volume		
2,049 m³		
Number of residents		
2 + 1		
Start of construction		
September 2006		
Completion		
May 2008		

Site plan

Gem

Whenever an architect builds a house for a designer, one would assume that the layout is not coincidental, that everything has its purpose and reason. This is not a prosaic fulfillment of a contract; rather, a dialog develops between the two as to what is made where and why and from what material. This was the case for this home on a southwest slope in the Swabian Alps.

From the street it shows a closed facade, an angular, resting bar with its gleaming white tiled exterior isolating it from the surroundings. However, the artifact opens toward the landscape on the valley side with a sweeping view: fragile metal profiles in front of the ceiling-high sliding doors and glass balustrades dissolve the mass of the building, as nothing was supposed to block the view. The solution for the sun shade is part of this: shimmering silver curtains, actually awnings, which are utilized to secure building scaffolding. However, the home is not a high-security prison. There is no fence to keep people away or to prevent them from peeking over the low wall enclosure toward the lower atrium with its entirely visible living quarters set around it. There are two entrances, leading to the jewelry shop to the right and the private quarters to the left.

The offices and workshop are located on the top level and surround the atrium, with a tree and water pool facing the lower floor. The opposite living area is open for guests, and skylights in the roof and a large round roof opening provide visual contact and illumination. Next to the staircase leading downward lies the comprehensively-appointed main bedroom with a high tower room as a retreat, accessible via a narrow staircase. Just below it in the same wing are the similarly generous bedrooms for children or guests.

The garden level takes up the slope, with its steps and platforms. An intense proximity to the landscape is provided by ceiling-high glass sliding doors. The top level protrudes up to 6 meters and forms a protected free space which can also be closed off with the silver curtains. They continue the contour of the floating building block. Only a narrow swimming pool gurgles from the gleaming fold.

Not everything is white and neutral. Intense colored areas, Canadian birch floor boards, a wall plaster with a high clay content, and a rammed earth wall at the rear of the living area provide a balance between experiment and closeness to nature.

Silver-colored, shimmering curtains made from tarpaulins used for construction scaffolds provide shade to the garden facade.

A closed gleaming white wall faces the street. The only protruding living space consists of the tower room.

The views are oriented clearly. All of the rooms facing the valley feature ceiling-high glazing.

Floor plan of tower room   scale
1:200

1	entry
2	dressing room
3	bathroom
4	bedroom/yoga
5	balcony
6	lavatory
7	atelier
8	kitchen
9	storage
10	technical
11	child/guest
12	kitchen
13	dining
14	pond
15	living
16	fireplace
17	wardrobe
18	pool
19	tower room

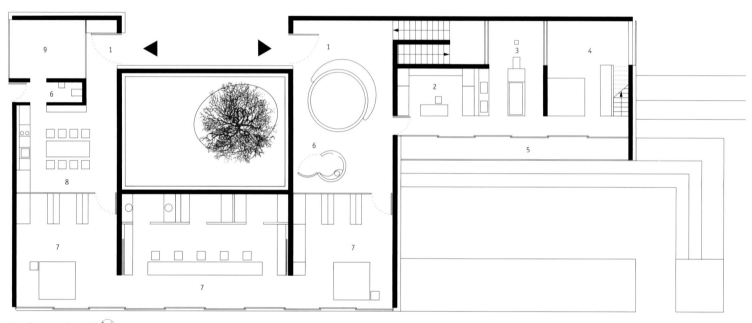

First floor   scale 1:200

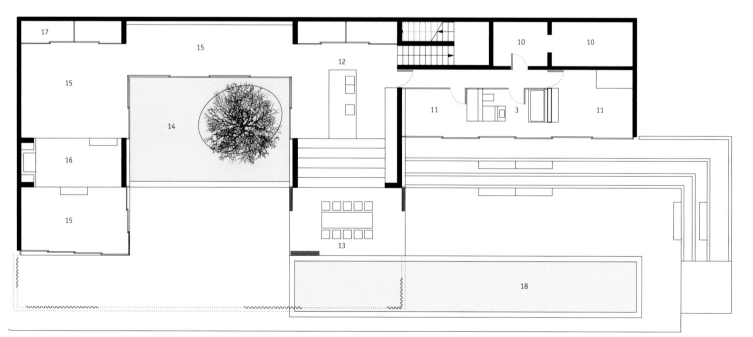

Lower floor/garden level   scale 1:200

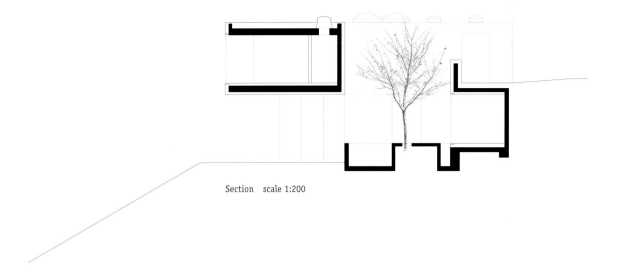

Section   scale 1:200

The variable definition of the room's
boundary is unusual. Dining area, pool,
glass facade, curtains, and terrace
interface and overlap.

The staircase features the use of color which is austere yet effective.

Apart from the atrium, circular skylights on the garden level provide illumination.

The owner's office lies next to the apartment (photo, opposite).

Home in Munich

4architekten

Lot type	Type of construction	slabs; kitchen with lacquered MDF boards, interior drawers solid walnut, countertop Nero Assoluto; library, wardrobe, sink of oiled walnut, dressing room and interior doors lacquered
freestanding	low-energy house, wood	
Lot size	frame construction with	
823 m²	laminated wooden board	
Covered area	ceilings; cellulose insula-	
189 m²	tion, ventilated and	
Living area	colored facade cladding;	**Primary energy**
286 m²	steel concrete basement;	**consumption**
Effective area	heat pump, energy cages,	35.9 kWh/m²a
101 m²	solar collectors, ventila-	**Heating energy**
Gross volume	tion system	**consumption**
1,505 m³	**Materials**	41.5 kWh/m²a
Number of residents	wood and aluminum win-	
2	dows with triple glazing,	
Start of construction	exterior with anodized	
July 2010	aluminum, interior with	
Completion	color-coated wood; bath-	
July 2011	rooms with unglazed stone	

Site plan

Splendid isolation

Living means staying. Heidegger's principle was taken literally in this case as the client's parental home used to stand on this lot, a simple house from the 1950s which was demolished for the new building. The neighboring homes are quite a bit larger; in this case the maximum allowed volume was not used. Both residents, a medical doctor and a humanities scholar, wished for a primarily introverted home which protects from the inhospitable surroundings.

Hence the home takes up the entire width of the lot with a garage on both sides bordering the building boundaries. A steel pergola faces southwards, and even more intimate is the Japanese-influenced interior patio with the building arranged around it in an angular style. Even the top floor contains only a perforated outer wall, which barely allows for a glimpse of the neighbors. Half of the southward-facing terrace is roofed so the cubature of the house closes to form a protective shell.

The floor plan is based on sound classic design which includes the dark walnut bookshelves reaching below the roof and lining the walls of the living and study areas. Next to the entrance area is a closed-off kitchen with a small breakfast corner; guests are hosted at the larger table in the

dining room next to the garden atrium. The contiguous living room is lowered two steps and takes up the entire width of the house. Between the fireplace consisting of a sizable natural stone block, the book shelves, and a grand piano, the elegant living culture is apparent.

On the first floor you reach a long, stretched out office room with the contiguous bathroom and bedroom. The basement contains a swimming pool which is illuminated by a glass band on the side of the house. Only the lower level is made of concrete, with a wood frame construction on top of it.

The owners emphasized the fact that they did not want a hut or block house character for their home, however, they also did not want to miss the comforting ambience of a wood construction home. The exterior bolted facade was painted with maintenance-free industrial paint. The gentle profiling of the horizontal panels meets frame-like window embrasures. Insulation is provided by cellulose. The inner shell consists of drywall screwed onto the wooden frames. The free walls are painted white, and the bleached oak parquet emphasizes the wood construction design.

The house is meant to protect the residents from the environment. This is why two flanking garages on the street side interrupt the view toward the garden.

An additional intimate space is provided by the atrium which reaches up to the roof edge.

The industrially painted and bolted facade does not exhibit the typical character of wood.

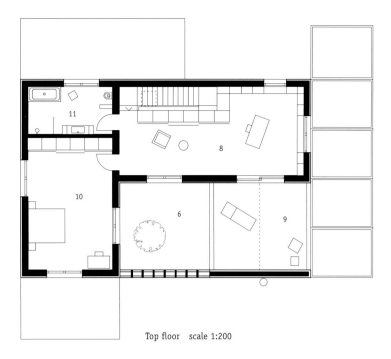

Top floor   scale 1:200

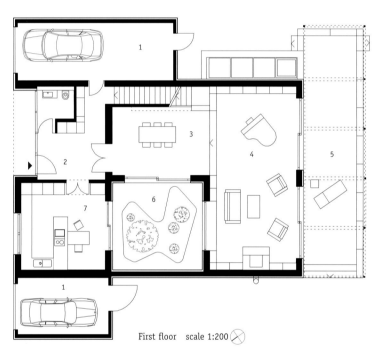

First floor   scale 1:200

1 garage
2 entry
3 dining
4 living/library
5 pergola
6 garden atrium
7 kitchen
8 office/library
9 roof terrace
10 bedroom
11 bathroom
12 lobby
13 pool
14 storage
15 utility room
16 technical

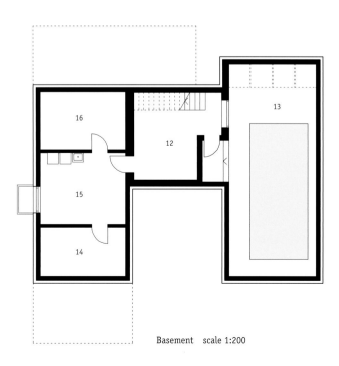

Basement   scale 1:200

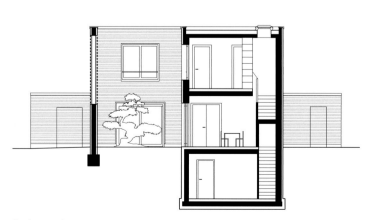

Section   scale 1:200

Apart from the breakfast corner in the kitchen, there is a dining room in the center of the house.

The living room receives light from both sides; through the garden atrium you maintain eye contact with the kitchen.

Home in Sargans (Switzerland)
Atelier–f architekten

Lot type	**Type of construction**
slope	solid concrete construc-
Covered area	tion, lightly sanded facade,
135 m²	interior: concrete and
Effective area	lightweight design, paint-
333 m²	ed with diluted lime
Number of residents	**Building cost home only**
3	740,000 CHF
Start of construction	**Building cost per m² of**
April 2008	**living area and effective**
Completion	**area**
November 2008	4,600 CHF
	Heating energy
	consumption
	227 MJ/m²

Site plan

Summit station

A consistently concrete home. It shows the crude material without fuss: solid concrete, 20 cm thick, with the marks of the standard formwork clearly visible. Even the fifth facade, the roof, is made from concrete sealed with liquid plastic to avoid the use of a different material.

When approaching the home, one is prepared for the main theme. Concrete garden walls which line the driveway of the sloping lot lead to the building. The entrance is accessed via a patio with a deep path along the mountainside. The outer facade is slightly sandblasted while the concrete walls, ceilings, and staircase are painted with a thin coat of lime slurry. The perimeter walls are insulated with XPS boards on the inside while the drywall is plastered white. The roof does not require an additional vapor barrier as the hard foam insulation of 100 mm thickness is sufficient. It is a home that explains itself through its prosaic construction. Only the welded white handrails of the curved staircase and on the balcony add a filigree disruption of its rectilinear design.

The footprint of the basement is more narrow than the floors on top of it, which saved on excavation costs and also resulted in a slight protrusion toward the downhill side. The floor plan of the first floor is divided into three parts by the supporting transverse bulkheads. The large garage at the front side was fitted with large windows to provide a harmonious facade and also allows for a later conversion for use as a living space without incurring high expenses. A guest/children's room is located in the central area behind the staircase, and the adjacent compartment contains the main bedroom with wardrobe/dressing room and bathroom. The tub stands in front of the window and offers a great view. The staircase leads to the living area, and here as well a discernible three-part division with corridor, kitchen/dining area, and living room is present due to the narrow balcony.

The view is obvious: a loggia as wide as the house with entirely glazed walls faces the valley.

The filigree railing does not obstruct the panoramic view.

The garage on the entrance level is glazed just like the adjacent rooms, allowing it to be converted into a living room.

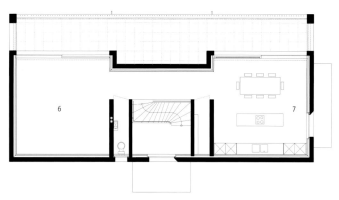

Top floor   scale 1:200

First floor   scale 1:200 ⊗

1 entry
2 bathroom
3 bedroom
4 guests
5 garage
6 living
7 kitchen/dining
8 storage
9 office
10 utility room

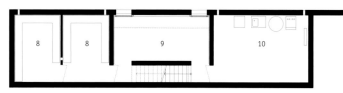

Basement   scale 1:200

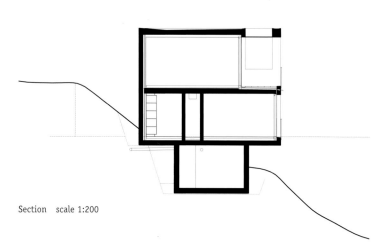

Section   scale 1:200

Kitchen and dining area are located on the top level.

Contrary to the strict threefold division of the floor plan, the concrete staircase — which also saves space — provides a distinctive harmony to the home.

The location on the sloping lot allows for bathing, even without curtains.

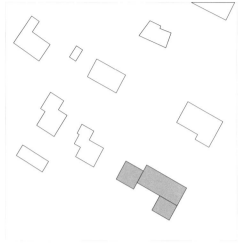

Site plan

Massive back, light front

The sloping lot lies at the edge of the village with an unobstructed view toward the southwest. The shape of the home is designed so it forms a clear break at the edge of the settlement. It stands in nature like an artifact. Its outer walls consist of coarse concrete with core insulation, and the inner shell is partially made with bricks. Slightly higher, at its back, is a house to which it reacts: its flat roof does not obstruct the other home's view, while on the other hand the facade is entirely closed toward the northeast; except for the garage gate there are only lateral entrances.

The cubature of the building breaks up toward the landscape, where the volume divides into projecting roofs, supporting walls, a wide staircase in front of the terrace, and naturally generous, ceiling-high openings. The architects did not want small windows facing all sides, rather, they projected a clear decision as to where you can look outside, where the light comes from, and where a protective wall should be located. A private orientation is conserved in spite of the lavish glazing of the terrace, which is treated as an interior patio.

The location on a sloping lot allowed for an additional living room facing the terrain on the lower level next to the obligatory basement rooms. The entrance is located at the inside corner to the garage. A clear access becomes obvious after stepping into the wide entry. The path along the glazed terrace leads to the dining area and kitchen and to the transverse living room. This is the bright "official" access. A staircase behind the wardrobe leads upstairs. Here the access is reversed — the upper corridor lies along the windowless rear wall of the home illuminated by light cupolas. It indicates that you are entering the personal retreat area.

The children's and parents' bedrooms are functionally organized, bathrooms and dressing rooms interlaced like a stacking game. They continue the three-dimensional denticulation which is visible from the outside, and the interior rooms become living architecture rather than a place to put furniture. The formal reduction is compensated by a tangible practical value.

The living space delimits the terrace
patio with a view, as a single-level porch.

The angle of the garage protrudes as a protective delimitation in front of the building toward the other side.

The architecture does not intend to block the view, nor to blend with the landscape. Nature remains close to the house which is intentionally designed as a "foreign object."

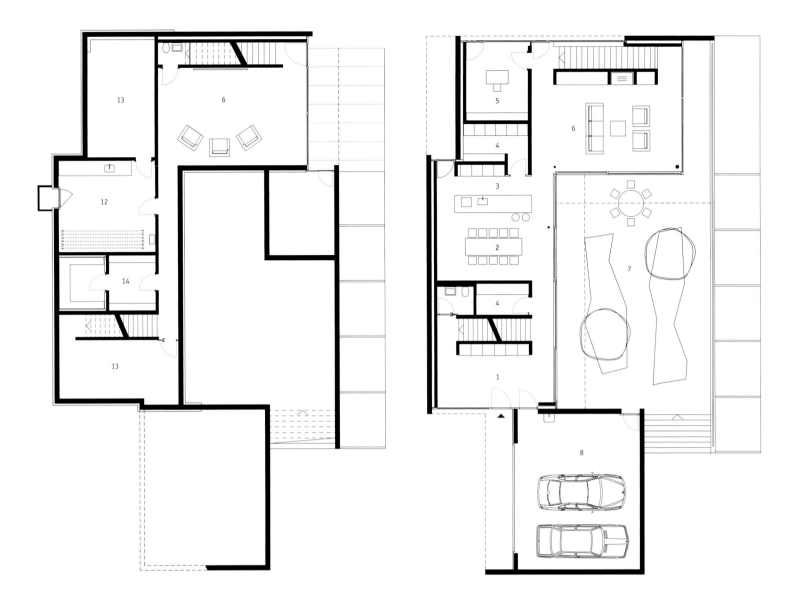

Basement   scale 1:200

First floor   scale 1:200 ⊗

The windows are not conventional everyday solutions. They are located only in areas where the view or the lighting is worth it, and then they are ceiling-high.

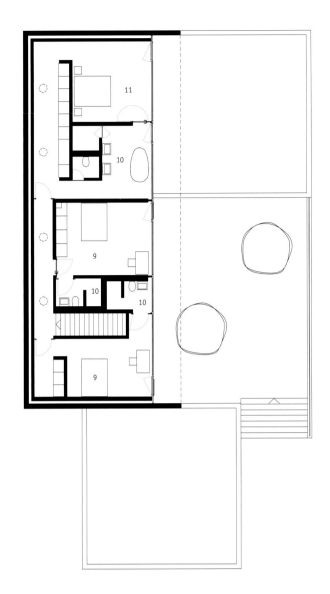

1 entry
2 dining
3 kitchen
4 storage
5 office
6 living
7 terrace
8 garage
9 child
10 bathroom
11 parents
12 utility room
13 basement
14 wine cellar

Top floor   scale 1:200

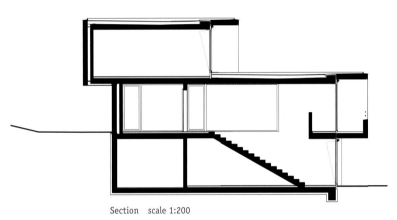

Section   scale 1:200

The living room and office are
accessed not via a dark corridor,
but along the terrace, passing
the dining area and kitchen.

Lot size
1,640 m²
Covered area
299 m²
Living area
140 m²
Effective area
327 m²
Gross volume
1,200 m³
Number of residents
2
Start of construction
2009
Completion
July 2010

Type of construction
two-layer construction
with interior insulation,
exterior: Petersen Danish
Brick (DNF-D91), interior:
Porotherm

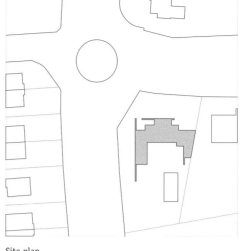

Site plan

A solid castle

The two architects Pieter and Thomas Bedaux work at the firm established by their grandfather in 1937. Not only are they continuing the family business, they also keep the architectural style of the founder alive as a legacy. This explanation should be provided in advance, because this house is not immediately recognizable as a new building. The characteristic entrance facade and the slate roof ridge which is delimited by chimneys on both sides is reminiscent of the living culture of our grandparents' generation. Only when you get closer do the fine details make it clear that the architecture has arrived in the present.

The location of the lot directly next to a noisy traffic circle was a determining factor for the design of the house. The premise was to shield the home without building a hermetic fortress. This was achieved by the construction of massive brick walls which stand in front of the entrance like a screen or which extend as protective flanks from the single-floor annexes at both sides. Only a few slits and windows interrupt the appearance. A shallow pool in front of the living area not only provides contemplative tranquility, but

also reflects additional light into the office space glazed with ceiling-high glass walls. Sound proofing on the first floor is provided via a generous foyer behind the brickwork wall as well as the entrance, auxiliary rooms, and garage. On the top floor, which is closed off toward the northern traffic circle, the bathroom and a long cabinet corridor under the roof provide isolation from the traffic noise.

The first floor frames the garden with pool in a U-shape, and its opulent glazing integrates the top floor. The living hall comprises both levels. From here you reach a bedroom with bathroom extending into the depth of the garden. Kitchen and dining area are clearly defined but not separate from the spatial flow. There is a separate access from the foyer for the top level for children or guests, however, there is eye contact to the hall via the gallery.

Thus the house has two faces, like the god Janus, faces that are connected to each other with a logical and diversified organization.

A home that shields itself against the noisy street with architectural rather than technical means.

The entrance lies deeply retracted behind a wall.

A high wall also protects toward the side, interrupted only by a window for the office.

A totally different surprise results from the garden side, which opens toward the garden and is entirely glazed.

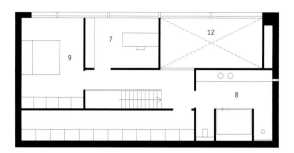

1	entry/hallway
2	utility room
3	garage
4	storage
5	kitchen
6	dining
7	office
8	bathroom
9	bedroom
10	pool
11	terrace
12	air space

Top floor   scale 1:200

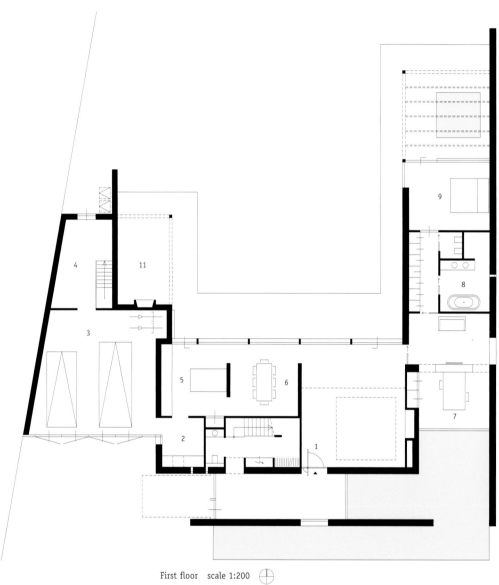

First floor   scale 1:200

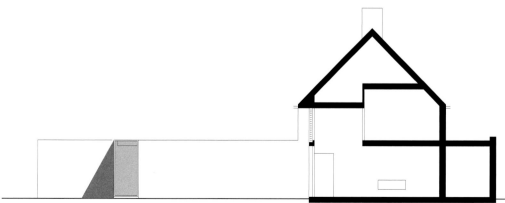

Section   scale 1:200

The office lies at an angle between two walls facing the street. A pool reflects light as a metaphorical break.

The same pool as seen from the air trap which functions as a noise barrier.

Home in Neustift (Austria)

Pauhof Architekten

Lot type	Type of construction, materials	geothermal system, low-temperature heating system with controlled living area ventilation and highly efficient heat recovery
slope	concrete for subterranean	
Lot size	areas and for the support-	
840 m²	ing vertical plates, wood	
Living area	for all volumes visible from	
295 m²	the exterior from the first	
Effective area	floor up. Exterior siding	
382 m²	and cladding for the atrium	
Number of residents	floor from flamed oak.	
4	Interior rooms: waxed oak,	
Start of construction	broken natural stone slabs,	
2005	exposed concrete, black	
Completion	terrace floor, bottle-green	
2008	mosaic, sisal walls	
	Energy consumption	
	28 kWh/m²a (low-energy	
	home) heated and cooled via	

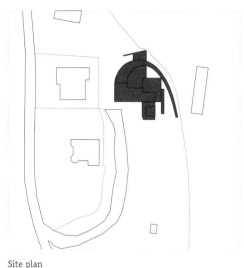

Site plan

Natural swing

Architecture that seems to arise from its conditions. But even if you don't register how topography, pathways, landscape, neighborhood buildings, building lines, lot boundaries, and favorite views have modeled the house, you sense that some sort of balance has been kept, as if the building which ends with a swinging gesture over the hill is a cryptic answer to all of the profane challenges.

At the end of the access driveway it leans at an angle into the steep hillside with its four floors; toward the north its rounded contour closes with a roof element "which the house, as if it were a large curve, throws over its shoulder, like a scarf" (Christian Kühn). At the entrance side its staircase, divided by a suspended wall, says that nothing is as it appears and that you will discover more than merely utilitarian enclosed space.

At the street level lies a high semi-public concrete studio gallery which receives light from the side and from above. Eye contact is maintained via the built-in office space of the owner one level farther up. The children's rooms line the quadrant of the gallery volume, and there is a guest room

with service cabinets. Most importantly, the two-level library hall starts here and leads to the living level via the interior run of the outer staircase, which features a circumferential band-like window with a priceless view of the landscape.

The rooms fold at angles with labyrinthine axes of movement and views around a terrace above the gallery. The gallery remains half-open under the roof shape which from here on swerves as a pergola into the vineyards. The kitchen features an open-air lunch/dining area facing south. A final staircase leads to the media room with a terminally overwhelming roof terrace.

The house is suspended by concrete slabs inside the ground, toward the slope as well as at its core; all of the visible volumes are added as wood frame construction elements. The facade is hatched with black flamed slats; the interior is surrounded with exposed concrete, natural stone, and waxed oak which exude warmth and personality. This impression is due to a cooperation with the Bozen artist Manfred Alois Mayr.

The essence of the house is its relation with the surroundings. Various terraces guide the view toward the landscape and not to the heavily-set houses in the neighborhood.

Far left: an open-air lunch/dining area next to the kitchen.

The suspended wood facade divides the entrance staircase.

1 entry
2 interior patio
3 interior patio gallery
4 gallery
5 basement
6 garage
7 foyer
8 child
9 sauna
10 guests

11 wardrobe
12 office
13 dining
14 living
15 terrace
16 bedroom
17 kitchen
18 atrium
19 media room

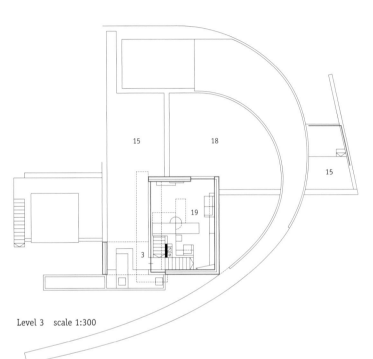

Level 3   scale 1:300

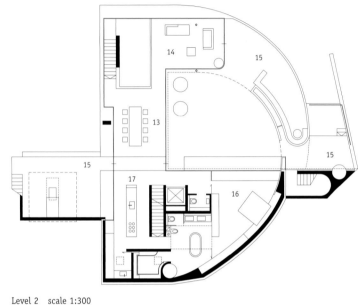

Level 2   scale 1:300

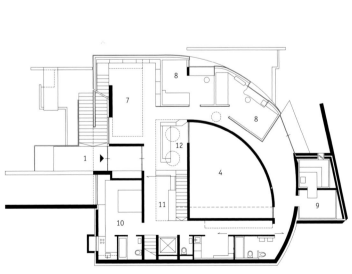

Level 1   scale 1:300

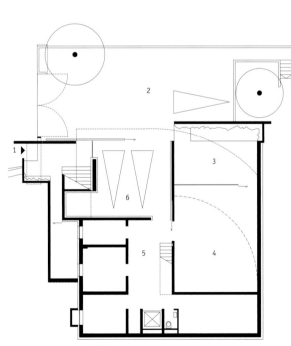

Level 0   scale 1:300

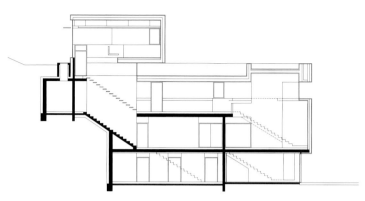

Section   scale 1:300

Studiously located band windows exhibit
the impressive landscape like a film strip.

Kitchen and dining area; the large table is still missing. The areas are delimited by a stone floor, marking the oblique connection between the terrace and the open-air grill area.

The workplace of the gallery owner is an immobile architectural element. Behind it you can see into the studio gallery.

The bathroom next to the main bedroom. Warm-colored waxed oak lines the room.

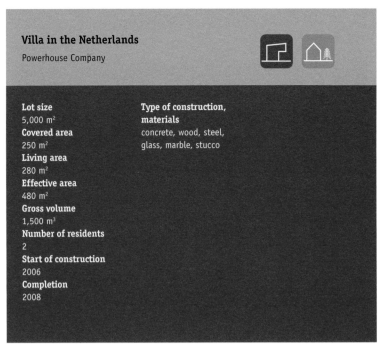

Villa in the Netherlands
Powerhouse Company

Lot size	Type of construction,
5,000 m²	materials
Covered area	concrete, wood, steel,
250 m²	glass, marble, stucco
Living area	
280 m²	
Effective area	
480 m²	
Gross volume	
1,500 m³	
Number of residents	
2	
Start of construction	
2006	
Completion	
2008	

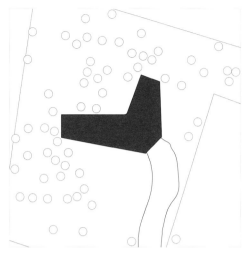

Site plan

Lightning blazing on house

This generous villa is located on a clearing of a forest in eastern Holland. The orientation of the Y-shaped building follows the sun and the views of the landscape. Due to the regional building code, half of the area of the home had to be located in the basement. This resulted in a clear two-fold division consisting of an upper "glass box" with furniture-like, built-in fixtures, and a "medieval underworld" with rooms cut from one single volume.

The northeast wing features two office spaces without direct sunlight and inside ceiling-high, built-in forms of walnut. Next to them is the music room and a small living area. The kitchen, oriented toward the southeastern sun, features slate fixtures. The large living room is divided into three private areas and faces westward, enclosed by concrete walls. In between, roofed terraces provide shaded open-air seating.

The lower level, on the other hand, contains intimate rooms with protective qualities. A ramp provides the sensitive transition between the levels. No flowing levels, rather, solid closed rooms with their bathrooms greet the resident down here. Illumination is provided via an interior patio or via the modeled garden terrain. The main bedroom is complemented by a wooden element, containing dressing room, bathroom, and its own staircase, while a 22-meter-long corridor with a seemingly endless row of built-in cabinets leads to the guest rooms. The third basement floor of the house contains the garage, with the cars being stage-produced as if in a theater.

The ceiling-high above-ground glazed building receives support and contour with a surrounding sharply-cut Travertin cornice which incorporates all of the walls and terraces. Its lines meet at the front sides of the three wings to form walls. The support structure, just like the window profiles, remains invisible. The required steel construction is hidden within the built-in furniture, such as a beam running through a book shelf of the study/office room. The glass walls are glued. A 4.50-meter-wide sliding marble door leads to the terrace. When open, the living space extends to include the landscape.

The outstanding qualities of the villa lie in the experience of entirely contrarian atmospheres. They span the gamut from tight and dark cavernous corridors to light-filled garden salons. This variety of spatial sensations can not be fully expressed using functional descriptions.

Living in this house consists of trying out different atmospheres. Or, simply enjoying.

The lower floor is illuminated with light patios. The car plays a fairly important role. It gets a flashy entrance with the garage as its stage.

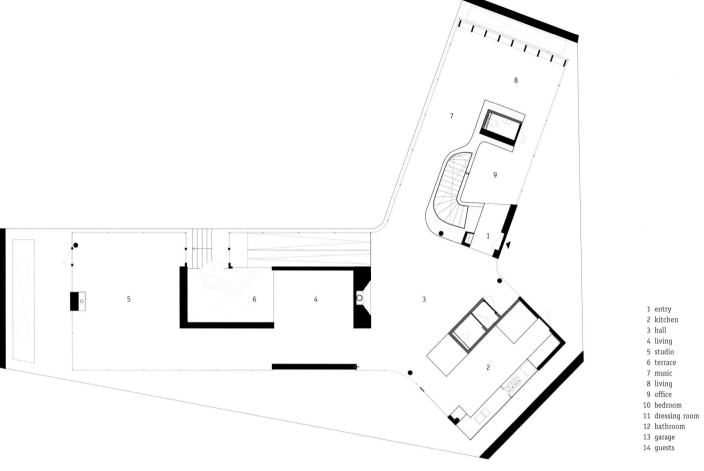

First floor   scale 1:200 ⊕

1 entry
2 kitchen
3 hall
4 living
5 studio
6 terrace
7 music
8 living
9 office
10 bedroom
11 dressing room
12 bathroom
13 garage
14 guests

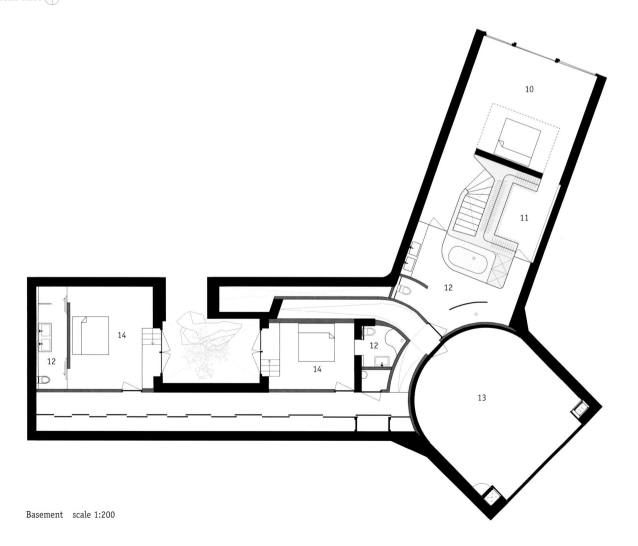

Basement   scale 1:200

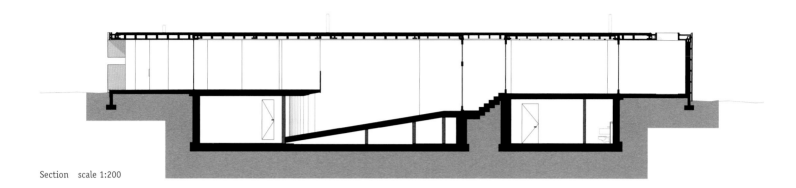

Section   scale 1:200

The glazed first floor features more private areas and functions, with a ceiling-high wooden form which surrounds the staircase and the guest lavatory.

The house appears to float as a closed band, without touching the forest floor (see pages 182/183). Between the roof projecting at the pendentives and the protruding base plate is the entrance and the terrace.

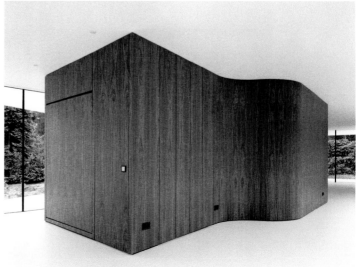

Home in Frohnleiten (Austria)
WEIchlbauerORTis Architekten

Lot size	**Total building cost**
2,582 m²	379,068 Euro
Covered area	**Building cost per m² of**
121 m²	**living area and effective**
Living area	**area**
295 m²	1.458 Euro
Effective area	**Energy requirements**
260 m²	28 kWh/m²a (low-energy
Built volume	house), heated and cooled
745 m³	via geothermal system,
Number of residents	low-temperature area
5	heating system with con-
Start of construction	trolled living area ventila-
2008	tion and highly efficient
Completion	heat recovery
2009	

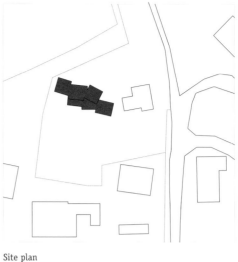

Site plan

Green, green grass of home

It seems as if, with this house, you first need to explain the view and not the floor plan. But both are inextricably interlinked. The design is difficult to describe since it follows a method which is hard to fathom. Rather than working out the client's specifications while respecting the required solutions the architects fed their computer with a randomly selected pattern. The goal was to develop a home which was free of pre-existing concepts, that is, to reduce the role of the planner as the originator and to leave it to an automated shape designer.

The description of this digital shredder, superimposing data and planning parameters from prior projects and arbitrary values from physics, medicine, and nutrition looks like a comedian's sketch for architectural wizard apprentices. The random section without scale was ultimately turned, scaled, zoomed, and converted into a house-like item.

Familiar elements like concrete staircases and simple plastic windows received different functions. The architects posited that the terms deter-

mine the function. Applying nonsensical parameters opened up a wealth of possibilities.

Surprisingly, the home for a family of five features a rather familiar layout. Three levels conform the living area. The entrance features a small economic sector where goat cheese is manufactured. Living room, dining area, kitchen on the first floor, bathrooms, main bedroom, and three children's bedrooms are described as essentially cubic-shaped boxes which are not stacked in orderly fashion, rather, they are fitted as if it were a castle of toy blocks about to fall over. In addition there are the non-walkable but partly supportive staircases reminding one of M. C. Escher, the windows which mimic the edge glazing as balustrades — and of course the bright green synthetic lawn which covers the spatial agglomeration on all sides.

The architecture does not follow any known images, any tradition — but when you are inside of it you are really at home. The absurd can actually be domesticated.

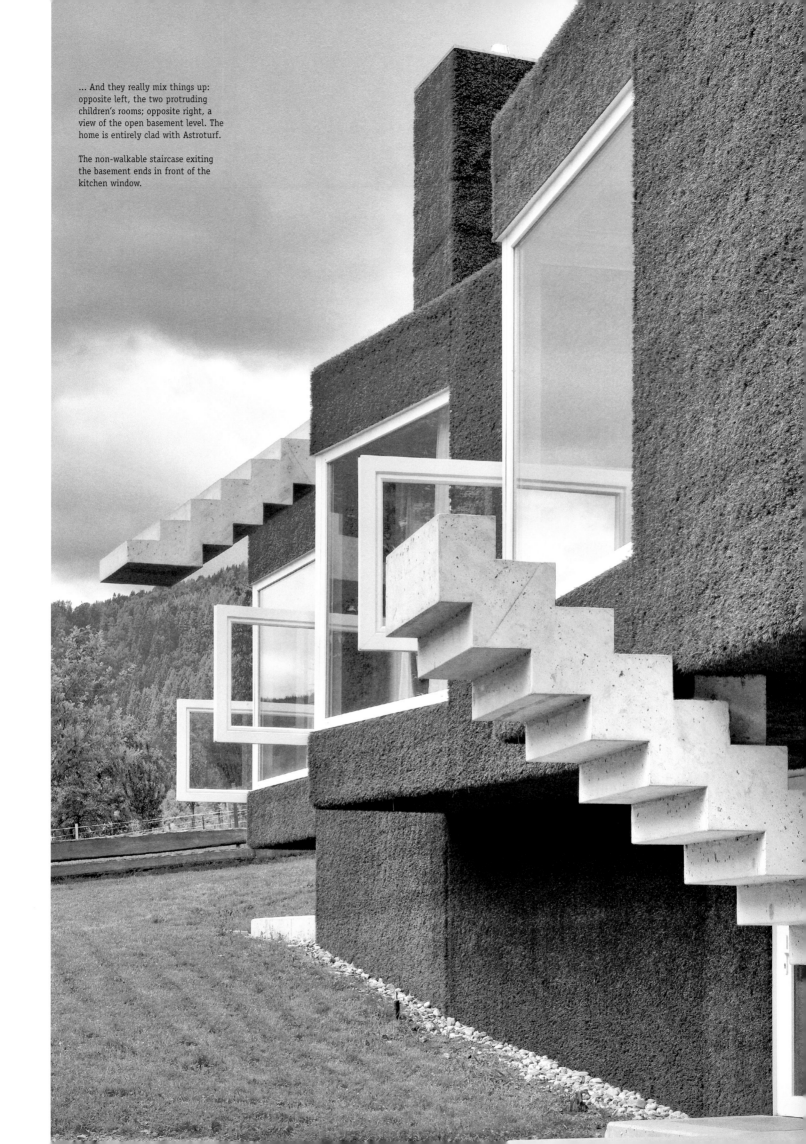

... And they really mix things up: opposite left, the two protruding children's rooms; opposite right, a view of the open basement level. The home is entirely clad with Astroturf.

The non-walkable staircase exiting the basement ends in front of the kitchen window.

Top floor   scale 1:200

1 entry
2 storage
3 kitchen
4 dining
5 living
6 terrace
7 parents
8 child
9 bathroom
10 utility room

First floor   scale 1:200

Section   scale 1:200

Basement   scale 1:200

View from the side of
the valley.

Misappropriation; a
closed glass door as
balustrade, a window
profile as a handrail.

Home in Seewalchen (Austria)

Architekten Luger & Maul

Lot type	Completion
freestanding, slope	July 2007
Lot size	**Type of building**
2,400 m²	concrete, insulated interior
Covered area	shell; facade: siding of
390 m²	horizontal planed boards,
Living area	interior with white plaster
225 m²	**Materials**
Effective area	concrete, stone, wood,
105 m²	glass, steel
Gross volume	
1,380 m³ with covered	
parking space	
Number of residents	
2	
Start of construction	
October 2005	

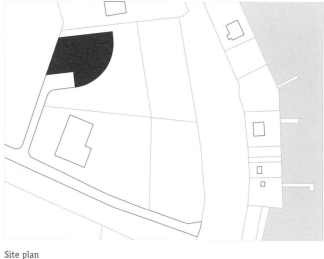

Site plan

Seascape with quadrant

"After all … building in the landscape has nothing to do with invisibility" was the final comment of Friedrich Achleitner referring to this home. This meant that the building at Lake Atter presents itself as a self-confident artifact inside the delicate landscape, while when viewed from above — contrary to the neighboring homes — it disappears inside the landscape and does not block the view. For those interested in architecture one might add that there is an Inkunabel by Ernst Anton Plischke in this neighborhood, the Gamerith House of 1933/34. The same client continues his commitment for building culture.

His home takes advantage of the only almost entirely flat level of the hilly property. Car parking spaces and utility rooms disappear at the property boundary toward the northwest. A glass passage which ultimately leads to the lower level and the garden at the rear connects with the main building, a flat, quadrant-shaped concrete body which faces the lake landscape with its round facade. The rooms of the living level reach out like spokes from a central entrance hall to the perimeter — two bedrooms with a common

bathroom, a living room with an adjacent dining area, and a kitchen at the back complete the layout. Terrace and protruding roof feature the circle segment as a sharp contour within the landscape. The lower level features a cut-in loggia and, pushing into the hillside, a sauna and utility rooms.

The building consists entirely of concrete with the insulation on the interior side. The exterior features the imprint of the horizontal concrete framework boards. No chamfer strips or joint profiles were used in order to avoid interrupting the monolithic appearance of the erratic geometric body. Materials are reduced to concrete, stone, wood, glass, steel, and white plastered interior walls. Select pieces of art and furniture harmonize with the austere architecture. The partially curved door panels do not interrupt the flow of the wall surfaces. The view of the landscape has no competition.

The home is heated with geothermal energy which is provided via deep perforations and a heat pump, and then routed to the floor heating system under the oak parquet.

Next to the covered parking space at the lot boundary, a glass passage leads into the house. It continues into the depth of the lower floor with a garden loggia and a sauna (see right).

The round facade faces Lake Atter. All of the rooms extend outwards and increase the section of the landscape. At the same time they collect light for the exhibited works of art.

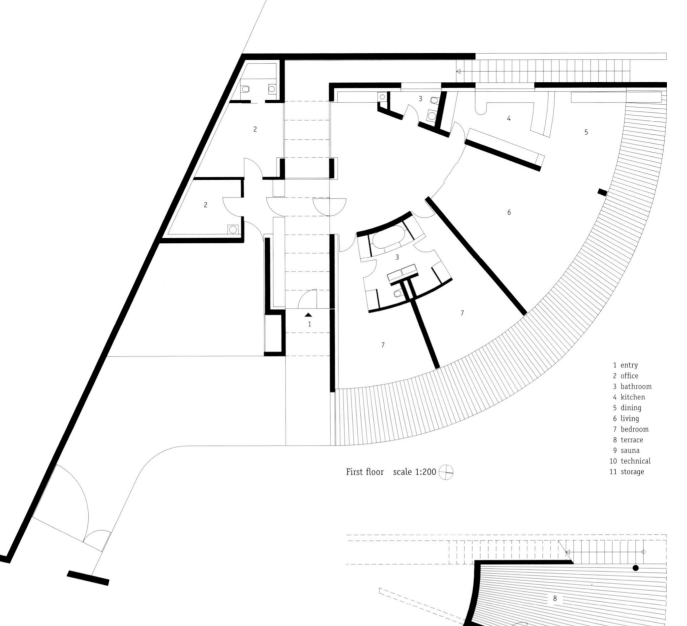

First floor   scale 1:200

1 entry
2 office
3 bathroom
4 kitchen
5 dining
6 living
7 bedroom
8 terrace
9 sauna
10 technical
11 storage

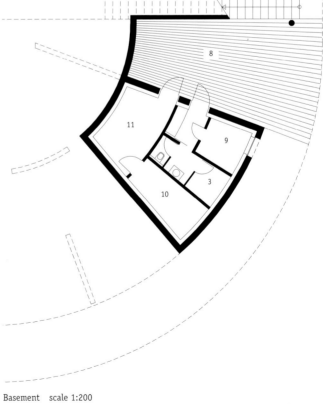

Basement   scale 1:200

A quadrant-shaped foyer conforms the exhibition area.
Left: view toward the glazed entrance passage.

The living area is closed off with a frameless glass portal.

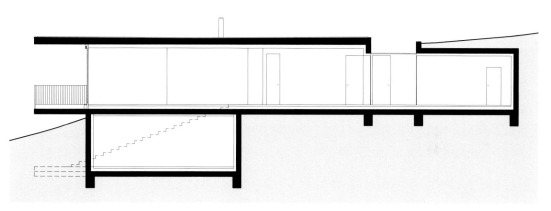

Section   scale 1:200

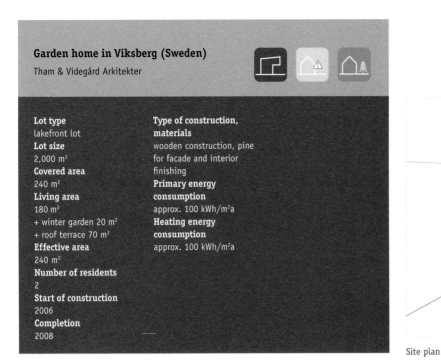

Garden home in Viksberg (Sweden)
Tham & Videgård Arkitekter

Lot type	**Type of construction, materials**
lakefront lot	wooden construction, pine for facade and interior finishing
Lot size	
2,000 m²	
Covered area	**Primary energy consumption**
240 m²	
Living area	approx. 100 kWh/m²a
180 m²	**Heating energy consumption**
+ winter garden 20 m²	
+ roof terrace 70 m²	approx. 100 kWh/m²a
Effective area	
240 m²	
Number of residents	
2	
Start of construction	
2006	
Completion	
2008	

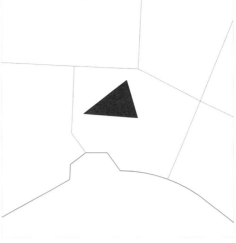

Site plan

Cubing the triangle

Architects have always been fascinated by even geometric forms. Mario Botta created a splash with them during the 1980s when postmodernism reached its peak. In this case the isosceles triangle of the home's footprint follows pragmatic conditions. A steep hill which limited the property left this very same area as a surface for building. A side effect was the possibility for a long facade facing south without having to accept a corresponding northern wall as is common for orthogonal layouts.

The owners wished to have a garden and gave up their home in the urban center of Stockholm to move to the countryside along Lake Mälar. This lake, west of the capital, is the third-largest in Sweden. The numerous bays, islands, and peninsulas are typical and many weekend homes line the partially undeveloped and pristine recreational area. The architects have interpreted the desire for a garden as a vertical addition where the interior and exterior rooms communicate and blend with each other.

All of the sides of the wooden home were clad with overly large trellises. They partially cross the windows where you would not want transparency (such as the bathroom). These rhombic lattice structures reach over the roof terrace where they result in an unfocused "natural" contour, particularly with the building's greenery.

After the funnel-shaped foyer with its corresponding auxiliary and storage rooms, an oblique staircase divides the living space of the otherwise undivided first floor. The outer walls approach the tip of the house which ends with a two-level winter garden. Its heat recovery contributes to the energy balance. The main bedroom over it features a balcony reaching into the glazed triangle. Two children's or guest rooms are located at the wide side of the building. From the roof terrace, secured with a simple wire mesh, you have a fantastic view of the hilly landscape at Lake Mälar.

The batten trellis brings the garden to the facade. The kitchen visually continues the concept: wood and green.

The staircase leads all the way up to an exit leading onto the roof terrace.

The geometry of the home takes advantage of the flat area inside the hilly topography.

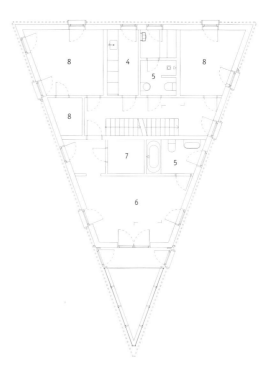

Second floor   scale 1:200

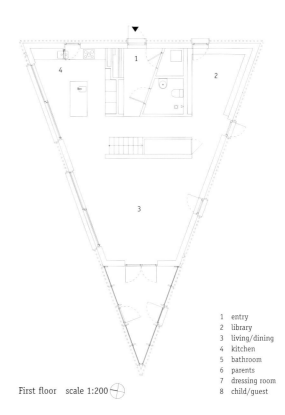

First floor   scale 1:200

1 entry
2 library
3 living/dining
4 kitchen
5 bathroom
6 parents
7 dressing room
8 child/guest

Section   scale 1:200

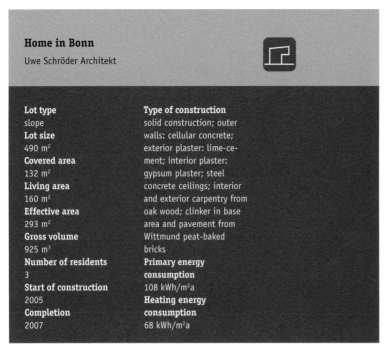

Home in Bonn

Uwe Schröder Architekt

Lot type	Type of construction
slope	solid construction; outer
Lot size	walls: cellular concrete;
490 m²	exterior plaster: lime-ce-
Covered area	ment; interior plaster:
132 m²	gypsum plaster; steel
Living area	concrete ceilings; interior
160 m²	and exterior carpentry from
Effective area	oak wood; clinker in base
293 m²	area and pavement from
Gross volume	Wittmund peat-baked
925 m³	bricks
Number of residents	**Primary energy**
3	**consumption**
Start of construction	108 kWh/m²a
2005	**Heating energy**
Completion	**consumption**
2007	68 kWh/m²a

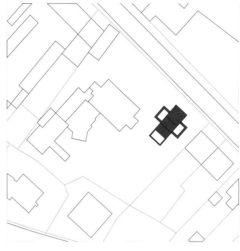

Site plan

Nice and orderly

This home stands at the foot of the Venus mountain in the Bonn neighborhood of Kessenich. Its vertical layout is staggered toward the hillside like a staircase, from three levels to the north down to one level to the south. It counters its rather shapeless context with its strict reason and announces its presence to the public space with only three distant narrow windows. The recessed entrance patio is lined with peat-baked bricks which push into the mountain, and it cuts the private parcel from the diffuse area lining the street. The noteworthy division of levels toward the garden side is marked by bands of clinker.

The patio is used as a parking space and begins the promenade through the home, which is conceived as a small city. The narrow entrance with a few steps following it can be thought of as the boundary to the private quarters. Toward the left is the staircase which pushes over the open eye, indicating that this is not the first path for visitors. Rather, it leads to an "interior exterior space" of the high central living hall lowered one step. From both sides it is flanked by terraces. Following the kitchen and dining area is another roofed garden area. The high masonry pedestal, the windows and

dark shutters of the flush built-in fittings are reminiscent of the facades belonging to a city square. The image of a public space is emphasized by the robust materials, the coarse plaster finishes, and the absence of visible installations such as switches and openings.

The top floor contains two symmetrical children's rooms of the same size. They are organized with built-in beds, cabinets, and writing desks; a common terrace connects them to the garden. There is an open shaft spanning the corridor behind the staircase, oblique to the long axis of the home, and shutters can be opened from the rooms, thereby converting the stairwell into a stroll through some Mediterranean alleyway. The main bedroom is located on the third floor and also features its own terrace.

But this does not complete the access to the house. The high room at the end of the staircase above the lower run is not left unused. Here we find a studio which is illuminated by grazing light only, a small working and thinking space for one person, perhaps for the chief of the lower-lying "city."

As a townhouse it stands close to the street, but the private quarters' separation from the public space is indicated by the narrow recessed entrance.

Brickwork bands conform decorative lines and indicate the staggered cubature.

From the rooms you can open up shutters toward the interior staircase — as is customary in the alleyways of Mediterranean villages.

Ziggurat: the building provides terraces toward the garden side, both at ground level and up high.

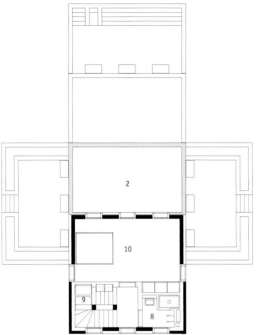

Third floor   scale 1:200

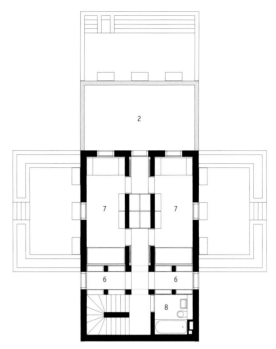

Second floor   scale 1:200

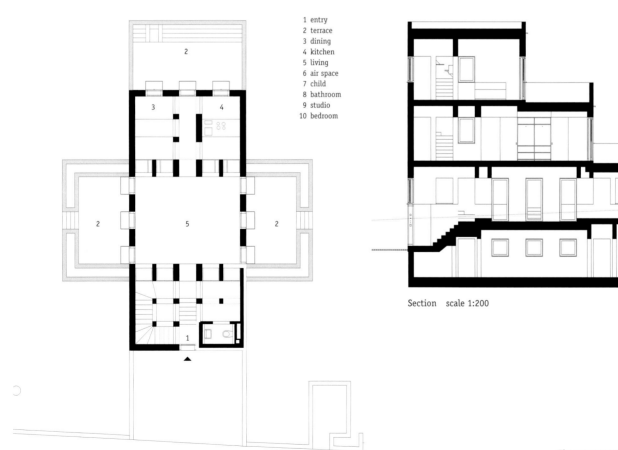

First floor   scale 1:200

1 entry
2 terrace
3 dining
4 kitchen
5 living
6 air space
7 child
8 bathroom
9 studio
10 bedroom

Section   scale 1:200

The masonry street pedestal continues
into the foyer, as if the visitor were
supposed to only gradually leave behind
the formal section.

Home in Sexten (Italy)

Plasma Studio

Lot type
freestanding
Lot size
263 m²
Living area
150 m²
Effective area
220 m²
Gross volume
566.41 m³
Number of residents
4
Start of construction
2006
Completion
2008

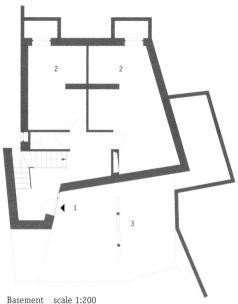

Basement   scale 1:200

Folded and visored

The single family home stands on a steep hill in the middle of the closed village center. The buildable area was limited, the exposed location at a through street was a concern, but at the same time the property offered a fantastic view across the mountain landscape and the historic center of the village toward the south. This resulted in the folded cubature which opens toward the southeast with large glazed surfaces and terraces, thereby expanding the compact interior space while at the same time screening it from curious looks with a second shell consisting of larch siding. These multiple folded facade surfaces, which feature the white plastered vertical building edges, place the home with its roof and its walls into the surrounding terrain. The support structure consists of brickwork reinforced with concrete pillars.

The volume is stuck inside the earth and protrudes, sustained by a V-shaped tubular support, across two parking spaces and provides a protected entrance. Here, at the basement level, a narrow staircase leads upwards. In order to entirely renounce non-essential areas, the staircase platform which reaches a functional core for fireplace, furniture, and an installation wall leads on to the kitchen, to the left, while the living area is reached to the right. The volume protrudes outward to make space for the dining area, and can be reached from the outside, while the open and tight throughway from the living room indicates a break. The long tongue of the terrace expands the area during the warm seasons and leads directly into the garden.

The upper floor is organized following this very same principle. Two children's rooms and the main bedroom are contained almost without any additional corridor space, the large one of which can be partitioned. The access to the two bedrooms is organized accordingly. Here once again a balcony lines the compact volume at two sides.

The house stands in the village and yet it has a nice orientation toward the mountain backdrop. The folded facade reacts to this paradox with its calculated incisions.

The terrace areas enlarge the compact interior space. The oblique angles indicate generous dimensions.

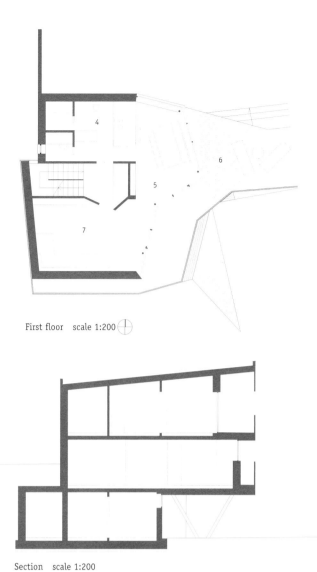

First floor   scale 1:200

Top floor   scale 1:200

Section   scale 1:200

1 entry
2 storage
3 parking spaces
4 kitchen
5 dining
6 terrace
7 living
8 child
9 parents
10 bathroom

Like a nest the terrace behind the wood siding expands the free space between the living space and the garden.

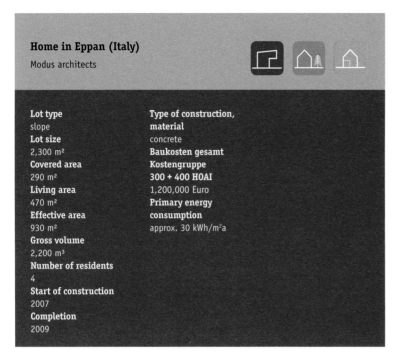

Home in Eppan (Italy)
Modus architects

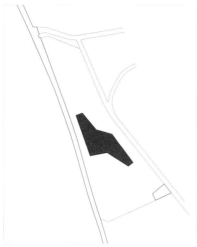

Lot type	Type of construction, material
slope	concrete
Lot size	**Baukosten gesamt**
2,300 m²	**Kostengruppe**
Covered area	**300 + 400 HOAI**
290 m²	1,200,000 Euro
Living area	**Primary energy**
470 m²	**consumption**
Effective area	approx. 30 kWh/m²a
930 m²	
Gross volume	
2,200 m³	
Number of residents	
4	
Start of construction	
2007	
Completion	
2009	

Site plan

Roof landscape

The architecture of this house is best understood from a distance, looking down from the rising vineyard landscape. Then you recognize the flat and inconspicuous roofs which barely top the vines and duck into the fertile hills. The model of the offset platforms looks like origami. The Z-shaped building block below lies compact and compressed, while at the same time it extends its slim wings into the narrow lot and provides a new view from any perspective.

The lively cubature connects with nature, the house and the garden blend into each other, the gentle hill continues on the inner level. At the same time a "natural" structuring of the functions results without the common elements under the large roof getting lost. The priceless views of the landscape are focused into the building's rooms.

The entrance looks closed and private. The official dining area with its living area lying three steps lower looks all the more inviting, though. The kitchen is located laterally in the northern wing of the building, and can be divided by a large sliding door. At its outer end lies the two-level-high dining room for the family. Large windows bring the landscape and the profile of the mountains into the home.

On the other side, facing southeast, are the bedroom, dressing room, and bathroom. In front of that a staircase leads into the wine cellar which has been placed here following an ancient custom. It opens toward an atrium and an intimate water garden.

The rooms on the upper floor contain a second living space, open toward the small family dining room. The large rooms are for the children and guests. A small apartment could be divided later on, which would require a bathroom to be given up and would mean extending the wine cellar staircase upwards. Although the house is based on the free geometry of the shapes, there are no pendentives and extra areas which are hard to furnish; each room finds its rectilinear order.

A low stone wall delimits the property on the outside and forms a small area at the entrance. The ramp to the underground garage is located along the narrow flank. The gardens at both sides of the house are similar but fulfill different functions: the main attraction to the north is a swimming pool consisting of natural stone; facing south, the garden is stacked upward ... just like the vineyards.

The entrance appears closed and silent, you have to pass a gatehouse.

From a distance you can see how the cubature of the house under the folded roof fits into the lively topography of the vineyards.

The house and the free space blend into each other. The living space is understood as a solid extension of the landscape; the garden features steps as if it were segmented with architectural fragments.

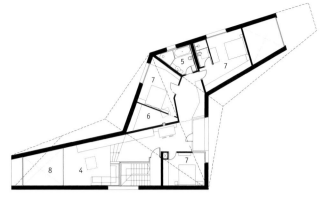

Top floor   scale 1:400

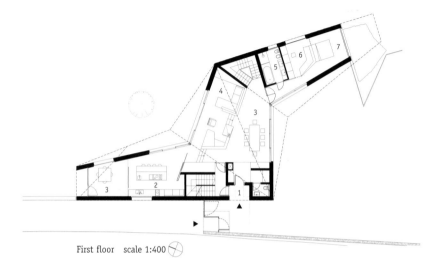

First floor   scale 1:400

1 entry
2 kitchen
3 dining
4 living
5 bathroom
6 dressing room
7 bedroom
8 gallery air space
9 garage
10 wine cellar
11 terrace

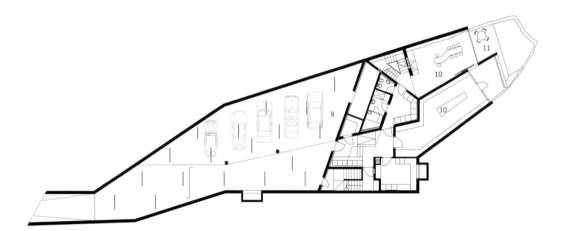

Basement   scale 1:400

Section   scale 1:400

The interior space changes between tight and large volumes without the cohesion getting lost. The family room is open toward the gallery.

The cellar for wine degustation lies below the main bedroom, following ancient customs. Illumination is provided by a small water garden.

Home at the Steuerberg in Kitzbühel (Austria)

splendid architecture

Lot type	Type of construction, materials	Building cost
slope	concrete construction,	1,450,000 Euro
Lot size	intermediate walls with insu-	**Building cost per m² of**
1,300 m²	lation and facade cladding	**living area**
Covered area	with original Tyrolean wood;	2,790 Euro
430 m²	windows; aluminum sliding	**Building cost per m² of**
Living area	doors; entrance hall facade:	**total effective area**
520 m²	aluminum	2,000 Euro
Effective area	post-and-beam construc-	**Heating requirement**
720 m²	tion; floors depending on	59.06 kWh/m²a
Gross volume	the area: oak floor boards,	**Heating energy**
2,900 m³	poured cement, carpet;	**requirement**
Number of residents	ceilings with coarse ex-	17.56 kWh/m²a
2	posed concrete; walls	
Start of construction	painted or with wallpaper;	
October 2009	doors with covered frames;	
Completion	high-quality lamps	
January 2011		

Site plan

Straight logs

It is a house which reacts in multiple ways to its surroundings. There is the steep hill where it must find support, its large area must be distributed, there are different functions to carry out, and the regional style of Tyrol should not be overlooked regarding new construction.

The architect divided the house into two sections which lie next to each other "like two logs of wood." By inserting them into the steep topography, and due to the contrary curving of the two building sections and their connection via a glass entrance hall, the new structures arrange themselves with the surroundings. At the same time the towering house offers fantastic views of the mountains as they have not been seen previously.

The lower floor is deeply anchored within the mountain with storage rooms and bathrooms, and contains two guest apartments. The entrance level, with a view toward the valley on top of it, contains the kitchen with its endless dining table and the main bedroom; the wing facing east with the underground garage in the back contains an office and a playroom. The main

attraction lies on top of it: from here you overlook the lower-lying tract. The library and the relaxation room with sauna keep the landscape within view. Below, between the logs so to speak, lies the shining center of the entrance hall, which is reminiscent of fire as the center of the divided house, and yet it conforms a formal prelude from where the functions spread out over the terrain like layers.

The three floor plans are certainly modern, as is the treatment with the ceiling-high window openings and corner glazing. The traditional Tyrolean building culture is paid homage in an unusual manner. The supporting concrete walls are clad with refurbished wood on top of the insulation. However, the slabs do not exactly trace the openings but are placed randomly. The home's edges also flirt with a restrained inaccuracy. The two resting "logs" are emphasized and the intervention into the landscape is retracted. The interior rooms partly feature recycled oak floor boards and the rough concrete is partially visible, contrasting with soft carpet — the walls are covered with ornamental wallpaper patterns which match the valuable chandeliers.

The two halves of the building lie next to each other like two logs, connected by a glass entrance hall.

The facade consists of old wooden boards
affixed to the concrete outer walls, and
plays with the regional motifs,
emphasizing them with irony.

The windows make it clear that a
comfortable home is hidden behind the
camouflage of wooden boards.

The higher "log" contains the living room with a view while the sheer endless sofa lining the rear angle offers front row seats.

The sauna features traditional objects.

1 patio	10 bedroom
2 entry hallway	11 living
3 office	12 library
4 bathroom	13 storage
5 underground garage	14 wellness
6 TV/playroom	15 guests
7 terrace	16 basement
8 dining/kitchen	17 technical
9 loggia	

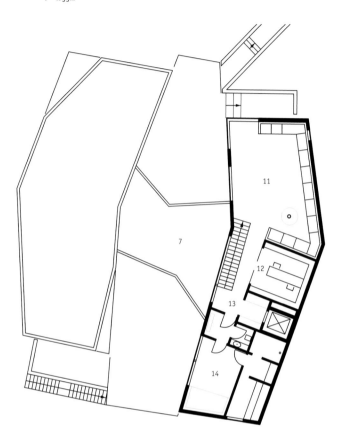

Top floor   scale 1:300

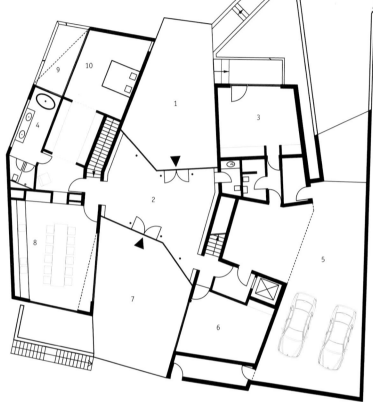

First floor   scale 1:300

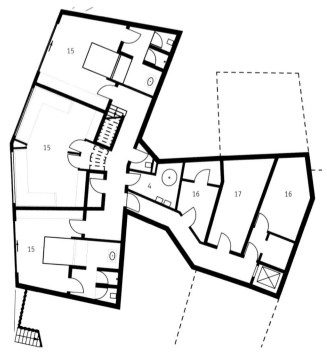

Basement   scale 1:300

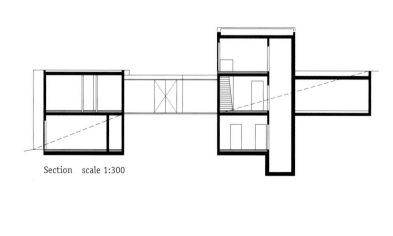

Section   scale 1:300

Home close to Stockholm (Sweden)

Johannes Norlander Arkitektur

Lot type	Type of construction
freestanding	concrete; roof: Kerto
Lot size	board-laminated wood
1,000 m²	**Building cost**
Covered area	300,000 Euro
160 m²	**Building cost per m²**
Living area	**living area**
130 m²	1,875 Euro
Effective area	
80 m²	
Number of residents	
1	
Start of construction	
2007	
Completion	
2008	

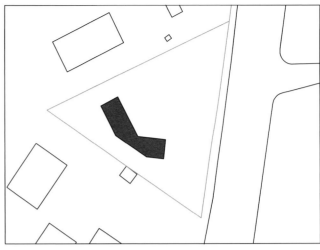

Site plan

Edge play

The house is unusual; you can imagine how the bourgeois middle-class neighbors living in their 1960s homes resisted its construction. (One of them actually went to court.) The case presented was the rather arbitrary one of Beautiful vs. Ugly, and it took a judge to rule in favor of the architect. The applicable building code was not altered. The narrow house of 4.60 m wide and 6 m high without a basement had to be fitted onto the sloping triangular lot.

The angle and the bow shape of the layout resulted from these limitations and the concept to provide a functional space which is open on the first floor despite its humble dimensions. The home is accessed via the kitchen with the dining corner for its single resident. Only the bathroom and toilet are separated, and the living area is adjacent to the narrowing at the building's approximate center toward the other side. A central fireplace not only heats the large room, which opens toward the top floor via a triangular ceiling cut-out next to the staircase, but its sculptural placement provides a caesura to the spatial flow.

At the top floor we encounter a gallery corridor with its small library and three bedrooms and/or office rooms. The filigree railing profiles maintain the view toward the first floor. Cement screed, white plaster, and light, white furniture demonstrate the absence of any luxury. The black wood stove is the visible and warming center. However, things are not entirely rustic, not at all. The concrete contains a floor heating system, and all of the rooms feature ventilation.

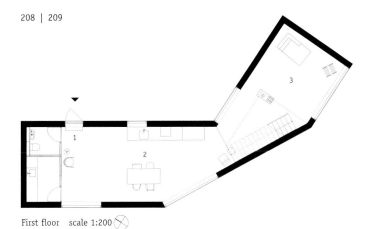

First floor   scale 1:200

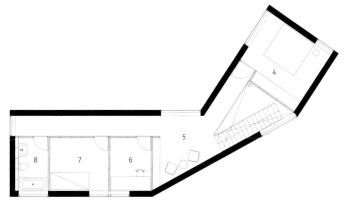

Top floor   scale 1:200

1 entry
2 kitchen/dining
3 living
4 bedroom
5 library
6 office
7 guest
8 bathroom

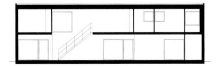

Section   scale 1:200

Due to its lack of foundation, and its oddly spaced windows of various sizes, the house's size is difficult to judge. Even its functions are hard to see.

Its unconventional shape results from a clever use of the lot's building area.

The tapered footprint provides a functional division on both floors without interrupting the spatial flow.

Aside from the decorative stove, there is a floor heating system under the screed.

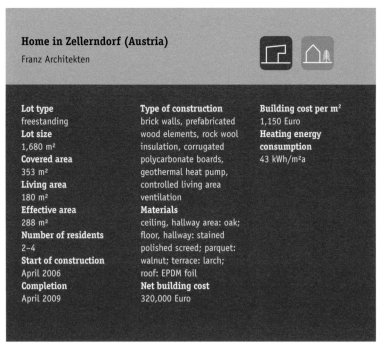

Home in Zellerndorf (Austria)
Franz Architekten

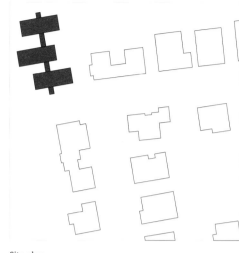

Lot type	**Type of construction**	**Building cost per m²**
freestanding	brick walls, prefabricated	1,150 Euro
Lot size	wood elements, rock wool	**Heating energy**
1,680 m²	insulation, corrugated	**consumption**
Covered area	polycarbonate boards,	43 kWh/m²a
353 m²	geothermal heat pump,	
Living area	controlled living area	
180 m²	ventilation	
Effective area	**Materials**	
288 m²	ceiling, hallway area: oak;	
Number of residents	floor, hallway: stained	
2–4	polished screed; parquet:	
Start of construction	walnut; terrace: larch;	
April 2006	roof: EPDM foil	
Completion	**Net building cost**	
April 2009	320,000 Euro	

Site plan

In triple time

The journey is the destination. In this case it is 35 meters long, a long glass hallway which the family members file through to occupy the home which is divided into three container-like boxes. The model for this idea is based on the traditional stretched farmyard, where the living quarters, auxiliary buildings, and stables are lined up under one common roof. Whether this structure for traditional small properties is based on narrow lots or whether the lot can be better used was not an issue here. The client grew up in such a farmyard home in the vineyards close to the Czech border, and this single-level type of building was particularly suited for build-it-yourself, with the help of friends and family.

The three boxes of 16.60 x 6.60 meters were made from brickwork on top of self-made strip foundations, and insulation was added onto the vertical coring bricks, followed by an OSB (oriented strand board) with black airtight foil and, as an iridescent continuation, translucent corrugated polycarbonate boards with a honeycomb structure. The family was able to mount this facade in about three weeks.

While the houses in the vicinity, from the 1970s, pile their functions up to the saddle roof, in this case the architect, a brother of the owner, placed them next to each other. The entrance lies facing south, marked by a defiantly protruding roof on the first box. This is where the promenade begins, and at first it runs through the unheated garage and a storage area with a workshop. Then the corridor takes on the function of a generous air trap, enters the second unit which contains the three-sided glazed living and dining area, and then reaches the last compartment, far away from the street, containing the main bedroom to one side and the children's rooms to the other. The bathroom and storage rooms are integrated as room dividers. The corridor, however, does not just end somewhere; it protrudes from the facade as a glazed curiosity and functions as a light-filled alcove, a reading room, or a playroom. There was sufficient space between the protecting living and bedroom pavilion to add a narrow swimming pool surrounded by a wooden terrace.

The rooms are fitted with a floor heating system, and warm water is provided by a geothermal collector and two heat pumps, complemented by controlled ventilation with heat recovery.

The home is closed toward the street. A long tunnel-like corridor runs through the garage and the workshop and receives daylight between the compartments.

The corridor ends as a curiously protruding glass alcove.

From looking at the photo, one could assume a vertical dark varnished facade siding. However, it consists of corrugated polycarbonate boards with a honeycomb structure which are screwed onto a black OSB board.

Living among the individual functional areas and their glazed connections is rather relaxed.

The last section is possibly the most restful: there was sufficient space for a narrow swimming pool.

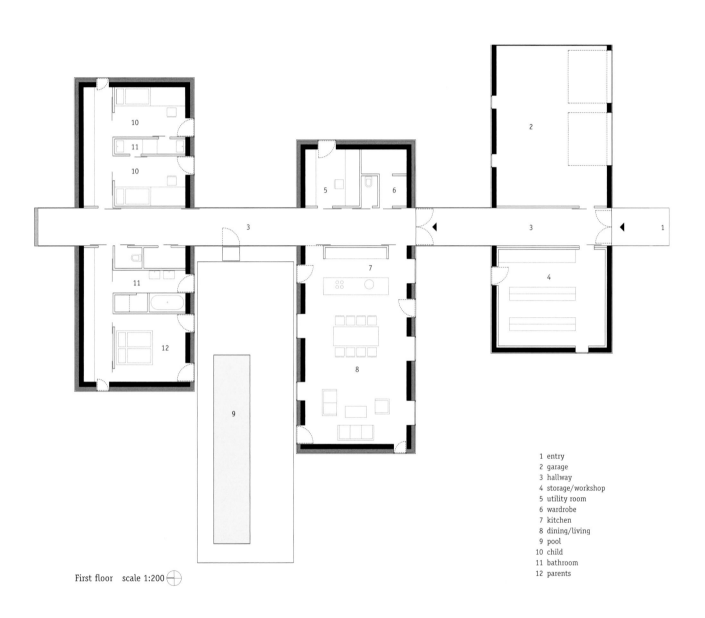

First floor   scale 1:200

1 entry
2 garage
3 hallway
4 storage/workshop
5 utility room
6 wardrobe
7 kitchen
8 dining/living
9 pool
10 child
11 bathroom
12 parents

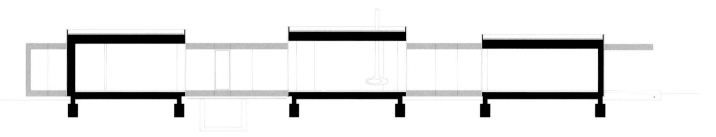

Section   scale 1:200

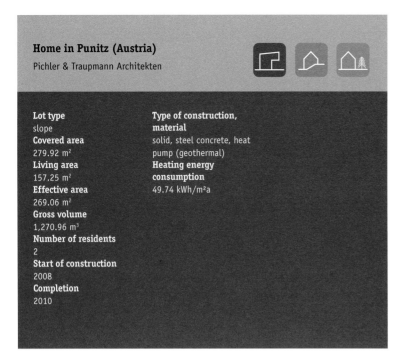

Home in Punitz (Austria)

Pichler & Traupmann Architekten

Lot type	**Type of construction, material**
slope	solid, steel concrete, heat
Covered area	pump (geothermal)
279.92 m²	**Heating energy**
Living area	**consumption**
157.25 m²	49.74 kWh/m²a
Effective area	
269.06 m²	
Gross volume	
1,270.96 m³	
Number of residents	
2	
Start of construction	
2008	
Completion	
2010	

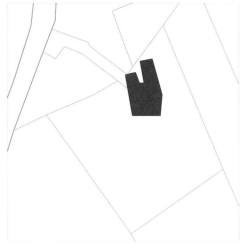

Site plan

Cut into the landscape

The clients wanted a comfortable home without wasting a lot of energy. The large and generously sized bathroom with a sauna next to the bedroom provides such comfort, as does the exterior pool of 3.50 x 10 meters. During the transitional seasons the pool is heated to 26° C via the existing home facilities utilizing excess heat provided by a geothermal heat pump.

This home with a north-south orientation lies in an agricultural area of the Burgenland, and its character was to be conserved. Hence the building inserts itself into the topography featuring a slight slope, and the driveway, consisting of a cut into the terrain, contributes to it. The embankment to both sides, lining the pathway, turns into a supporting wall which eventually reaches the height of the entrance level. This souterrain is only perceived as a full floor when standing in the niche of the entrance. The garage and utility rooms for technology and installations are located here. The single-floor sections of the building were fitted with greenery on the roof; its angle takes up the slope and transfers the moderate height onto the interior rooms.

A tapered staircase leads from the entrance hallway to the first floor which opens to both sides of the staircase like the blades of a pair of scissors. At the intersection is the kitchen and a central dining table facing east, and toward the west is the living room with an adjacent study. From here you reach a guest room with a bathroom, on top of the stairwell's balustrade shaped like a gallery. On the opposite side, separated by three steps, lies the master bedroom. A high glazing provides the visual contact to the continuity of the rooms.

The angular building — with its slightly crossed horizontal and vertical surfaces which cause the light to model a dimensional sculpture — continues to the pool area. The interesting detail here is that this technology works without chemical treatment. A biological filter unit with tubing running through gravel/quartz sand and a phosphate filter provide algae-free water. A second circuit removes suspended particles. The filter unit has a spillover which allows the water to seep away. The pools remain full during the year and a robot takes care of cleaning the walls. There are several open-air seats with wooden floors around the pool, in front of the kitchen, and at the staircase close to the guest room.

A protected resting place results from the supporting wall against the hillside.

The pool was determinant. It is
connected to a biological filter unit.
The design of the garden continues
the free lines of the home.

Arrangement in the green: the body
of the building pushes into the
sloping lot while the horizontal
walls shifted against the vertical
seem to mirror the dynamics.

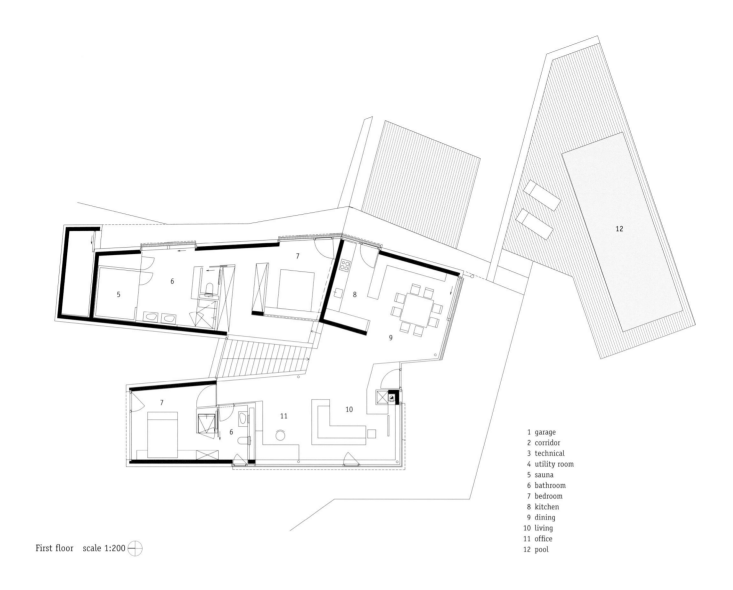

First floor   scale 1:200 ⊕

1 garage
2 corridor
3 technical
4 utility room
5 sauna
6 bathroom
7 bedroom
8 kitchen
9 dining
10 living
11 office
12 pool

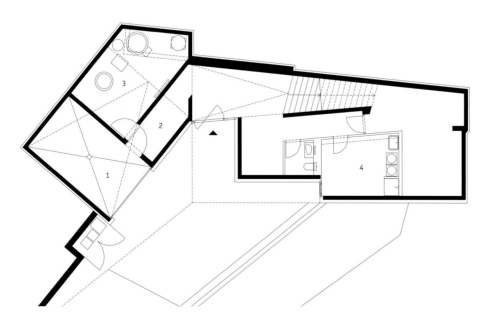

Basement   scale 1:200

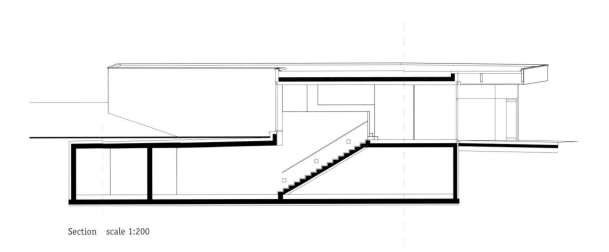

Section   scale 1:200

The bathroom and sauna are adjacent to
the bedroom. A low window provides a
visual connection to the living area.

Home in Utrecht (Netherlands)

Rocha Tombal Architecten

Lot type	Type of construction
freestanding	lime-sand bricks and steel;
Lot size	fitted with polystyrene,
775 m²	plaster; top floor: ready-
Covered area	mixed concrete with wood
188 m²	frame, roof: wooden con-
Effective area	struction
240 m²	**Building cost**
Gross volume	410,000 Euro
927 m³	**Building cost per m²**
Number of residents	1,716 Euro
4	
Start of construction	
March 2008	
Completion	
March 2009	

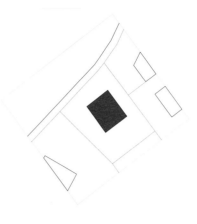

Site plan

Windows as intent and imagination

Basically this is "Nicholas' house," at least the local building plan says so. However, the architects found a lot of wiggle room as to design, and they converted the nondescript specifications into an architectural beacon. The lattice wood facade of the home emphasizes the planar look like two-dimensional mockups, with the various protrusions providing the third dimension. The display cabinet–like windows and roof snorkels are arranged so that they provide particular views of the surroundings but not to the neighbors. They can be comprehended as a resonance, as an image of their interior function, not really as obligatory apertures which are supposed to provide a harmonious look.

The center of the home, the eat-in kitchen, is located at the rear side. It is accessed via a diagonal corridor which runs past the children's rooms through the first floor. The outer wall opens below the eave with a ceiling-high glazing, since the direct connection to the garden was important for the owners. In counterpoint to the disturbance caused by the corridor a staircase runs with its last step standing freely in the room, in a shaft leading up to the roof. A small foyer lies to the left and leads to the upper living room, with its large ceiling-high bay windows with gables and a light shaft in the roof. The bedroom, bathroom, and study are somewhat secluded due to this layout. The large vertical pane over the eave is part of the study.

The untreated cedar siding of the facade continues on the roof surfaces. Instead of a visible gutter the facade turns into the slanted roof as an angular surface. Some of the wood siding can be removed for cleaning. The plasticity seems as if it were a folding game, and the shell fits the cubature uniformly. The masonry is conventional and where required — for example, at the alcoves — a steel structure is added.

A house which plays with its dimensions. Evenly hatched surfaces cover the walls and the roof.

The windows protrude like counterpoints and guide the views so they don't show the stuffy neighborhood homes.

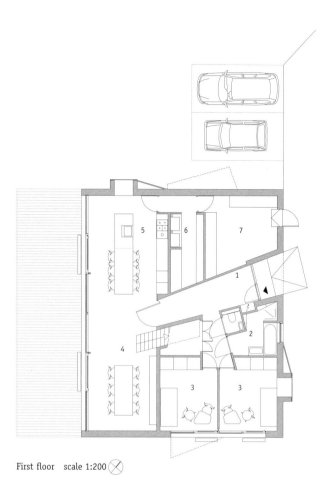

First floor   scale 1:200 ⊗

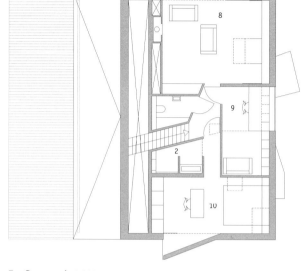

Top floor   scale 1:200

1 entry
2 bathroom
3 child
4 dining
5 kitchen
6 storage
7 room(s)
8 living
9 study
10 bedroom

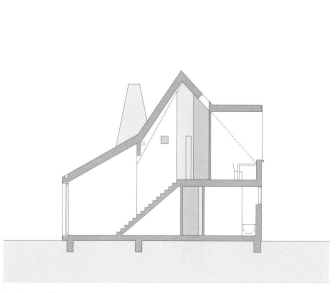

Section   scale 1:200

The trumpet-shaped light snorkels are not arbitrarily placed sensational items; rather, they correspond to the interior organization of the layout.

The eat-in kitchen and the lower living room feature a considerable height. The staircase leading to the private quarters disappears inside a portal-like access.

Home in Cologne

Johannes Götz und Guido Lohmann

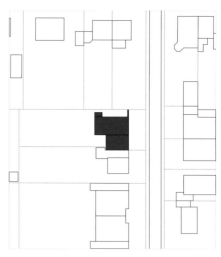

Lot type	Completion	Primary energy
gap, attached at one side	June 2008	consumption
Lot size	**Type of construction**	59 kWh/m²a
816 m²	solid construction; ceilings:	**Heating energy**
Covered area	steel concrete; walls: brick-	**consumption**
173 m² (house)	work; classic perlin roof	46 kWh/m²a
Living area	**Materials**	
182 m²	clinker base; plaster on	
Effective area	insulated masonry; tiled roof	
300 m²	**Baukosten gesamt**	
Gross volume	**Kostengruppe**	
1,358 m³	**300 + 400 HOAI**	
Number of residents	625,000 Euro	
3	**Building cost per m² of**	
Start of construction	**living area and effective**	
September 2007	**area**	
	3,400 Euro / 2,100 Euro	

Site plan

Cozy labyrinth

This home shows how attractive rooms can be developed with much finesse inside rather humble buildings. It replaces an existing house in the Cologne district of Lövenich, located on a street with most of the buildings being from the 1950s. The typical features of the one-and-a-half floor houses are the steep saddle roofs with gables or eaves. The design picks up these features as direct influences.

The house with a full basement builds on the neighbor's garage, with identical profile, and it therefore determines the street facade. The basement sticking out over the floor level of the lot lifts the first floor into the mezzanine level. At the same time it conforms, with its clinker base with the garage and the lot access, a horizontal unit running the entire width of the house, providing a stable support for the vertical volume with the pointed gable roof.

The house is accessed via a patio at the northern side, accompanied by the neighbor's high trees. The height of the foyer is 3.30 meters and quite im-

pressive, and from here you reach the dining area and center of the home a few steps further up. The first floor features an open design except for the kitchen, and the transitions between the different areas are clearly defined via floor and ceiling offsets. Since the client owns a few large-format paintings the task was to match openings and calm wall areas for hanging and illuminating the paintings.

The kitchen is flanked by a patio which is invisible from the street, and — glazed ceiling-high at two sides — it also illuminates the dining area. The adjacent living area opens up toward the garden with a large window which keeps the garden house and a gravel-covered and a wooden floor rest area in sight, like a picture frame.

The oblique single-run staircase accesses the top floor at the northern side. A corridor leads through the rooms and provides unlimited overhead height. The steep roof characterizes the rooms and provides a generous vertical proportion.

From the outside, the house with its pointed gable appears humble and fits into the area's 1950s building style.

The interior presents a well-thought-out spatial concept which assigns a function to every corner — in this case the open-air lunch/dining area next to the kitchen.

The garden facade with the large window.
The dormers provide height to the corridor
of the roof level.

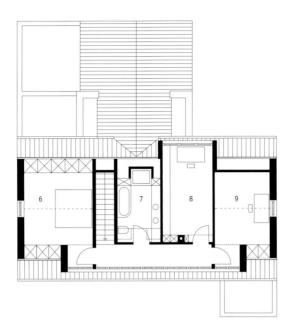

Top floor   scale 1:200

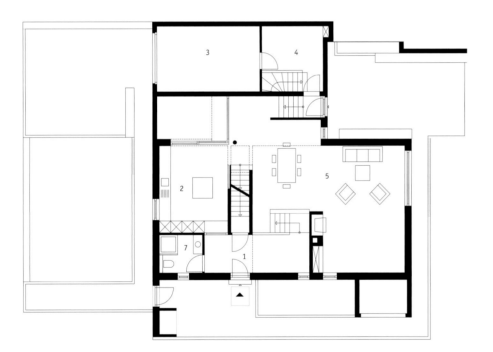

First floor   scale 1:200 ⊕

1   entry
2   kitchen
3   garage
4   utility room
5   dining/living
6   parents
7   bathroom
8   office
9   guest

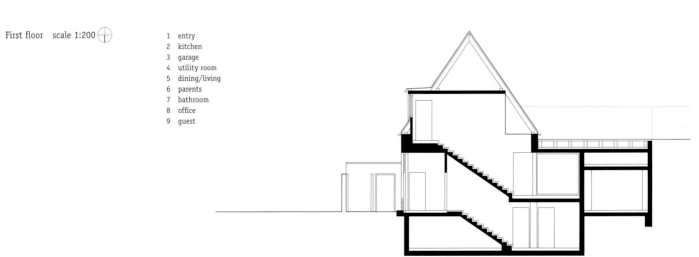

Section   scale 1:200

The dining area is centrally located. At the front left is the living room's fireplace.

The oblique staircase divides the kitchen from the dining and living areas.

Another premise of the design was to provide wall spaces in the small house to fit the client's large-format paintings.

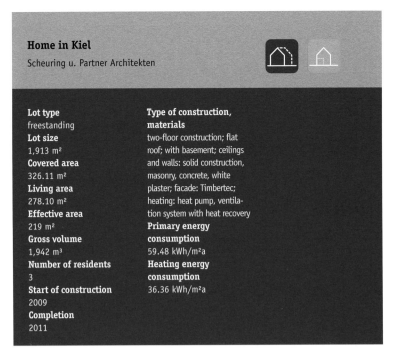

Home in Kiel

Scheuring u. Partner Architekten

Lot type	**Type of construction, materials**
freestanding	two-floor construction; flat
Lot size	roof; with basement; ceilings
1,913 m²	and walls: solid construction,
Covered area	masonry, concrete, white
326.11 m²	plaster; facade: Timbertec;
Living area	heating: heat pump, ventila-
278.10 m²	tion system with heat recovery
Effective area	**Primary energy**
219 m²	**consumption**
Gross volume	59.48 kWh/m²a
1,942 m³	**Heating energy**
Number of residents	**consumption**
3	36.36 kWh/m²a
Start of construction	
2009	
Completion	
2011	

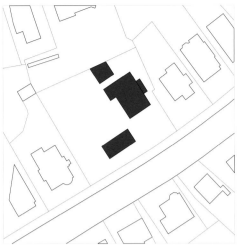

Site plan

Building on top

The clients had purchased a small single-floor house built in the 1950s. The idea was to take down the hip roof and to set a glass box on top of the existing first floor in order to extend the living area. However, as planning progressed it became clear that the old structure would have to be supported with steel beams and this would have affected the original idea.

Therefore, the decision was made to also demolish the first floor and to keep only the basement. Except for the angular staircase and the load transfer of the new walls, an entirely new building was created which reversed the original concept: the first floor now appears as a glass substructure which supports the top floor and which, thanks to the new construction, can protrude over the terrace. A guest house results in place of the former garage. Toward the garden is a broad alignment and equilibrium of the two building units, which are complemented by the new garage set at an angle.

This results in a protected interior area. The elevated terrace is due to the the previous basement ceiling. It is clad with Timbertec panels, and concrete steps lead to the lawn. The facade of the home is clad with coarse, silver-gray varnished larch panels.

The footprint follows the contour of the basement; only the vestibule with a wardrobe protrudes from the facade. This is where the access pathway clad with concrete sleepers connects. The living hall reaching below the roof does not show any signs of the humble former structure. The center of the open living level is a freestanding fireplace which separates the dining area and the seating group. Only an office (with its own entrance) remains separate. The top level features a central open fitness area flanked by the children's and the main bedroom. Bathrooms and staircase are separated by a long corridor which continues the inconspicuous zoning from the first floor.

Everything is lined up: the access path is made from concrete sleepers, the facades are clad with larch wood panels.

The fireplace marks an
invisible zoning
between the dining
and living area and
the foyer.

The raised terrace
platform is due to the
height of the
basement ceiling of
the demolished house.

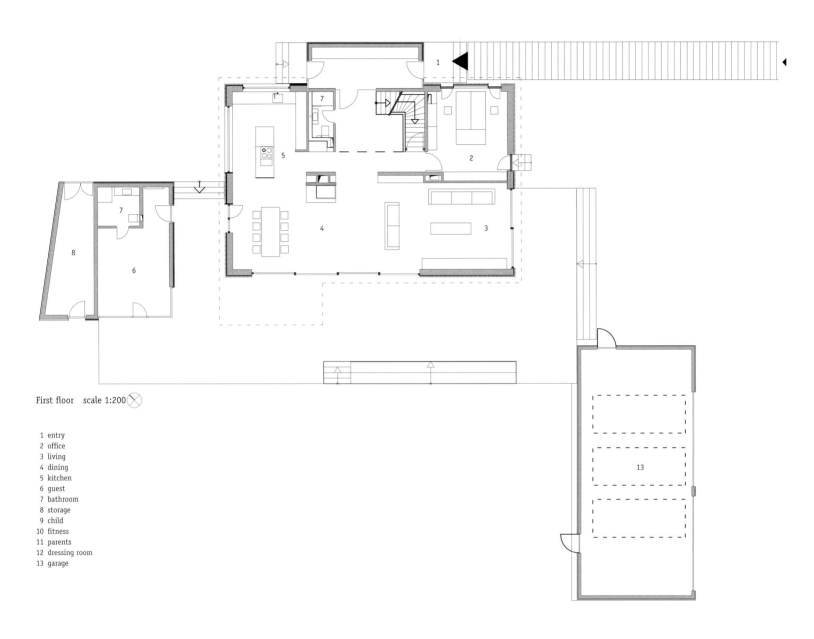

First floor   scale 1:200 ⊗

1 entry
2 office
3 living
4 dining
5 kitchen
6 guest
7 bathroom
8 storage
9 child
10 fitness
11 parents
12 dressing room
13 garage

Top floor   scale 1:200

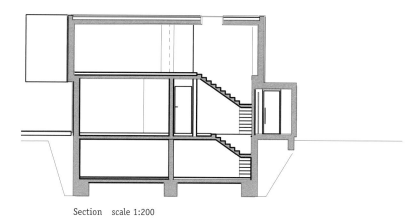

Section   scale 1:200

The entrance hall with a gallery on top of
it leaves no trace of the former humble
home on whose footprint the construction
was continued.

Home in Aarhus (Denmark)

Wienberg Architects

Lot type	Type of building
between traditional single family homes in the out-skirts of Aarhus	wood frame construction; facade: black varnished spruce boards; screed floors; interior: oak panels
Lot size	**Building cost per m² of living area**
928 m²	new construction: 12,500 Dkr
Covered area	renovation: 7,000 Dkr
187 m²	
Number of residents	
3	
Start of construction	
September 2007	
Completion	
May 2008	

Site plan

Continuation by other means

A simple small home of 87 square meters of living area was renovated and expanded to provide an attractive living environment for a family of three. The neighborhood consists of traditional single family homes. There are pine trees, gingkos, and rhododendrons. There are only a few traces of the old house left apart from the rectilinear contours; white paint, inside as well as outside, provides some clues. The extending building elements are clad with black varnished spruce boards. The two trapezoid expansions performed as wood frame constructions provide an entirely new face to the house. There is a nice balance between the sharp lines of the "architectural hardware" with materials like concrete and steel by fitting out the spaces with warm-toned wood, leather upholstery, and hides, complemented by light-colored curtains and soft illumination.

The home is accessed via a protective entrance loggia under the terrace. After a smallish corridor with wardrobe and guest lavatory and with a view of the kitchen, you reach an L-shaped ambulatory, illuminated by a light patio. Bedrooms and an additional bathroom are fitted into the old foot-print, and the main bedroom is illuminated via the small atrium.

The new building is reached via two concrete steps leading into the pentag-onal annex for kitchen and dining area. From here you reach the new main room via a portal-like opening a few steps lower, which is entirely clad with oak veneer. This "living cave" is lined by a bench and one side features a built-in bookshelf. The windows and their size and location are based on the existing trees. The oblique opening in the ceiling catches the eye, provides additional light from above, and elicits curiosity as to where the stairs leading over the seating bench might lead. Initially they lead past a narrow opening into the main bedroom, then at a right angle upstairs to an addi-tional room which continues the book shelves. A ceiling-high glass sliding door provides a view of the terrace, which features an intimate open-air area with a black varnished wooden balustrade, just like the facade.

The annex complements the small rectangle of the home with new contours, towering over it and adding a large terrace deck.

The entrance lies below this new protected open-air seating; the obliquely angled expansion, a wood frame construction, is clad with dark varnished spruce boards.

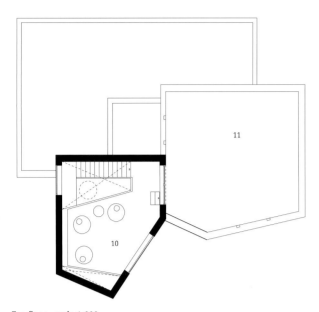

Top floor   scale 1:200

The living space comprises two levels and is clad entirely with oak veneer to conform a comfortable living cave.

The cave is lined by a surrounding bench on the first floor. It connects the kitchen/ dining area and main bedroom.

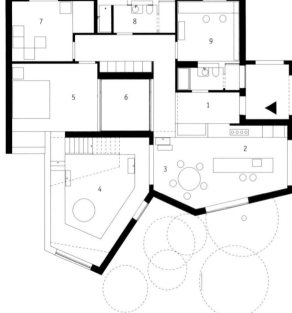

First floor   scale 1:200

1 entry
2 kitchen
3 dining
4 "living cave"
5 bedroom
6 atrium
7 child
8 bathroom
9 office
10 living
11 terrace

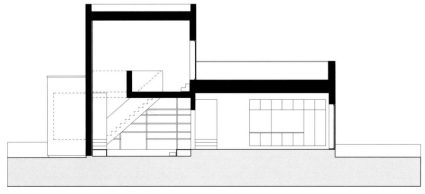

Section   scale 1:200

Home in Charrat (Switzerland)

clavienrossier architectes

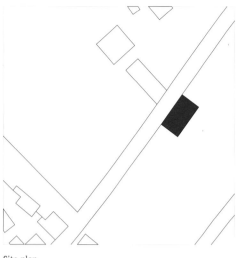

Lot type	Type of construction,
slope	materials
Lot size	base: stone wall; outer
345 m²	walls: colored concrete;
Covered area	larch window frames
142 m²	**Total building cost**
Living area	600,000 CHF
363 m²	**Building cost per m² of**
Effective area	**living area and effective**
230 m²	**area**
Gross volume	2,600 CHF
1,050 m³	1,652 CHF
Number of residents	
4	
Start of construction	
2009	
Completion	
2010	

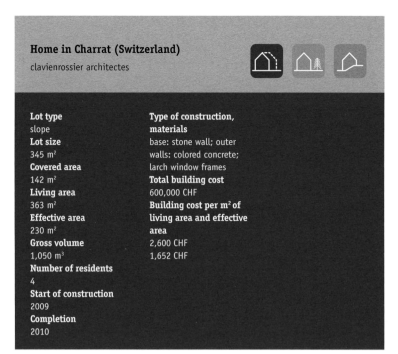

Site plan

Architecture with superstruction

The house clearly indicates that it is a new construction. On its footprint at the edge of the village stood a barn made from quarrystone which would have been too large for the intended home if refurbished. So only the areas which were easy to retrofit, the basement and the simple living rooms, were conserved; the rest was demolished. The integrated bosses keep the building on its site, and it stays within its grown surroundings of vineyards, stone walls, and, finally, the Alps. Ultimately this solution also contributed to lowering the cost. The effective area is reduced from 320 to 230 square meters.

The architects wanted to provide a strong contrast between the remaining foundation and the complementing construction. The new volume which replaces the saddle roof consists of colored concrete walls. The applied oxides match the color of the tuff found in the area. The massive construction corresponds with the historical masonry with its 60-centimeter-thick wall.

This also made it possible to build the new facades independently. Small vertical windows were recovered from the barn, and the offset addition responds with a single opening toward each side which frames the view of the landscape. The thickness of the concrete walls allowed for a distinct chamfer which improves the incidence of light. The outer walls provide an ever-changing play of light and shadow during the day.

The old entrance level contains storage and utility rooms, the laundry, and (of course!) the wine cellar. The staircase along one of the quarrystone walls leads to the new square living room on the upper floor. A white shelf balustrade lines the wide ceiling opening. Behind the rough stone bulkhead lies a kitchen unit, and from here a narrow staircase along the dividing wall of the main bedroom leads into the new roof level with additional bedrooms. So the kitchen becomes the center where all of the paths cross. There are no corridors; all of the pathways are located alongside the outer walls, from room to room, from window to window.

A house that stays. The remaining basement was expanded with a smaller annex, and the old stone walls connect the modern annex with the location.

While the historical foundation appears closed, the windows with the folded and colored concrete walls emphasize the view of the landscape.

The light incidence is improved because of the chamfer.

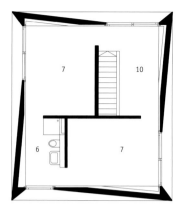

Third floor   scale 1:200

The living room as such begins on the middle level. A quarrystone wall separates the kitchen and living room where a white shelf wraps around the staircase.

On the other side, a narrow staircase leads to the upper bedroom level. Instead of corridors all of the rooms are connected with a passageway.

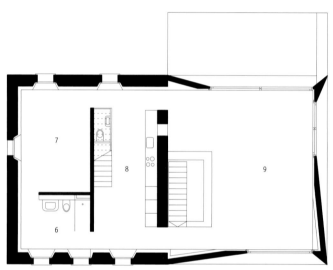

Second floor   scale 1:200

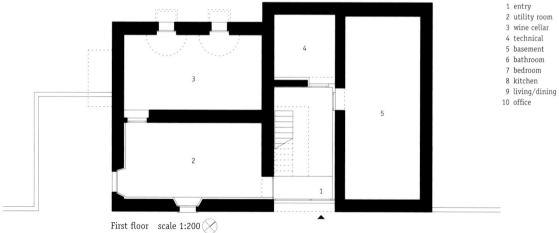

First floor   scale 1:200 ⊗

1 entry
2 utility room
3 wine cellar
4 technical
5 basement
6 bathroom
7 bedroom
8 kitchen
9 living/dining
10 office

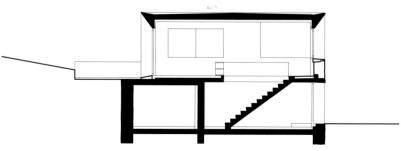

Section   scale 1:200

Home in Aalen

(se)arch Freie Architekten

Lot type	Type of building	Primary energy
northern slope	wood frame construction	consumption
Lot size	insulated with cellulose;	19.4 kWh/m²a
576 m²	laminated wood ceilings;	**Heating energy**
Covered area	basement from steel con-	**consumption**
203 m²	crete and lime-sand bricks	29.4 kWh/m²a
Living area	**Materials**	
312 m²	cedar shingles, wood-alu-	
Effective area	minum windows	
368 m²	**Total building cost**	
Gross volume	550,000 Euro	
1,605 m³,	**Building cost per m² of**	
with 1,314 m³ heated	**living area and effective**	
Number of residents	**area**	
4	1,763 Euro	
Start of construction	1,495 Euro	
2007		
Completion		
2008		

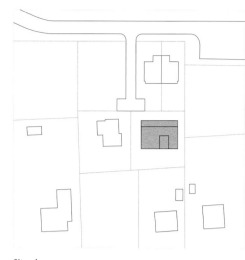

Site plan

Interlocked order

The property is accessed via a short cul-de-sac from the north and rises toward the south, which required particular attention toward the relationship with the surroundings. This was implemented on all levels with "green rooms." They are created via open volumes which are cut out from the three-level cube reaching into the flat hillside.

The lower level, which is accessed from the protected corner under the protruding living level next to the garage, contains the office of the home-owner. A narrow glass ceiling strip provides illumination and it also opens toward a small terrace at the retreating eastern side. The dark depths contain the basement and utility rooms.

The concept of intersecting recessed volumes continues upwards, on the one hand via two terraces facing south with different depths; a gallery opening connects the two living levels as well, and also contributes to distribute heat. The staircase reaches the kitchen and dining area, and the power plant of the home stands in front of the oriel-like living room: a sizable wood stove. Not only does it heat the entire home via the roof cutout, it also feeds about 70% of its heat into the floor heating system. The logs, stored in a niche, atmospherically emphasize the heating design. The northeastern corner of the home contains the main bedroom. It is accessed from the living room or along a cabinet corridor close to the kitchen, so open living can be freely interpreted. Sliding doors, including those in front of the bathroom area, provide either privacy or the usage of the flowing rooms.

The game with the offset volumes continues on the second floor. This allows for both children's rooms to be extended by their very area toward the outside onto a balcony or a loggia if the weather allows for it. The corridor opens up downwards to form wide intermediate spaces which can be used for play or work, whenever you want to retreat without being entirely cut off from family life.

The lower floor consists of concrete and masonry. On top of it lies a wood frame construction with 30 cm of cellulose insulation. The facade is clad with cedar shingles. Solar panels support the energy concept with its CO_2-neutral heating system.

From the entrance corridor you first reach an office on the lower level. A glazed ceiling strip provides illumination.

A small terrace makes for fun work — and allows for a later conversion into a room.

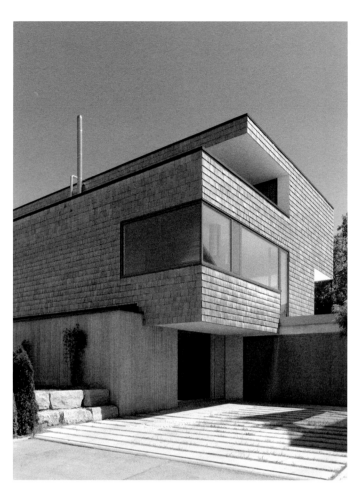

The entrance lies under the protruding top floors.

The garden side shows the slick interplay between building spaces and empty spaces. Unusually deep recesses break up the volume and provide protected open-air areas.

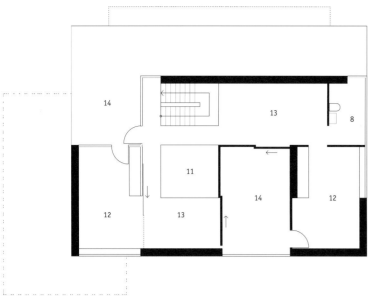

Top floor   scale 1:200

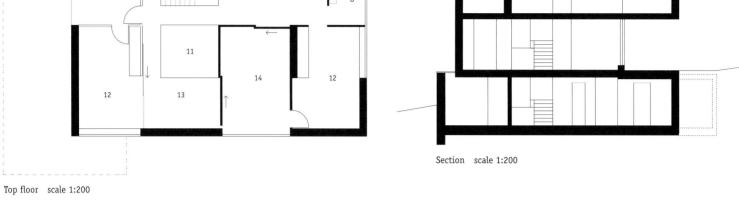

Section   scale 1:200

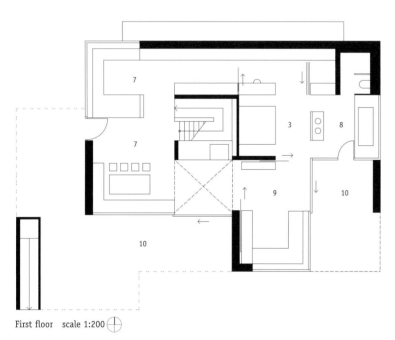

First floor   scale 1:200 ⊕

1 entry
2 office
3 bedroom
4 technical
5 storage
6 garage
7 kitchen/dining
8 bathroom
9 living
10 terrace
11 air space
12 child
13 gallery
14 balcony/loggia

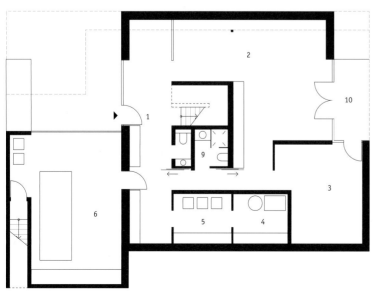

Basement   scale 1:200

A sizable wood stove stands in the center of the home. Sliding doors and an open ceiling design allow for heat to circulate if required.

Home with granny flat at Ritten (Italy)

Sabina & Klaus Valtingojer Architekten

Lot type freestanding **Lot size** 4,200 m² **Covered area** 289 m² **Living area** 428 m² **Effective area** 615 m² **Gross volume** 2,800 m³ **Number of residents** 5 **Start of construction** May 2006 **Completion** August 2008	**Type of construction** basement, first and second floor: solid construction; attic: wood beam framing with prefabricated wall elements; roof with steel support construction and filling with wood beams **Materials** wood windows: oiled Siberian larch; sliding shutters; steel frames, panels made from cedar wood can be turned electrically; terraces: steel frame with beams and slatted larch frame; floors: larch in living and bedrooms, natural stone in	bathrooms, hallway and stairwell; facade: plastered masonry and ventilated cedar wood facade; roof: flat roof with extensive greenery; heating system: wood pellet heating **Total building cost (Kostengruppe 300 + 400 HOAI)** 1,300,000 Euro **Building cost per m² of living area and effective area** 1,246 Euro **Heating energy consumption** 37 kWh/m²a

Site plan

Playrooms

The house in Ritten stands at the promenade leading from Oberbozen to Klobenstein. This high-lying plateau has been traditionally populated with chalet-type wooden vacation homes or masonry villas belonging to city residents. The new building is based on both types of construction, consisting of two units pushed into each other. The whitewashed core with the main rooms faces approximately southward, and a contiguous corner clad with cedar wood contains smaller rooms and utility rooms toward the north and west. The tension between the two shells is due to the slight overlap and the large terraces which indicate the transition between inside and outside, between grown landscape, swimming pond, and solid building. Due to this feature the home also appears to be lower. The open-air seats on each level connect the load-dissipating building walls like elements of a stacking game. The recurring motif of cedar wood blades emphasizes the look of privacy.

Aside from the generous apartment on the first and the top floor, there is a granny flat for family members or friends on top of it which is accessed via a roofed exterior staircase. A sweeping terrace is the main feature here.

The quality of the main apartment is determined by the variety of the rooms (living room, billiard/pool room) and the continuum of the living area. Dining area and the upper living space are separated by a red fireplace which is apt for grilling, and a second stove at the outer wall contributes to heating and the general atmosphere. The room continues into the top floor to a surrounding gallery. The adjacent children's room features a glazed balustrade. The interior fitting is made from white oiled larch wood.

The swimming pond is lined inconspicuously by a plant basin which takes care of water filtration. For the six parking spaces the house was extended with a private underground garage. The driveway is clad with a rock formation, and a tunnel leads into the lower level. On the same level is a media room and a collection of wellness equipment.

The top bedroom level is accessed via the living room gallery or, inconspicuously, via the exterior staircase.

Two steps and a red grill fireplace separate the living and dining area.

The sizable building volume is diluted with balconies, terraces, blinds, and windows.

This results in attractive pathways and various correspondences with the garden area, which includes a pond with a separate swimming pool.

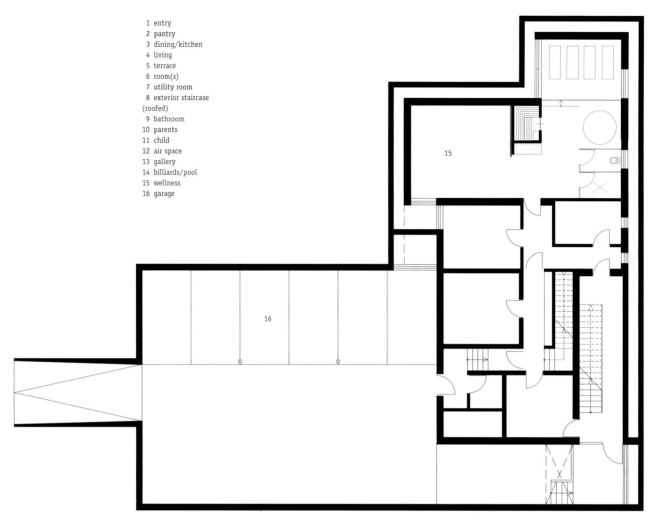

1 entry
2 pantry
3 dining/kitchen
4 living
5 terrace
6 room(s)
7 utility room
8 exterior staircase
(roofed)
9 bathroom
10 parents
11 child
12 air space
13 gallery
14 billiards/pool
15 wellness
16 garage

Basement   scale 1:200

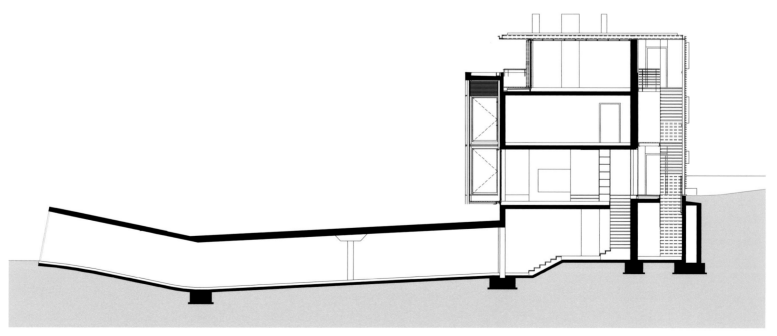

Section   scale 1:200

First floor   scale 1:200

Top floor   scale 1:200

Attic   scale 1:200

Apart from the bathrooms of the
bedrooms, the lower level
features a wellness area.

Villa in Cologne

Axel Steudel

Lot type	**Type of construction**
freestanding	solid construction; insulat-
Lot size	ed masonry walls, both
1,014 m²	sides plastered, first floor
Covered area	with clinker finish; con-
225 m²	crete ceilings
Living area	**Materials**
274 m²	exterior: raked plaster,
Effective area	clinker, wooden windows;
123 m²	interior: oak parquet,
Gross volume	slate, lacquered wood
1,877 m³	**Primary energy**
Number of residents	**consumption**
2	94.28 kWh/m²a
Start of construction	**Heating energy**
2007	**consumption**
Completion	46.68 kWh/m²a
2008	

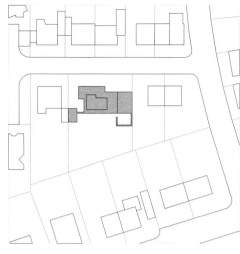

Site plan

A house providing tranquillity

The floor plans of this villa remind one of the grand villas as they were built at the beginning of the 20th century. However, the functions are completely different — there are no small rooms for servants — but the play with symmetry and asymmetry, the hierarchy of the pathways and the increasing privacy of the rooms, are part of the repertoire of classic living culture. The building develops from floor plans characterized by stylish usability.

The surrounding construction from the post-war era shows no common features except for the building line facing the street, and a similar depth. There used to be a simple small duplex on the lot, but only its garage was preserved. The advantages of the building site are its usable width and its ideal orientation toward the south. Hence the new construction is built parallel to the street in order to delimit the garden.

The house actually consists of two units. Two office rooms connected via an internal staircase lie facing the street with a separate entry at the garage driveway. A granny flat could be easily fitted with a bathroom, guest lavato-

ry, kitchen, and basement access, or the large apartment could be extended by adding this area.

The main entrance lies protected under a portal-like recess at the center of the building which dominates the entire width of the lot. It marks a place, an address. A foyer with a wardrobe and lavatory welcomes the visitor as a functional vestibule, and a broad double door indicates the living area. The kitchen can be accessed via a lateral entrance and also leads into the basement.

A diversified layout of rooms leads to the bedrooms with bathrooms via an office gallery; farther up a staircase leads to an attic room lined by terraces and featuring a bathroom and a yoga room.

A dark clinker pedestal provides a horizontal line. The ambition of craftsmanship is palpable. On top of it rests the white-plastered upper and mezzanine floor. The bricks are continued with the outer walls, and the carport which transitions into a garden patio creates a uniformly generous estate.

The classy functionality of the floor plan is outstanding. The entrance gives the impression of a protected private address.

Details characterize places; in many cases it is just a column, a ledge, or a niche, as in the living room.

A bright office space can be fitted over the wardrobe via a broadened corridor. The bedrooms are accessed from this mezzanine gallery.

The architecture dissolves progressively toward the garden with freestanding columns, walls, and annexes.

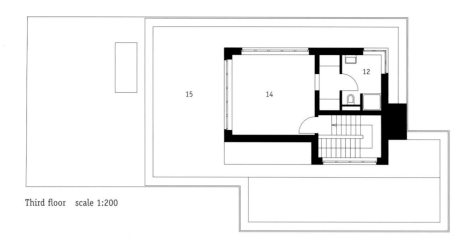

Third floor   scale 1:200

1 entry
2 wardrobe
3 utility room
4 carport
5 herb garden
6 roofed terrace
7 kitchen/dining
8 living
9 garage
10 office
11 bedroom
12 bathroom
13 dressing room
14 room(s)
15 terrace

Second floor   scale 1:200

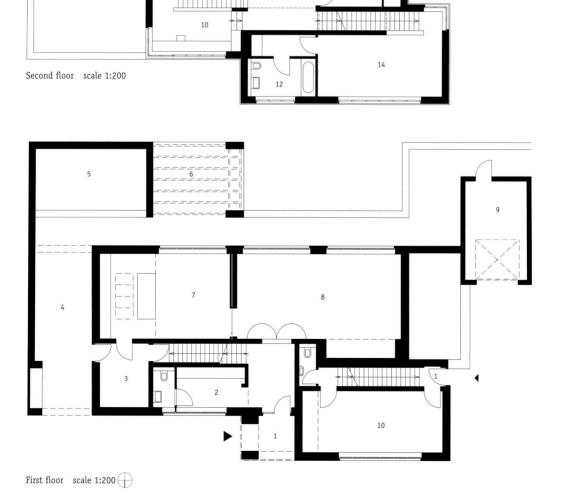

First floor   scale 1:200

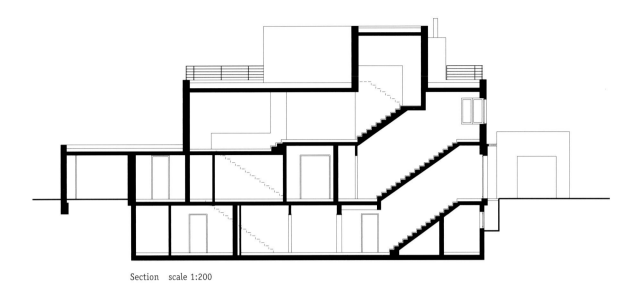

Section   scale 1:200

The dining area continues outside. The columns could eventually form the base of a pergola.

Lot type in a traditional neighbor- hood, surrounded by new homes **Lot size** 500 m² **Living area** 210 m² on two levels **Office area** 85 m² **Cubature** 855 m³ **Number of residents** 4 **Start of construction** December 2006 **Completion** May 2007	**Building cost** 650,000 Euro **Building cost per m²** 900 Euro **Building cost office** 110,500 Euro **Building cost office per m²** 1,300 Euro **Type of construction** concrete strip foundations, insulated concrete ele- ments and floor heating with polished concrete ceiling, hot-rolled mounted steel construction with box girder profiles. Steel outer cladding; exterior facade: corrugated metal sheets;	Bolted Perfoprofil steel sheet metal; thermically separated steel walls; rock wool insulation; sheet metal profiles; installa- tions: air heat pump (cooling and heating), floor heating on first floor; energy supply for apart- ment: electrical

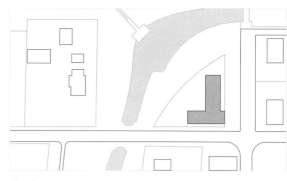

Site plan

Steelwork

The home is located on a street with old properties from different epochs, from farms to the typical small houses from the 1940s ("Apeldoornse Hueskes") with adjacent homes from the '80s and '90s. The new steel structure continues this leap in time, a concept featured by the architects and their three similar steel homes in the vicinity.

The construction without basement rests on ten individual footings. The support structure consists of hot-rolled box section profiles with mounted steel sheets insulated with rock wool. The wind bracings are partially visible. The lightweight construction was coated with black weatherproof off-shore-quality corrugated sheets wherever the facade does not feature ceiling-high glazing. Its energy contribution adds to the output of an air heat pump which distributes hot or cold air under the ceilings via airsocks. In addition the floors feature a heating system as well. This allows for spontaneous or planned control when adjusting to climatic conditions. A control unit keeps track of the air quality (temperature, humidity, and CO_2 level). The top floor ceiling consists of exposed trapezoid sheet metal profiles. The exterior walls are also clad with sheet metal, only interior walls feature drywalls. Special coated glass provides protection from the sunlight, blinds can be lowered, and in addition some of the interior walls are painted black.

The T-shaped building combines living and work while the vertically joined building units strictly separate the functions. The entrance lies on the first floor under the frame-mounted office tract while the exterior staircase leads to the separate architecture office wing. The private home consists of two levels, and an obliquely placed staircase divides the kitchen from the dining/living section. During the warm seasons the facade in front of it can be completely removed so that you can almost reach the exterior from the top floor. A large storage room lies behind the entrance and houses the washing machine, dryer, and freezer.

On the top floor the staircase leads to a corridor with a children's and guest room, each at its own end. A bathroom and the main bedroom flank the stairs, connected to each other.

The architecture office is divided into two sections which are separated by the staircase, coffee kitchen, and lavatory.

The architecture office is located on the top floor of the obliquely-placed building unit.

The vehicles are parked below. The windows are located to provide for the privacy of the family.

If you open the ceiling-high glass sliding doors, the staircase almost leads to the exterior (photo, opposite left).

Despite the strict architectural aesthetic, the children can create their own living environment (photo, opposite right).

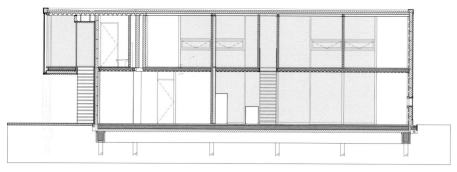

Section   scale 1:200

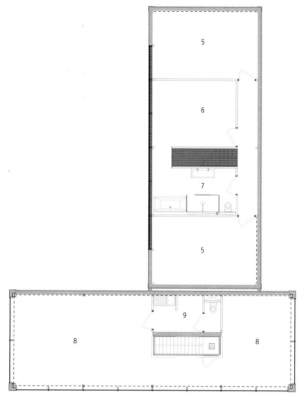

Top floor   scale 1:200

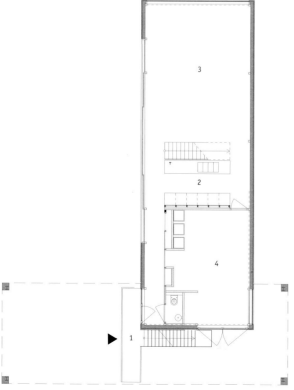

First floor   scale 1:200

1 entry
2 kitchen
3 living/dining
4 storage
5 child/guest
6 parents
7 bathroom
8 office
9 coffee kitchen/
lavatory

The dining area with its industrial lights appears wear-resistant. The utility systems are visible everywhere.

Home in Reischach at Bruneck (Italy)

Pardeller Putzer Scherer Architekten with

Joachim Rubner

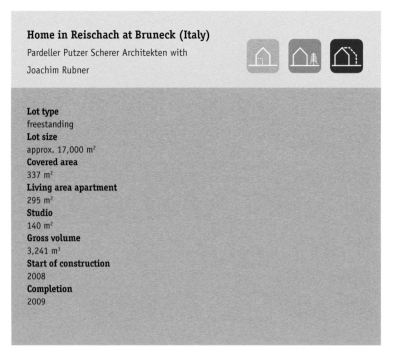

Lot type
freestanding
Lot size
approx. 17,000 m²
Covered area
337 m²
Living area apartment
295 m²
Studio
140 m²
Gross volume
3,241 m³
Start of construction
2008
Completion
2009

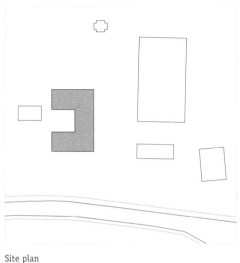

Site plan

Holding court

It is a large home which reacts to the location, local culture, and history without lowering its sights with regards to the resident's comfort. The "firber" patio is regarded as a "closed patio," a historical term which transferred the indivisibility of the property to the heirs. Its typology corresponds to that of a paired patio or yard, so it consists of two separate buildings for the home and the remaining functions. The current owner, proprietor of a wood construction company, does not utilize the farm property, but he wanted to make it his residence and intended to conserve the characteristics of the former residence. The existing stable is a good example of local carpentry; however, the home itself was younger and less valuable so it was demolished and replaced with a new construction.

It stands at the same spot where its predecessor stood to conserve the spatial tension between the homestead and the stable. However, the L-shaped building appears to be larger due to the two-level studio and exhibition room in front of it. At first sight it could be a patio with three sides. Its small bakehouse, carefully restored, a private chapel, and a fenced farming garden conform a traditional farm ensemble which, however, does not

intend to be a farm house museum. Once you discover the recliners inside the inner patio you realize the respectful and sublime progression into the present time.

The rooms are located on two levels over a sizable storage basement. Living is oriented toward the south and the west across the yard. A walkway and balconies line the triple-glazed glass fronts, with its larch wood columns of two stories in height incorporating the exhibition building. The outer facades with the roofs reaching up to them are executed as closed and coarsely plastered wood frame walls; a few windows provide views of the landscape.

After passing the wind protection protruding from the eastern side you come to a hall reaching into the edge of the building with the staircase. Kitchen and utility rooms traditionally greet the visitor, while the living room with the studio and library is located on the other side. The top floor features the functional layout of children's and parents' rooms with their respective corridors, lined by built-in cabinets on the outer side.

The new building is based on the regional typology of farm houses. The living section wraps around an interior patio with its L-shape; the third side is closed off with a studio and exhibit building.

Old-fashioned reminiscence: at the entrance next to the kitchen lies a *Zirbelstube* (a paneled "parlor") with a tiled stove.

A carefully restored bakehouse, a fenced farming garden, and a private chapel (not seen in photo) are part of the building ensemble.

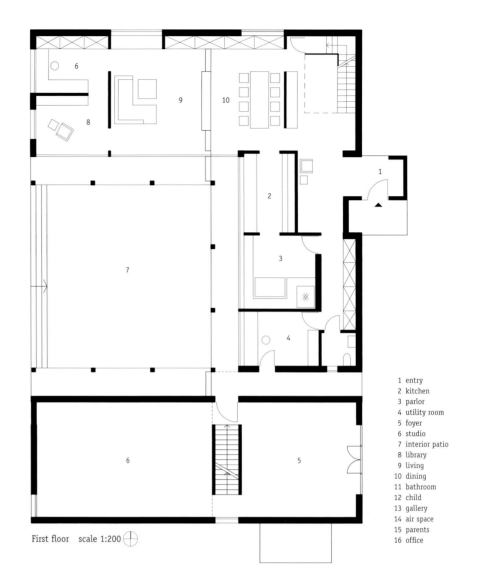

1 entry
2 kitchen
3 parlor
4 utility room
5 foyer
6 studio
7 interior patio
8 library
9 living
10 dining
11 bathroom
12 child
13 gallery
14 air space
15 parents
16 office

First floor   scale 1:200

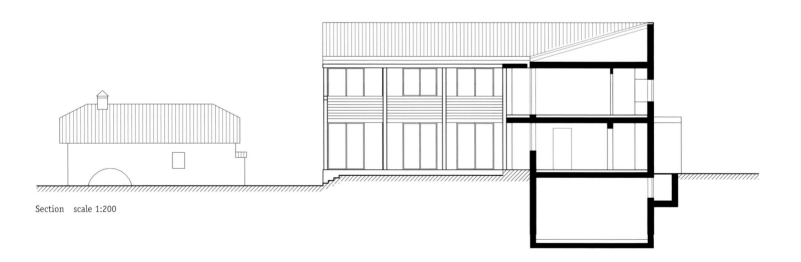

Section   scale 1:200

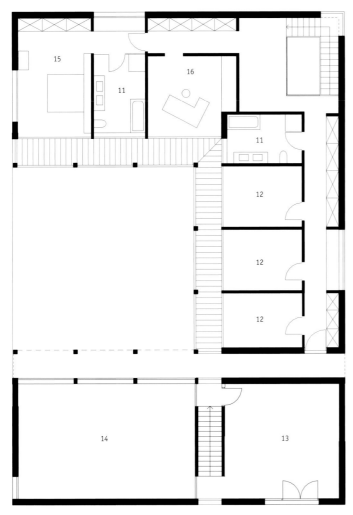

Top floor   scale 1:200

The kitchen in front of the
Zirbelstube exhibits contemporary
comfort without nostalgic
innuendo.

Beds with a view: the main
bedroom's long window at the foot
of the bed provides an excellent
view of nature.

Home with vacation apartment in Caputh

Anja Kaie, redthread

Lot type	**Start of construction**	**Baukosten gesamt**
slope facing west at the	November 2008	**(Kostengruppe 300 + 400**
edge of the village close to	**Completion**	**HOAI)**
forest	June 2009	493,000 Euro gross
Lot size	**Type of construction**	**Primary energy**
906 m²	first floor and top floor	**consumption**
Covered area	with wood frame construc-	33 kWh/m²a
218 m²	tion with cellulose, interior	**Heating energy**
Living area	with additional installation	**consumption**
230 m² (250 m² with	level; ceilings: solid wood	17.5 kWh/m²a
terraces and sauna at 25%)	ceilings from laminated	
Effective area	wood; basement: brickwork	
345 m²	from lime-sand bricks,	
Gross volume	super insulation blocks	
1,050 m³		
Number of residents		
4, with up to 3 guests in		
the vacation apartment		

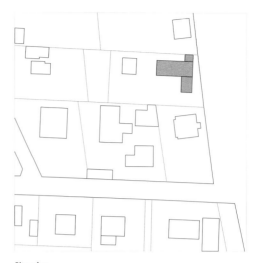

Site plan

Turning point for building

Sometimes the references between homes are invisible. This one is in the immediate vicinity of Albert Einstein's summer home built in 1929 by Konrad Wachsmann, which the city of Berlin gifted to the great physicist for his fiftieth birthday. Wachsmann later became famous through his main preoccupation, industrial prefabrication, which he experimented with by first applying it to wood construction. Some 80 years later, this new architecture responded to today's challenges of modern, ecologically manufactured wooden homes with low energy requirements.

The support structure consists of decoupled framed walls with an additional installation level. Insulation is provided by cellulose. The entire assembly only took two days. The outer cladding consists of black varnished trapezoid Douglas fir profiles accented with brown larch wood boards. A heat pump with geothermal heat from a deep perforation, a thermal solar system, and a ventilation with heat recovery complement the modern home technology. Wachsmann today, in a way.

The perfect southern orientation is part of it. Ceiling-high windows provide a passive heat input during winter. The angular shape of the house takes care of protecting the home's privacy on the terrace and the pool. The protective eastern wing at the street side without a basement contains the office and roof sauna. Following the terrain toward the west is a vacation apartment for three people set into the masonry lower level.

The main apartment allows for experiencing the slightly sloping terrain with steps between the living room and the dining area. The ceiling is recessed over the dining area which results in the top level belonging to it atmospherically because of the gallery. Generous rooms with bathroom and dressing room are located here. The children's room can be extended with the playroom corridor and the sauna terrace.

Interior and exterior intertwine the functionality, and the home organizes the living experience. Even the bicycles have a roofed parking space.

Cohesion: all of the functions including the
pool are concentrated in one building.

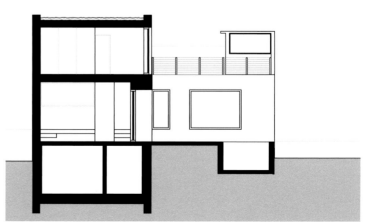

Section   scale 1:200

Wellness on two levels. The sauna on the
roof terrace, and a generous bathroom and
the pool in the garden.

The room reaches under the roof over the
dining area.

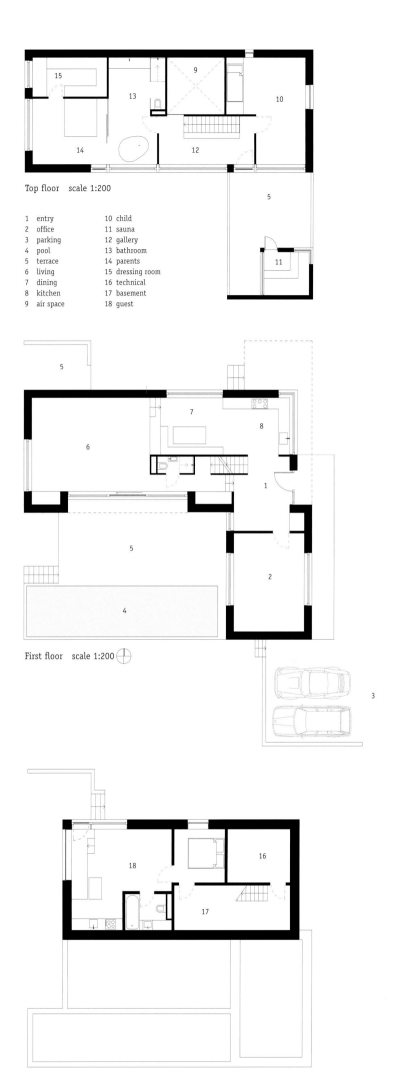

Top floor   scale 1:200

1	entry	10	child
2	office	11	sauna
3	parking	12	gallery
4	pool	13	bathroom
5	terrace	14	parents
6	living	15	dressing room
7	dining	16	technical
8	kitchen	17	basement
9	air space	18	guest

First floor   scale 1:200

Basement   scale 1:200

Lot type
slope
Lot size
4,560 m²
Covered area
183 m² and 84 m²
Effective area
403 m² with installations
and garage
Number of residents
4 and 2 employees
Start of construction
October 2008
Completion
July 2010

Type of construction
exposed concrete base-
ment, lightweight con-
struction with steel and
wood, wooden ceilings
Materials
facade: Eternit Aurea
large-format boards, par-
tially printed; partially
black acrylic glass; black
thinly-coated PV modules,
textile exterior roller
blinds; roof: Monoskin
large-format Eternit boards
providing shade for the
roof for passive cooling, 16
m² of water collectors,
black thinly-coated PV

modules; electric car
battery storage, water storage, prepared for fuel cell
operation
**Building cost per m² of
living area and effective
area**
2,950 Euro

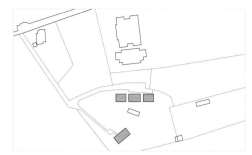

Site plan

The aggregate

This property on a sizable lot consists of a house for living and one for working, actually two buildings which form a single unit, just like farm buildings do. The owners, a family with two children, call it "future evolution house" since they are basically self-experimenting with future living and technology concepts. The architectural habitat includes an electric car in the garage. First and foremost it is an experiment as it is uncoupled from the urban surroundings and conforms a luxurious exception: its results and solutions cannot be readily applied in a general sense. However, according to the ideas of the owner, some of the elements can be transposed to large and dense ensembles as "mental architecture."

Both buildings can be read as examples for living. A steel construction which is extended or replaced by timber framework sits over a concrete sloping floor, in the case of both houses. This lightweight construction allows for changing the outer walls and replacing them with newer facade materials. The two ashlars consist of fiber cement boards or glazed walls with an exterior sun protection. The topic is living in nature. Technology is

not hidden away — water collectors are placed on top of the roof, thin polyvinyl foils are integrated into the facade. A block-type thermal power station is in preparation. Music, heating, and illumination are controlled via an iPad.

The floor plan of this case study home based on 1960s architecture is flexible and allows for later retrofitting. Storage and utility rooms are located next to the garage in the short base of the home. The long living level is located over it, and consists of ceiling-high heavy doors which allow for closing off the areas if you want to be left undisturbed. To the right of the entrance is the children's place, and to the left you reach the living area called a lounge by the owners. Here you can have an old-fashioned fire popping and crackling, or enjoy an informal meal on high stools which brings the family together. Downstairs the mobile residents can use the escape route to the garage. The last compartment contains the main bedroom and bathroom. The owner states that his family provided the architect with an opportunity to investigate social relationships.

A wide wooden terrace connects
the artificial technological
futuristic home with the present.

Part of the ecological living experiment is the work area within calling distance: the office is located in a neighboring second building.

Case Study 2010. The modular concept of the home does not hide its technological features. It seems to float over the garden landscape.

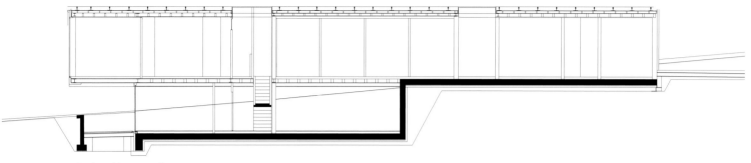

Section of home   scale 1:200

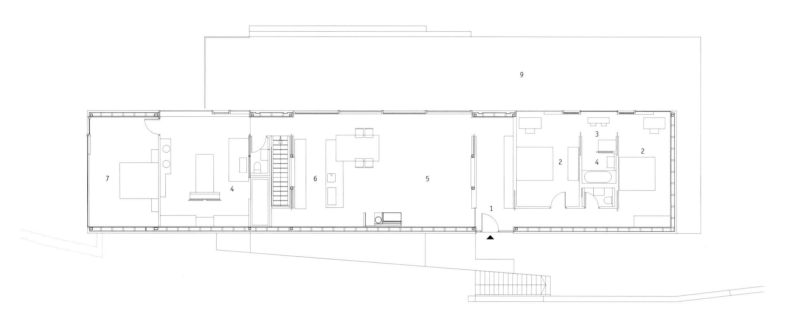

First floor of home   scale 1:200

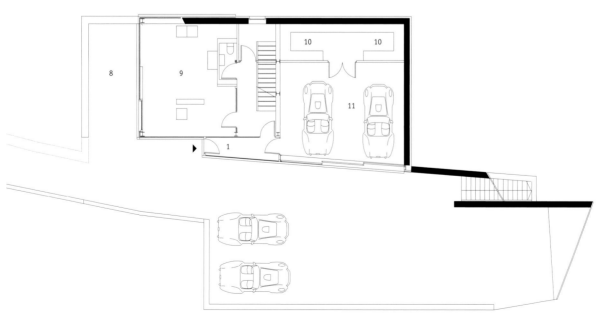

Basement of home   scale 1:200

1 entry
2 child/guest
3 tea kitchen
4 bathroom
5 living
6 kitchen
7 bedroom
8 terrace
9 technical
10 storage
11 garage
12 office
13 apartment

First floor office   scale 1:200

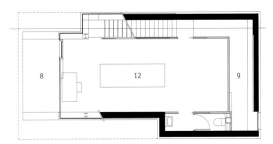

Basement office   scale 1:200

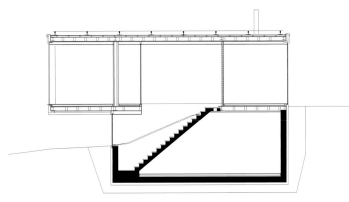

Section office   scale 1:200

The electric car is part of
the energy concept. Here
it is being fueled, and
when not in use it serves
as energy storage for the
house.

Even eating is not just
another affair. The family
takes care of that rather
informally, sitting on high
stools in their "lounge."

Home in Lochau (Austria)

Baumschlager + Eberle

Lot type	**Type of construction**
slope	in-situ concrete, insula-
lot size	tion, wood facade
1,565.55 m²	**Materials**
Covered area	floor, wall, ceiling: IPE,
514.91 m²	lapacho
Living area	**Heating energy**
407.5 m²	**consumption**
Effective area	40 kWh/m²a
556.60 m²	
Gross volume	
2,971.62 m³	
Number of residents	
4	
Start of construction	
August 2009	
Completion	
December 2010	

Site plan

Grand game of doubles

The contract for this villa with a view over Lake Constance simply stated: "Single family home consisting of two separate units." The smaller object located to the west and slightly lower is conceived as a guest house for tenants who can also utilize an office. Actually there is a third building too, attached on the eastern side via an arcade to the main house, sticking out like a finger into the landscape. Its upper edge terminates at the level of the sloping lot, and the wellness area of the residence is hidden under it. At the center of this U-shaped ensemble is a garden patio over a large underground garage. It is staggered downwards with a castle-like attitude to the rhythm of steps and bosquets.

The main building is accessed from a lower level where the sauna and a series of utility rooms are located in the depths of the mountain. Staircase and elevator lead to the "bel étage" whose center dominates the living room, flanked at one side by an office area with library and at the other by dining room and kitchen. A counter with a stove in the garden completes the amenities. The facade recedes facing the lake and provides space for a loggia.

The bedroom, cabinets, dressing room, and bathrooms one level up are placed around a more private living space with training gear. Here as well the main attraction is a loggia with a view of the lake.

The support structure of this complex consists of concrete, however, it remains invisible. The all-encompassing ironwood siding — actually South American lapacho, a high-quality, heavy hardwood — does not follow a primary structure. The scale is provided by the 10-centimeter-wide terrace floor boards which characterize the facades of all sides. The standardized boards were laid out around the building like a box, with a tolerance of 4 mm without any waste, and then joined at the edges with elaborate box joints. The windows are also custom-made. They are flush on the inside and conform the facade with their protruding lintels and ledges. Instead of visible aluminum weatherboards an invisible groove and a tube drains the rainwater. The theme of wood continues inside with built-in furniture, staircases, and oiled oak parquet. Traditional look and innovative construction combine to form long-lived architecture.

The terrace is continued with the grand vegetation, flanked by the guest wing (left) and the pool house (right).

The entrance to the main building is designed as a proprietary entree at the garden level.

From the living room loggia you enjoy the sweeping view over Lake Constance. A pool in the garden invites a quick refreshing plunge; a sauna is fitted under it.

The accesses to the two houses are separate. They share the facade consisting of oak which encloses the buildings like a case.

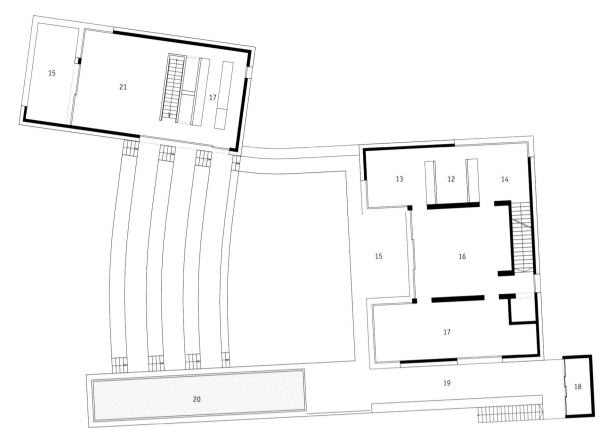

Second floor   scale 1:250

1 entry
2 wardrobe
3 wine cellar
4 workshop/utility room
5 technical
6 wood storage
7 arcade
8 garage
9 pool utility
10 sauna
11 room(s)
12 bathroom
13 office
14 library
15 loggia
16 living
17 kitchen
18 garden shower
19 garden kitchen
20 pool
21 living/dining
22 guest
23 hobby
24 bedroom
25 dressing room

First floor   scale 1:250

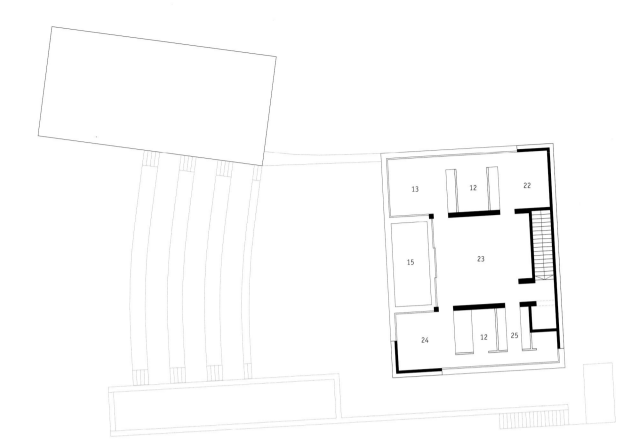

Third floor   scale 1:250

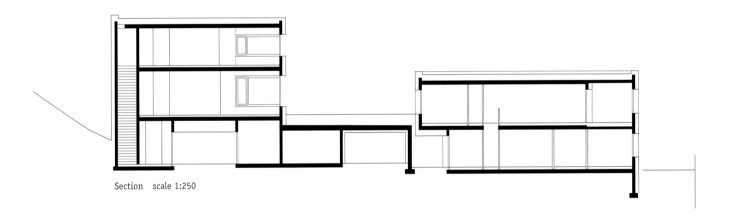

Section   scale 1:250

The professional kitchen in the main building is complemented by a "garden kitchen."

The central living room with the adjacent library and office to one side, and the kitchen and dining room to the other.

Architects and Photo Credits

4architekten
Dom-Pedro-Straße 7
D-80637 Munich
info@4architekten.de
www.4architekten.de
Photos, pp. 156, 157, 159:
Christian Hacker, Berlin

aa.ar
Atelier d'architecture Alain Richard
assistants: Alain Richard, Jean-Philippe
Possoz, Monique Bronlet, Matthieu Loncke,
Eléonore Delecour, Frédéric Brausch
Luc Mabille
Place Coronmeuse, 14
B-4040 Herstal
atelier@aa-ar.be
www.aa-ar.be
Photos, pp. 128, 129: Alain Janssens, Liège

aeby aumann emery architectes sàrl
assistants: Patrick Aumann, Emile Aeby,
Stéphane Emery
Route de la Fonderie 2
CH-1700 Fribourg
aumann@aae-architectes.ch
www.aae-architects.ch
Photos, pp. 51, 52, 53 top: Thomas
Jantscher, Colombier; pp. 50, 51, 53 bottom: Corinne Cuendet; Clarens

anako'architecture
Olivier Cheseaux Architecte HES
assistants: Jacques Frossard, Manu Crettaz
Pradelaman 14
CH-1971 Grimisuat
info@anakoarchitecture.ch
www.anakoarchitecture.ch
Photos, pp. 94, 95, 97: Thomas Jantscher,
Colombier

Architekt DI Bernardo Bader
Steinebach 11
A-6850 Dornbirn
mail@bernardobader.com
www.bernardobader.com
Photos, pp. 114, 115: Adolf Bereuter, Dornbirn

ARTEC Architekten
Bettina Götz + Richard Manahl
assistants: Gerda Polig, Johannes Giselbrecht, Michael Murauer
Am Hundsturm 5
A-1050 Vienna
goetz.manahl@artec-architekten.at
www.artec-architekten.at
Photos, pp. 86, 87, 88, 89: Bruno Klomfar,
Vienna

atelier-f architekten
Kurt Hauenstein Dipl.Ing. Architekt ETH SIA
assistants: Daniel Jäger, Murat Ekinci
Kirchgass 1
CH-7306 Fläsch
architektur@atelier-f.ch
www.atelier-f.ch
Photos, pp. 160, 161, 162, 163

atelier st
Gesellschaft von Architekten mbH
project team: Silvia Schellenberg-Thaut,
Sebastian Thaut | Architekten BDA
assistant: Marion Mendler
Kochstraße 28 | Fabrikgebäude
D-04275 Leipzig
info@atelier-st.de
www.atelier-st.de
Photos, pp. 118, 119: Werner Huthmacher,
Berlin

Architekturbüro Jakob Bader
Amalienstraße 14a
D-80333 Munich
architekturbuero@jakobbader.de
www.jakobbader.de
Photos, pp. 116, 117: Kai Arndt, Munich

Baumschlager + Eberle
Lochau ZT GmbH
Dietmar Eberle, Jürgen Stoppel
Objekt 645, 4. Stock
A-1300 Vienna Airport
office@be-lochau.com
www.baumschlager-eberle.com
Photos, pp. 264, 265, 267: Roland Halbe,
Stuttgart

Bedaux de Brouwer
Architecten BV BNA
Ir. Thomas Bedaux, Ir. Pieter Bedaux
Dr. Keyzerlaan 2
NL-5051 PB Goirle
post@bedauxdebrouwer.nl
www.bedauxdebrouwer.nl
Photos, pp. 168, 169, 171: Michel Kievits,
Breda

Bembé Dellinger
Architekten und Stadtplaner GmbH
assistant: Benjamin Saupe,
Tobias Zimmermann
Im Schloss
D-86926 Greifenberg
mail@bembe-dellinger.de
www.bembe-dellinger.de
Photos, pp. 76, 77, 79: Angelo Kaunat,
Wals-Siezenheim

Bergmeisterwolf Architekten
Gerd Bergmeister Arch., Michaela Wolf Arch.
Domplatz 20
I-39042 Brixen
office@bergmeisterwolf.it
www.bergmeisterwolf.it
Photos, pp. 58, 59, 61: Günter Richard
Wett, Innsbruck

Bottega + Ehrhardt Architekten GmbH
Giorgio Bottega, Henning Ehrhardt,
Christoph Seebald
project manager: Anja Richter
Senefelderstraße 77A
D-70176 Stuttgart
info@be-arch.com
www.be-arch.com
Photos, pp. p. 22, 23, 25: David Franck,
Ostfildern

Buchner Bründler AG Architekten BSA
Daniel Buchner, Andreas Bründler
project manager: Jenny Jenisch
assistants: Rino Buess, Beda Klein
Untengasse 19
CH-4058 Basel
mail@bbarc.ch
www.bbarc.ch
Photos, pp. 142, 143, 145: Dominique Marc
Wehrli, Unterengstringen

Caramel Architekten ZT GmbH
assistant: Kolja Janiszewski
Schottenfeldgasse 60/36
A-1070 Vienna
kha@caramel.at
www.caramel.at
Photos, pp. 136, 137, 139, 140, 141:
Hertha Hurnaus, Vienna

clavienrossier architectes hes / sia
Valéry Clavien, Nicolas Rossier
41, rue de Neuchâtel
CH-1201 Geneva
info@clavienrossier.ch
www.clavienrossier.ch
Photos, pp. 234, 235, 237: Roger Frei,
Zurich

Courage architecten BNA
Lars and Christa Courage
Veenhuizerweg 207
NL-7325 AL Apeldoorn
post@courage.nl
www.courage.nl
Photos: Pieter Kers: pp. 250, 251 top; Petra
Appelhof: p. 251 bottom; COURAGE architecten: pp. 252, 253

Döring Dahmen Joeressen Architekten
project manager: Dipl.-Ing. Architekt Christian Schardt
Hansaallee 321
D-40549 Düsseldorf
info@ddj.de
www.ddj.de
Photos, pp. 18, 19, 21: Manos Meisen,
Düsseldorf

dreibund architekten BDA
Olaf Ballerstedt, Thomas Helms, Rene Koblank
Maxstraße 7
D-44793 Bochum
mail@dreibund-architekten.de
www.dreibund-architekten.de
Photos, pp. 36, 37, 39: Fabian Linden, Bochum

EM2 Architekten
Kurt Egger,
Gerhard Mahlknecht,
Heinrich Mutschlechner
assistant: Arch. David Stuflesser
Rienzfeldstraße 30
I-39031 Bruneck
info@em2.bz.it
www.em2.bz.it
Photos, pp. p. 130, 131: Guenter Richard
Wett, Innsbruck

Franz ZT GmbH
Hornbostelgasse 3/2/32
A-1060 Vienna
office@franz-architekten.at
www.franz-architekten.at
Photos, pp. 210, 211, 213: Lisa Rastl,
Vienna

Fuchs, Wacker.
Stefan Fuchs, Thomas Wacker,
Architekten BDA
Am Westkai 9a
D-70327 Stuttgart
buero@fuchswacker.de
www.fuchswacker.de
Photos, pp. 80, 81, 83: Johannes Vogt,
Mannheim

Gassner & Zarecky
Architekten und Ingenieure
Partnerschaft BDA
assistants: Arch. Kathrin Wilhelm,
Arch. Danjiel Schneider, Arch. Birgit Bachmann
Leonardo-da-Vinci-Straße 17
I-39100 Bozen
studio@pps-arch.it

Johannes Götz and Guido Lohmann
assistant: Thorsten Schmitz
Hardtstraße 8
D-50939 Cologne
info@johannesgoetz.com
www.johannesgoetz.com
Photos, pp. 222, 223, 225: Jan Kraege, Cologne

Niklaus Graber & Christoph Steiger
Architekten ETH/BSA/SIA Gmbh
Alpenstrasse 1
CH-6004 Lucerne
mail@graberundsteiger.ch
www.graberundsteiger.ch
Photos, pp. 46, 47, 49: Dominique Marc
Wehrli, Regensdorf

Heide & von Beckerath Architekten BDA
Tim Heide, Verena von Beckerath
assistants: Henrike Kortemeyer (project
architect), Jürgen Krafft, Sarah Humpert
Kurfürstendamm 173
D-10707 Berlin
mail@heidevonbeckerath.com
www.heidevonbeckerath.com
Photos, pp. 100, 101: Maximilian Meisse, Berlin

Hein-Troy Architekten
DI Matthias Hein
assistants: Bernd Rommel (planning),
Günther Obermair (bid, site management)
Kirchstraße 2
A-6900 Bregenz
office@hein-arch.at
www.hein-arch.at
Photos, pp. 84, 85: Robert Fessler,
Lauterach

h i e n d l _ s c h i n e i s
architektenpartnerschaft_augsburg-passau
Am Schanzl 10
D-94032 Passau
Fabrikstraße 11
D-86199 Augsburg
buero@hiendlschineis.com
www.hiendlschineis.com
Photos, pp. 122, 123: eckhart matthäus_
em-foto_augsburg

Höller & Klotzner-Architekten
Thomas Höller, Georg Klotzner
assistant: Thorsten Hein
Cavourstraße 95
I-39012 Meran
info@hoeller-klotzner.com
www.hoeller-klotzner.com
Photos: Ulrich Egger, Meran: p. 75 right; Robert
Fleischanderl, Vienna: pp. 72, 73, 75 left

Jeuch Architekten
Patrik Jeuch, dipl. Architekt FH
assistant: Karin Bertoli, dipl. Architekt ETH,
Sergio Peratoner, project manager,
Reto Lindenmann
Dachslerenstrasse 11
CH-8702 Zollikon
architekten@jeuch.ch
ww.jeuch.ch
Photos, pp. 90, 91, 92: Sandi Kozjek, Zurich

Kaestle Ocker Roeder Architekten
Marcus Kaestle, Andreas Ocker, Michel Roed-
er
Hölderlinstraße 40
D-70193 Stuttgart
mail@kaestleockerroeder.de
www.kaestleockerroeder.de
Photos, pp. 150, 151, 153, 154, 155:
Brigida Gonzalez, Stuttgart

Architektin Anja Kaie
Am Waldrand 7
D-14548 Schwielowsee
post@redthread.de
www.redthread.de
Photos, pp. 258, 259: Anja Kaie, Schwielowsee

Johannes Kaufmann Architektur GmbH
Sägerstraße 4
A-6850 Dornbirn
office@jkarch.at
www.jkarch.at
Photos, pp. 106, 107: Norman A. Müller,
NAM Architekturfotografie, Dornbirn

Ken Architekten BSA AG
Jürg Kaiser, Lorenz Peter, Martin Schwager
Badenerstrasse 156
CH-8004 Zurich
mail@ken-architekten.ch
www.ken-architekten.ch
Photos, pp. 42, 43, 45: Hannes Henz, Zurich

Klumpp + Klumpp Architekten
Prof. Hans Klumpp + Julia Klumpp,
M. (Eng.), Dipl. Ing. (FH)
Engelhornweg 21
D-70186 Stuttgart
stuttgart@klumpp-architekten.de
www.klumpp-architekten.de
Photos, pp. 102, 103, 105: Zooey Braun,
Stuttgart

köppen strauch, architekten
Tobias Köppen, Günter Strauch

assistant: Derya Saglam-Kahraman,
Mehmet Kahraman
Konkordiastrasse 38
D-40219 Düsseldorf
info@koeppenstrauch.de
www.koeppenstrauch.de
Photos, pp. 132, 133, 134, 135: © Tomas
Riehle / arturimages, Bergisch-Gladbach

Architekten ETH SIA BSA
KUNZUNDMÖSCH GmbH
Leonhardstrasse 38
CH-4051 Basel
mail@kunzundmoesch.ch
www.kunzundmoesch.ch
Photos, pp. 26, 27, 29: Tom Bisig, Basel

LA'KET ARCHITEKTEN GmbH
David Lagemann, Tim Kettler
assistant: Ben Joscha Grope
Arnoldstraße 16
D-22765 Hamburg
info@laket.net
www.laket.net
Photos, pp. 98, 99 : Ralf Buscher, Hamburg

L/A
Liebel Architekten BDA
assistants: Steffen Kainzbauer,
Frank Weinschenk
Richard-Wagner-Straße 14a
D-73430 Aalen
buero@liebelarchitekten.de
www.liebelarchitekten.de
Photos, pp. 30, 31: Michael Schnell,
Essingen

Lohmann Architekten BDA
In der Ahe 1
D-27356 Rotenburg/ W.
info@lohmann-architekten.com
www.lohmann-architekten.com
Photos, pp. 54, 55, 57: Marco Moog,
Hamburg

Architekten Luger & Maul
ZT GmbH
Bauernstraße 8
A-4600 Wels
office@luger-maul.at
www.luger-maul.at
Photos, pp. 188, 189, 190, 191: Edith
Maul-Röder, Wels

meck architekten
Prof. Andreas Meck;
project management: Francesca Fornasier

Kellerstraße 39
D-81667 Munich
office@meck-architekten.de
www.meck-architekten.de
Photos: Fotograf Elias Hassos, Munich: p. 111,
113; Stefan Müller-Naumann, Munich: p. 110, 112

MODUS architects
dott. arch. Samuel Minesso, Sandy Attia
Via Fallmerayer, 7
I-39042 Brixen (BZ)
info@modusarchitects.com
www.modusarchitects.com
Photos, pp. 200, 201, 203

PAUHOF Architekten
Michael Hofstätter / Wolfgang Pauzenberger
art: Manfred Alois Mayr
assistants: Dipl. Ing. Barbara Kolb,
Dipl. Ing. Hendrik Seibel
Ramperstorffergasse 2/10
A-1050 Vienna
office@pauhof.com
www.pauhof.com
Photos, pp. 172, 173, 175, 176, 177:
Matteo Piazza, Milan

Muck Petzet Architekten
Muck Petzet, Sarina Arnold
Landwehrstraße 37
D-80336 Munich
sekretariat@mp-a.de
www.mp-a.de
Photos, pp. 32, 33, 35: Future Documenta-
tion/EO, Munich

Susanne Nobis
assistant: Björn Siedke
Am Fichtenhain 9
D-82335 Berg
Su.nobis@t-online.de
Photos, pp. 62, 63, 64, 65, 66, 67: Roland
Halbe, Stuttgart

Johannes Norlander Arkitektur AB
Norlander Projekt AB
Brogatan 2
SE-413 01 Göteborg
studio@norlander.se
www.norlander.se
Photos, pp. 208, 209: Rasmus Norlander, Zürich

Pardeller Putzer Scherer Architekten
with Arch. Joachim Rubner
www.pps-arch.it
Photos, pp. 254, 255, 257: Antonio
Maniscalco, Milano

pichler._architekt[en]
architekt dipl. ing. günter pichler staatl.
befugter u. beeideter ziviltechniker
A-8775 Kalwang 142
Atelier Vienna
Zentagassen 45.3
A-1050 Vienna
office@pichlerarchitekten.at
www.pichlerarchitekten.at
Photos, pp. 124, 125: © pichler architekt-
t[en]

**Pichler & Traupmann Architekten
ZT GmbH**
project management: Barbara Aull (manage-
ment), Mario Gasser, Peter Schamberger,
Jürgen Schneeberger
Weyrgasse 6/4
A-1030 Vienna
office@pxt.at
www.pxt.at
Photos, pp. 214, 215, 217: Lisa Rastl,
Vienna

PLASMA studio
Eva Castro, Holger Kehne, Ulla Hell
assistants: Angelika Mair, David Preindl,
Daniela Walder
Lanerweg 18
I-39030 Sexten
mail@plasmastudio.com
www.plasmastudio.com
Photos, pp. 198, 199: Cristobal Palma,
Santiago de Chile

Powerhouse Company
Nanne de Ru
Design: Nanne de Ru, Charles Bessard,
Alexander Sverdlov
Team: Nolly Vos, Wouter Hermanns,
Anne Luetkenhues, Bjørn Andreassen,
Joe Matthiessen
Westzeedijk 399
NL-3024 EK Rotterdam
office@powerhouse-company.com
www.powerhouse-company.com
Photos, pp. 178, 179, 181, 182, 183:
Bas Princen, Rotterdam

Rocha Tombal Architecten
Ana Rocha and Michel Tombal
assistants: Iwona Wozniakowska, Enrique
Otero Neira, Elena Cabrera Vacas
Nieuwpoortkade 2A-110
1055 RX
NL-Amsterdam
info@rocha.tombal.nl
www.rocha.tombal.nl

Photos, pp. 218, 219, 220, 221: Christian
Richters, Münster

Doris Schäffler Architekt
Clausewitzstraße 5
D-10629 Berlin
dschaeffler@gmx.de
Photos, pp. 68, 69, 70, 71: Christian Gahl,
Berlin

**Scheuring u. Partner
Dipl.-Ing. Architekten**
Claudia Hannibal-Scheuring,
Prof. Andreas Scheuring
Statthalterhofallee 10
D-50858 Cologne
buero@scheuring-partner.de
www.scheuring-partner.de
Photos, pp. 226, 227, 229: Werner Huth-
macher, Berlin

**UNIV.-PROF. DIPL.-ING. UWE SCHRÖDER
ARCHITEKT BDA**
assistants: Stefan Dahlmann (project
management), Till Robin Kurz
Kaiserstraße 25
D-53113 Bonn
office@usarch.de
www.usarch.de
Photos, pp. 194, 195, 197: Stefan Müller,
Berlin

(se)arch Architekten gbr
Prof. Stefanie und Stephan Eberding
Frei Architekten BDA
assistant: Frank Stasi
Christophstraße 40
D-70180 Stuttgart
team@se-arch.de
www.se-arch.de
Photos, pp. p. 238, 239, 241: Zooey Braun,
Stuttgart

SFA – Simon Freie Architekten BDA
with Claudia Pfeiffer
assistant: Yvonne Schindler
Falbenhennenstraße 17
D-70180 Stuttgart
buero@simon-freie-architekten.de
www.simon-freie-architekten.de
Photos, pp. 108, 109: Brigida Gonzales,
Stuttgart

spaceshop Architekten GmbH
Alleestraße 11
CH-2503 Biel
info@spaceshop.ch
www.spaceshop.ch

Photos: Stefan Weber, Nidau: pp. 126, 127
left; spaceshop Architekten, Biel: p. 127
right

splendid architecture
Architekt Stephan Schmid, Nina Schmid
Große Johannnisstraße 13
D-20457 Hamburg
message@splendid-architecture.com
www.splendid-architecture.com
Photos, pp. 204, 205, 207: Ralf Buscher,
Hamburg

Axel Steudel Architekt
assistants: Andreas Dittrich, Jan Horst-
mann, Rudolf Kuntz
Aachener Straße 637
D-50933 Cologne
kontakt@axelsteudel.de
www.axelsteudel.de
Photos, pp. 246, 247, 249: Christian Eblen-
kamp, Rietberg

team 51.5° architekten

Prof. Dipl. Ing. Architekt Swen Geiss
Dipl. Ing. Franziska Wagner
Charlottenstraße 13
D-42105 Wuppertal
s.geiss@team51-5.com
www.team51-5.com
Photos, pp. 120, 121: Selina Pfrüner,
Cologne

Tham & Videgård Arkitekter
Bolle Tham, Martin Videgård
assistants: Fredrik Nilsson, Lukas Thiel,
Erik Wåhlström, Johan Björkholm,
Dennis Suppers
Blekingegatan 46
SE-116 62 Stockholm
info@tvark.se
www.tvark.se
Photos, pp. 92, 193: Åke E: son Lindman,
Bromma

Valtingojer Architekten
Sabina & Klaus
assistants: Dipl. Ing. Nils Bohn, outer
design: Freilich Architekten, Sebastian
Gretzer
Rennweg 69
I-39012 Meran
info@valtingojer.com
www.valtingojer.com
Photos: p. 243: Giovanni Franchelucci,
Rome; pp. 242, 245: Richard Becker, Stein-
heim

Weichlbauer Ortis
Reinhold Weichlbauer, Albert Josef Ortis
Mauritzener Hauptstraße 3
A-8130 Frohnleiten
office@ortisbau.at
www.ortisbau.at/architektur.html
Photos, pp. 184, 185, 187

Wienberg architects
Mette and Martin Wienberg
Havnegaden 24, stuen
DK-8000 Århus C
mette.wienberg@gmail.com
www.wienbergarchitects.dk
Photos, pp. 230, 231, 232, 233: Jacob Ther-
mansen

wild bär heule architekten AG
assistants: Corinne Hufschmid, Irene Kessler
Baurstrasse 14
CH-8008 Zurich
info@wbh-architekten.ch
www.wbh-architekten.ch
Photos, pp. 164, 165, 166, 167: Roger Frei,
Zurich

Hans Peter Wörndl
assistants: Walter Härtig, Alexander Karaiva-
nov (submission plans and renderings),
Max Gangler (factory plans), Waldemar Oster
(Details and construction mgmt.), Culum
Osborne (interior and concept diagrams,
facades), Adrien Jacques le Seigneur (model
construction), Elisabeth Semmler (organiza-
tion, magistrate)
Grundsteingasse 37
A-1160 Wien
hpwoerndl@gmail.com
Photos, pp. 260, 261, 263: Klaus Vyhnalek,
Pressbaum

zelle_03
manuela fernández langenegger
Collaboration with: M. Moll (Ausführung)
Hindenburgstraße 30
D-72622 Nürtingen
kontakt@zelle3.de
www.zelle3.de
Photos, pp. 146, 147, 149: Reiner Blunck,
Tübingen

Photo, page 4 left:
Manos Meisen, Düsseldorf

Photo, page 4 right:
Hannes Henz, Zurich

Photo, page 5 left:
Johannes Vogt, Mannheim

Photo, page 5 right:
Kai Arndt, Munich

Photo, page 6 left:
Michel Kievits, Breda

Photo, page 6 right:
Cristobal Palma, Santiago de Chile

Photo, page 7 left:
Jan Kraege, Cologne

Photo, page 7 right:
Pieter Kers

Images, page 8: Guido Harbers, *Das freiste-hende Einfamilienhaus von 10–30.000 Mark und über 30.000 Mark*; Munich, 1932

Photo, page 10:
Roland Halbe, Stuttgart

Photo, page 12:
akg-images, View Pictures Ltd

Photo, page 13 left:
Mercedes-Benz Classic

Photo, page 13 right:
Getty Images, A. Y. Owen

Photo, page 14 left:
Getty Images, John Philips

Photo, page 14 right:
akg-images, Jürgen Raible

Photo, page 16:
Arno Lederer, Stuttgart

Photo, p. 17, 1st row left:
Michael Schnell, Esslingen

Photo, p. 17, 1st row right:
Fabian Linden, Bochum

Photo, p. 17, 2nd row left:
Bruno Klomfar, Vienna

Photo, p. 17, 2nd row right:
Eckhart Matthäus, Augsburg

Photo, p. 17, 3rd row left:
Reiner Blunck, Tübingen

Photo, p. 17, 3rd row right:
Weichlbauer Ortis, Frohnleiten

Photo, p. 17, 4th row left:
Werner Huthmacher, Berlin

Photo, p. 17, 4th row right:
Antonio Maniscalco, Milan

Photo, back cover, left:
Hannes Henz, Zurich

Photo, back cover, right:
Hertha Hurnaus, Vienna

Other Schiffer Books on Related Subjects:

Contemporary Kitchens: A Style Portfolio, Melissa Cardona, ISBN 978-0-7643-2399-7

Contemporary Villas, David Strahan, AIA, Katharine Kaye McMillan, Ph.D., & Patricia Hart McMillan, ISBN 978-0-7643-3774-1

The Contemporary Log Home: Solid Wood Homes for Residential Living, Marc Wilhelm Lennartz, ISBN 978-0-7643-4330-8

Cover design by Danielle Farmer
Type set in Steiner/ITC Officina Sans

ISBN: 978-0-7643-4847-1

Printed in China

Published by Schiffer Publishing, Ltd.
4880 Lower Valley Road
Atglen, PA 19310
Phone: (610) 593-1777; Fax: (610) 593-2002
E-mail: Info@schifferbooks.com

For our complete selection of fine books on this and related subjects, please visit our website at www.schifferbooks.com. You may also write for a free catalog.

This book may be purchased from the publisher. Please try your bookstore first.

We are always looking for people to write books on new and related subjects. If you have an idea for a book, please contact us at proposals@schifferbooks.com.

Schiffer Publishing's titles are available at special discounts for bulk purchases for sales promotions or premiums. Special editions, including personalized covers, corporate imprints, and excerpts can be created in large quantities for special needs. For more information, contact the publisher.

Project notes: Dr.-Ing. Wolfgang Bachmann
Project management: Tina Freitag, Bettina Springer
Editing: Katrin Pollems-Braunfels
Cover design: independent medien-design
Layout: hackenschuh communication design
Site plans: Jens Schiewe

All other plans were provided by the architecture firms.

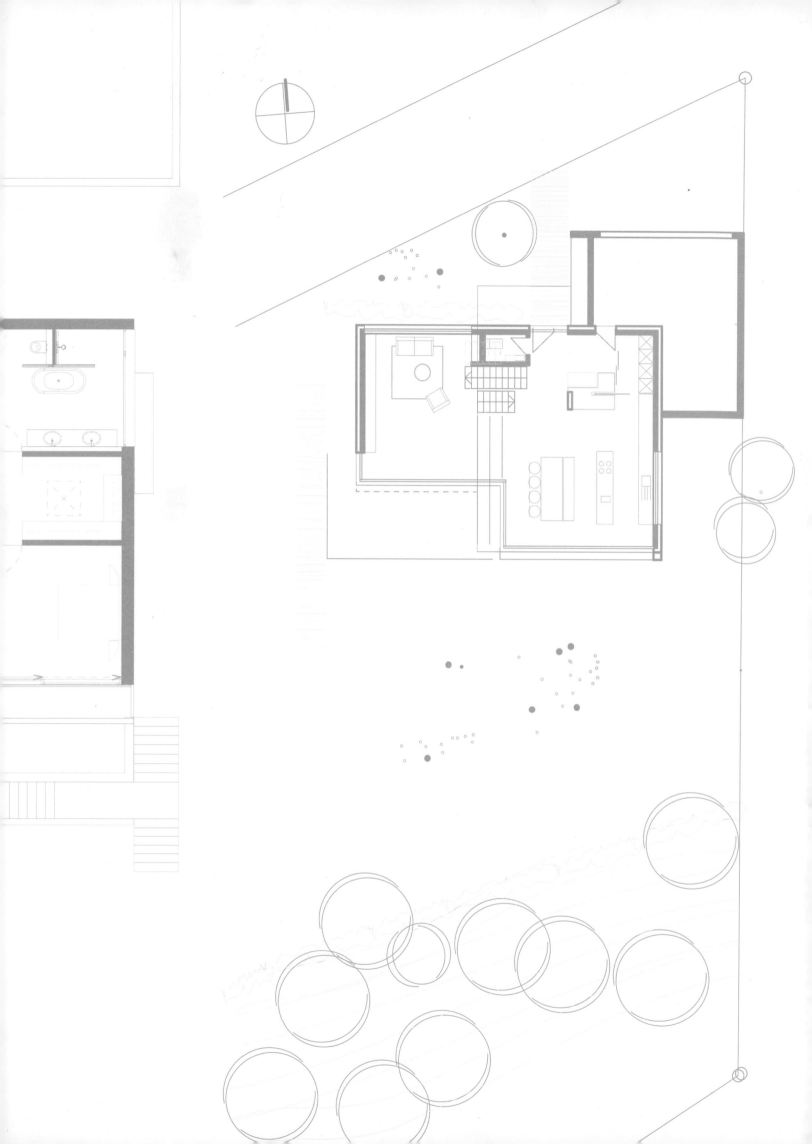